COME SWING WITH ME

Come Swing with Me

MY LIFE ON AND OFF THE TOUR

by DOUG SANDERS

with LARRY SHEEHAN

Doubleday & Company, Inc.
Garden City, New York
1974

A portion of Chapter 6 of this book appeared originally in *Golf Digest* in December 1973.

Library of Congress Cataloging in Publication Data

Sanders, George Douglas, 1933-
    Come swing with me.

      1. Sanders, George Douglas, 1933-   2. Golf.
I. Sheehan, Larry, joint author.   II. Title.
GV964.S28A32   796.352′092′4 [B]
ISBN 0-385-05631-1
Library of Congress Catalog Card Number 73–9174

PHOTO CREDITS:
University of Florida Photographic Service Department   3
Wide World Photos   2, 7, 9, 23
Dave Patterson, *Golf Digest*   10
U.P.I.–Compix   4, 5, 17, 18
Lester C. Nehamkin   13, 15, 16
All other photos, courtesy of the Sanders family

Contents

COME SWING WITH ME

1 / Hagen, Hogan, and Me

Up in Massachusetts a couple of years ago, a fan gave me the eagle eye as I walked on the practice green before a tournament round. He must have seen me play before, because after a while he called out in a dry Yankee twang.

"Gettin' a little gray up on top, ain't you, sonny?"

A little gray? My hair resembled an Alpine snowfield.

"Yes, sir, I am," I replied. There was no good reason to renew the Civil War just then. "And I've enjoyed every goddam minute of it."

I have been scolded, preached at, pointed to, prayed for and whispered about for things I have done, in golf or business or love. Somebody once told me that with all my faults I should have been born an earthquake.

I have been pitied for things I have not done—notably not

making a thirty-inch putt in the 1970 British Open. You may recall my handing over that major championship to Jack Nicklaus, Inc., on the seventy-second green at St. Andrews, Scotland, on international television. Actually I did not hand it over. Jack won it fair and square in the play-off round the next day. But my little stab at the cup remains the shortest missed-putt-to-win in the history of the world's four classic golf events.

I don't need scolding, because whatever's gone wrong in the past has been at my expense, no one else's. And to balance every vice of mine, I've tried to develop a virtue—which is the only way for natural man to get along in society, anyway.

I certainly don't deserve pity. In fifteen years I won twenty important pro tournaments, nearly a million dollars in prize money, and I don't know how many friends and fans from all walks of life from all over the world. I beat the best golfers on tour, knew some rare and beautiful ladies, and kept my money in circulation. A country boy would say those were fair consequences of being able to play a game halfway decent.

I did not achieve in those years the kind of historical success a dedicated athlete would wish. There were some lasting records. I was—and remain at this writing—the last golfer to win a major professional tournament as an amateur. I was only twenty-two when I won the Canadian Open in July 1956, six months before turning pro. I also won back-to-back tournaments in four different years—1961, 1962, 1965, and 1966.

Most satisfying, though, has been the fact that my personality seems to have gained for me greater acceptance even than my playing record. I am happy in my friends and my fun and my travel. And in spite of some business fiascos, I really have made some money, not just in endorsements and exhibitions (which come to any consistent winner), but in the stock market, in real estate and travel ventures, and various other enterprises introduced to me by golfing contacts—often people I have been willing to meet and fool with when some other pros couldn't take the time to be nice.

So I am fixed well enough, today, to provide for my family, buy drinks for my friends (a friend is the person on your right in the saloon), and generally to persist in my bad habits for as long as I want to, and in the style I am accustomed to, which is first class. In fact long ago I decided that if I can't go first class, then the hell with going at all.

I don't mean to philosophize at length or suggest other people improve their lives—or get worse, depending on how you look at what I say. Character reform was frowned on in my home town of Cedartown in Polk County, north Georgia, possibly because it interfered with the local specialties, gambling and whiskey running. The town was fairly active in the sex arena too, when I was growing up. It was a kind of Peyton Place Dixie-style. Preachers and politicians had plenty to talk about and hardly anyone to listen.

My own politics, by the way, are simple: Any man with money in his pocket and love on his mind has to be a reasonably good citizen.

Walter Hagen, the prince of golf in the Roaring Twenties, would say to harried friends, "Take it easy, relax. Stop to smell the flowers." The phrase was engraved on his coffin when "the Haig" died in 1969, that's how much it meant to him.

I believe some people actually stop to count the boulders in their way. I've tried not to. That's why, when I look back, I don't see much in my career or in my non-golfing pursuits, as crazy and mixed-up as some of it has been, to worry at or pine over. I do see a fair amount that may be funny or revealing about the high places and tight spots I've been in, and about the various characters I have met.

I see some things that may even help people get more out

of who they are and what they do, whether it's love, friendship, work, games like golf, or just plain fooling around.

That's mainly what I would like to share with readers of
this book. A couple of the boulders, maybe, but mostly the
flowers and the laughs.

First, I want to show you how I see my own career in terms
of the golf in America in the past few decades.

My prime years on tour really bridged two major epochs
in the game, and also saw a thorough transformation in the
character of life on tour.

The postwar epoch dominated by Ben Hogan, Sam Snead,
Byron Nelson, and Jimmy Demaret died out. In that earlier
time, of which I only had a glimpse, tournament purses were
small, organization was casual, behavior was individualistic.
Pros traveled in groups between tournament sites, stayed in
one or two favorite hostelries in the town nearest the course,
and tended to gather in the evenings to swap stories, make
toasts and deflate each other's putting theories.

It was an era of practical jokes, impractical apparel, stiff
rivalries, and solid friendships. Life was supposed to be fun.
Business was simple too. Deals were made with handshakes,
not in twenty-page contracts signed in triplicate.

All this had begun to change when I came on tour. I suppose
golf boomed for the same reasons a lot of things boomed, because the nation was prosperous and sure of itself and had
leisure time to kill. Also from 1952 to 1960 we had in Dwight
D. Eisenhower—Ike—a keen golfing President to publicize the
sport as no Madison Avenue ad campaign ever could have
done. Masses of people were stimulated to play by his example,
or by the convenience of the powered golf cart, or by the
romance of the game as they saw it on color TV.

Pro golf became a popular and market-worthy spectator
sport and overnight received a fat injection of money. In 1957,

when I played my first U.S. event as a pro, there were thirty-two Professional Golfers' Association tournaments worth $820,000. In 1970, the year I lost the British Open to Nicklaus, there were forty-seven events valued at $6,200,000. Forty-five million dollars was awarded to the PGA pros in official money in those fifteen years. If the era of Walter Hagen and Bobby Jones in the 1920s was called the Golden Age, then the era of my time on tour became at least a gilded one.

Many of the old guard stayed into the 1960s to benefit from the new affluence and to carry on some of the older traditions and rivalries. There was Snead, Dutch Harrison, Tommy Bolt, Julius Boros, Doug Ford, Dow Finsterwald (the pro I beat in the play-off for my 1956 Canadian Open title), the Hebert brothers, Art Wall, Gardner Dickinson and others.

But the weight of public attention, and most of the prize money, began to shift to the brilliant younger players coming up. Arnold Palmer and Billy Casper arrived in 1955, Ken Venturi and Tony Lema in 1956, and Gary Player and Bruce Crampton, the two outstanding foreign-born players of the time, in 1957. The cast of major characters in the new Gilded Age was not really complete until Dave Hill turned pro in 1959, Nicklaus in 1962, Tom Weiskopf, in 1965 and Lee Trevino in 1966, but in the meantime tour life changed.

Though few noticed and even fewer seemed to care (I didn't notice, and it wasn't until later that I cared), some of the pleasanter values and habits of the older era began to wither away. Tour organization improved and gallery control increased. Player behavior was policed more rigorously, and golf fans had a harder time seeing a shot made. More pros tended to travel and make lodging arrangements independently, so group feeling declined. Social life became more cliquish and sophisticated. In former times practically everyone on tour was the graduate of some caddie yard or other, and mixing was easy. Now golfers appeared with degrees in economics, law, theology, or business administration. And they actually knew their subjects—they had not cheated and connived through college as many athletes in my time did, present company not excepted! Anyway there was a greater variety of backgrounds on tour and it made for social and cultural barriers that were brand new.

Fun became harder to have, I think. Jimmy Demaret caught the spirit of the previous era when he once observed, "It's only when you're broke that you can enjoy life." But in the old days not every stroke was weighed in gold—after the first few finishing spots in any given tournament in his era, the cash awards were insignificant. Later pros would have said, "It's only when you're in the Top 60 (the list of pros who do not have to qualify for tournament berths every week) that you can enjoy life."

Not that tour life became outright dull. I did my part, for one thing, though I was periodically upbraided by fellow pros and by outsiders who felt golfers were not in the entertainment business. "What are we doing then," I used to say, "fixing plumbing?" And there were other extroverts to support my view, including Porky Oliver and Bo Wininger, both gone now, unfortunately, and virtually forgotten except by those who experienced their wit and humor firsthand. There was Al Besselink, my favorite gin rummy partner, impulsive and handsome, now working as a club professional in Las Vegas—a match made in heaven if there ever was one. Once when Bessie was down to his last nickel, he bought five one-cent pencils with it and started signing tabs. He also beat me into the pages of the old exposé magazine, *Confidential*, when he started dating movie star Terry Moore. Then there was Tony Lema, who died in an airplane crash in 1966 when he was rounding into form not just as a top player but as an engagingly warm and forthright fellow. And there were others too. And there is still Lee Trevino, full of cheer and charity with a smile the size of a sombrero.

Really I am not talking about individuals so much as atmosphere. The Gilded Age had money and gifted players and extraordinary performances. Tour life did not become dull, but finally it seemed to lose some of its heart. The winner's champagne began to flow with a little too much calculation toward the end of my prime playing years, as though the act were a commercial message now, and not that secret celebration of man and fan that the true sports figure always seeks to honor.

Young players arriving on tour in recent years have been criticized for having personalities as machinelike as their putting strokes. I don't think this is true. In fact they are the ones who are going to put the heart back into pro golf, if anyone is. Modern pressures combined with a media that tends to play the same old tunes have simply obscured or ignored the potential of the newcomers. It isn't easy for a fellow to express himself freely if he is worried about upsetting wife, sponsor, tournament official, agent, attorney, orthopedic surgeon, or accountant. That's like trying to get through a busy intersection with a car full of back-seat drivers. But with poise and practice it can be done, and I for one am betting on the reappearance of good feelings and funny business on tour.

So much for the history lesson, which ended up sounding like a gripe. I meant it simply as a backdrop for saying that my own development on tour was erratic and not without misgivings about the way *I* did things, and worries about the sometimes contradictory needs and desires that drove *me*. I had two bad slumps. One was a short but rough, confused period in 1959, the other was a seemingly endless time when I went without winning for over three years, finally reasserting myself in the Bahamas Open in December 1970.

Of course slumps are supposed to teach you the pleasure of peaks, so to speak, but no one ever realizes that until they are over. I will save the gory details on my two slumps—neither was caused simply by some technical problem in my golf game—for later. For now I will just say that it was during the slumps that I became most aware of the conflicting drives within me. If I had to name the opposing sides in the psychological dogfights that took place, I would dub one side "Hagen" and the other side "Hogan." Hagen was the spirit of fun and laughter, Hogan the desire to win.

Sometimes Hagen and Hogan had terrible arguments in the damnedest places. I would be trying to enjoy myself in a restaurant, forgetting about how long it had been since my last victory, when the fight would start:

HOGAN: You little cotton-picking blockhead. Go home to bed.

HAGEN: Are you kidding? We haven't even ordered dinner. Hey, junior! Wine list, please!

HOGAN: You're teeing off at 10:10 A.M., that's less than 12 hours from now. Go back, get some rest.

HAGEN: I don't need any rest, I'm still young. By the way, how do you like the young lady I'm with?

HOGAN: Never mind the girl. Think of the tournament. Go over the course in your mind. Think of winning. Win, *win*. WIN!

HAGEN: All right, I will, but first things first.

HOGAN: What now?

HAGEN: I want to smell the flowers.

Or I might be relaxing in a hot bath after a round, nursing a drink, contemplating a missed putt or misjudged approach, and all of a sudden another debate would roar in my head:

HOGAN: You lost twenty yards off the tee between the first and last holes today, do you know what that means?

HAGEN: Too many parties this week.

HOGAN: This *week?* You went to three last night alone. You're not just burning the candle at both ends. It's lit in the middle too!

HAGEN: Well, I had some fun. Did you see me give that boy on number twelve a dollar? Did you see his expression?

HOGAN: Never mind the galleries.

HAGEN: On thirteen I kissed a sixty-year-old lady. On sixteen, I signed my name on somebody's visor.

HOGAN: Forget autographs, forget the galleries.

HAGEN: But I like people, I can't help it.

HOGAN: Then join Actors Equity. At this rate you'll never make a living playing golf again.

Sometimes my Hogan would finally get his way. I would decide to bear down. Now my Hagen would be the one who was insulted.

HAGEN: What have you stopped drinking for?

HOGAN: I've stopped drinking until I win again. I'm not going to touch anything but orange juice.

HAGEN: Orange juice? Are you crazy? Do you want to get Vitamin C poisoning?

HOGAN: I told you I'm not drinking until I *win.*

Finally I would win, but that would start another battle:

HAGEN: Now we certainly can relax.

HOGAN: Don't think about last week's victory. Keep it going when you got it going. Every week is a brand-new contract.

HAGEN: Take off. Acapulco is lovely this time of year.

Of course the real Walter Hagen was more serious about winning than my "Hagen," and the real Ben Hogan was more relaxed about life than my "Hogan." Yet even in real life they were distinctly different models for a young man to consider in managing his own development.

I admired Hagen most of all for his gallantry with people. He produced the effect of the actor John Barrymore, his contemporary, in that people felt better just going out to see him.

He was a stylist in everything he did. He rode in a Rolls or a Duesenberg, smoked cigars and drank champagne, called all the girls in his galleries "Sugar," and ignored class divisions. The old-time pros in Britain had never been allowed inside clubhouses. They often washed up after a round in tin basins set up in drafty tents. The Haig changed all that. "What the hell," he would say, and march straight into the members' bar and order a round of drinks.

Hagen was the first golf pro to make a million and to spend it, they used to say. He picked up tabs, underwrote the misfortunes of friends, spoiled his caddies. He loved parties, clothes, and kids. As an unschooled blacksmith's son, he was inclined to make mistakes in his use of the language—I am the same way—but he was theatrical all the same, magnetic. "He could draw audiences just by hailing a cab, or buying a paper," his old friend Fred Corcoran once recalled.

Above all Hagen loved to celebrate. He once teasingly announced that he preferred the British Open, which he won four times, to the U.S. Open, which he won twice, because winning abroad gave him a whole week on ship to drink champagne coming home. He was a scrambler and a gamesman, too: he burst into the locker room at the 1927 PGA and asked, in the presence of the likes of Gene Sarazen, Tommy Armour, and Lighthorse Harry Cooper, "Which of you guys is coming in second this week?" Sure enough, Sir Walter won his fourth of five PGA Championships that week.

Ben Hogan won in major championship play but not without a massive exertion of intelligence and will. To pay Hogan $25,000 for a week-long lesson—if one was determined to play golf as well as possible—would be a bargain because he became so knowledgeable about the golf swing in the course of his career. He was and remains one of the few golfers who never crosses over on a shot—that is, his right hand never overcomes his left hand in the swing. This is the ideal way to play golf, in my opinion, because the clubface remains on target throughout the stroke. It was in any case a method that Hogan perfected only after years of intense self-examination and relentless practice.

I also believe Hogan found the best way to excel at stroke play—the modern game—which is to attack the golf course and forget about the rest of the field. In fact, forget about the rest of the world. I played a few practice rounds with Ben prior to a U.S. Open one year and had a chance to ask him about his way of building concentration to such a pitch.

In the course of our talk, he said, "If I could just walk out and practice, then go straight to the first tee, play my round, go in, take a shower, have a beer and then go home, I'd play in tournaments every week. But I can't just do that. I always feel cooped up by people when I play in a tournament. I feel there's no place to escape to."

Some time later we played a casual round at Colonial. Besselink and I decided to take on Hogan and another Texas pro, Shelley Mayfield.

"Let's make it a $500 Nassau," Bessie announced on the first tee.

"Are you kidding?" I said, grabbing the Golden Greek, as he was called in those days, and pulling him to one side. "You do not attack The Hawk in his nest."

Sure enough, every time Hogan hit the ball that round the pin got in his way. He missed six easy putts and still shot 66. "Bessie," I said at the end of the round, "we would have lost $40,000 if we had played it your way."

In 1956, I was paired in a pro-am at Seminole, the exquisite Florida layout where, in fact, Hogan often played and practiced in his prime, with a tiny South African who was making his first professional appearance in America. His name was Gary Player. I sized him up, as others would do, and concluded that Gary had an uphill battle on tour. He had a scrawny frame and a somewhat raggedy swing, I felt. I remember his sand play was awfully good—he had studied under his countryman Bobby Locke, the short-game player par excellence—and that he was boyishly earnest about everything.

We became friends and when our separate schedules permitted, spent time together off the course. It was a few months later, during a tournament in Baton Rouge, Louisiana, that we had a conversation that in retrospect strikes me as remarkable.

We were having dinner in a restaurant and I asked him in the middle of it, "Look here, laddie,"—I was making fun of the way he spoke to his caddies—"if somebody offered you $250,000 in cold U.S. currency right now, what would you do? Would you take it and go back home? Or would you stay here, and try to win one of our major championships?"

Player shrugged and replied, "I'd try for the majors."

"Shoot!" I exclaimed. "I thought at least we'd have a *discussion* on the subject!" In fact I was surprised, and maybe a little awed, by the speed and conviction of his answer. He was as poor as I was, if not more poor, and in those days it was ridiculous to even think you could earn a quarter of a million dollars in pro golf. I thought, "The young man is off his rocker."

Obviously Gary was nothing like crazy. Somehow he had already faced the question on his own and answered it in favor of commitment to victory. He, too, was a great admirer of Hogan and, like Hogan, he would go on to win all four "major" championships—the U.S. and British Opens, the Masters, and the PGA Championship.

Hogan and Hagen—even today I feel myself drawn to both of them, as a boy is drawn to a favorite uncle. In a way, I tried to copy both, and finished being something else—myself. But the argument within me will probably go on for a long time to come.

2 / *Tilting with the "Major" Titles*

Long after the 1970 British Open, a man came up during an exhibition match in St. Paul, Minnesota, and thrust a piece of cloth at me.

"It's the flag from the eighteenth at St. Andrews," he explained. "I stole it after the play-off. It's a souvenir."

"Well, you can keep it," I said, trying to get away from this grim reminder. "I don't want any part of it!"

"But will you sign it for me?"

He stuck a pen at me and finally I wrote with some difficulty on the rough red fabric as follows:

> From riches to rags—
> You have the flag
> And I have the memories.
> —Doug Sanders

I want to reconstruct that missed putt at the British Open because it cost me so much sleep and got so much attention, and also because it sheds light on my play in the other "classic" events too. I don't represent Avis but I have become an expert on the subject of coming in second. I have been a shot out of the U.S. Open once, one shot, two shots, and three shots out of the PGA Championship three consecutive years, and two shots out of the Masters one year.

Maybe a golfer does not fully appreciate winning a big tournament unless he has already lost one by a narrow margin. If that is true, when I win my first major championship, I am going to need a network television special to explain how I feel.

But the British Open, where I have been runner-up twice, has become my sentimental favorite among the big four. I like it the way a child might enjoy visiting a quirky old aunt who wears floppy hats and swears a lot. (On that basis, I guess I would describe the PGA as a beefy pioneer woman, the U.S. Open as a severe New England banker's daughter, and the Masters as a willowy and wicked southern debutante. All very sexy in their own ways, I hasten to add.)

The British Open atmosphere is special with all its accents, the smells of sharp whiskey and pints of ale, and stories about blinkin' Willie hitting a bloomin' niblick into the whins. The crusty old caddies are straight out of Dickens, the golf writers talk like professors of history and the officials have more dignity than Georgia undertakers.

Most of all I like the old links on which the tournament is always staged. You need character to play some of the uncanny lies you get, and real spirit to escape from the bunkers or the savage seaside grasses. As the South African golfer Harold Henning said of the rough at Muirfield: "You take a search warrant to get in, and a wedge and a prayer to get out." And you need courage on the greens—when you stroke those lightning putts you've got to do it with nerve-ends only.

I usually play well over there because I can keep my drives in the fairway better than most players, I read the wind about as well as a hound-dog, and I know how to skip, hit, bump and run the ball like it's on a Yo-yo string.

The English and Scottish galleries are naturally reserved and, in the Open, they are kept even more remote from the players than galleries in most U.S. tournaments. I'm not tempted to cut up so much and it probably improves my concentration when I compete over there. I'm not sure the Britons would get my jokes anyway.

All this to explain why in July of 1970, I would take the trouble to fly over there at my own expense to try to qualify to play in the Open.

That in itself had some people scratching their heads. Of course there are pros who would not spend their own money on a Mother's Day card, let alone passage to Britain. And there are others who just don't feel comfortable traveling outside the U.S.A.—I think they think all foreigners carry the plague. Probably there are still others who would not want to risk the indignity of failing to qualify in these circumstances.

Not me. I had first competed in Britain in 1956, when I made a run at the British Amateur title. When I played in my first Open, I felt at home right away. Like a dozen or so other American pros, including Arnold Palmer, whose back-to-back wins here in 1960–61 put the event back on the map as far as the American public was concerned, I've always thought it was not just fun but a privilege to take part in the world's oldest golf championship.

Anyway I did not get an automatic starting berth in 1970 because of my playing record. This was when I had not won a title in three years. I had gone from sixth in 1967 to fifty-sixth in 1969, in world money rankings. After most of a decade within the top ten money winners each year, I was now out-

side the American PGA's Top 60 list. I was in rabbit territory
—a rabbit is a player who scraps for a tournament berth in
Monday qualifying rounds. Actually I had so many invitations
and exemptions, as a former winner in various tournaments,
that I never had to try to qualify for a regular tour event. But
emotionally I felt like a bunny.

My slump had been mainly the result of several nagging
personal problems. Among other things, I had been fighting
for custody of my young son, trying to pry my dream house
from an owner reluctant to sell it, and organizing an annual
program to raise money for my college scholarship fund. Combined with my habitual vices, these matters had me running
around like a stuck pig.

By the time I went over to Scotland, though, the problems
were pretty much settled. And my game was back in running
condition though few had bothered to notice. In fact a lot
of people had written me off. I was burned out, they said.

I qualified easily and played the first three chilling, blustery
days of the tournament in six strokes under par, with rounds
of 68, 71, and 71. I seemed to be the talk of "Open Week."

On the last day, I felt and played just as well. In fact as we
walked to the eighteenth tee of the Old Course at St. Andrews,
I was convinced all my personal and professional difficulties
were over. I was feeling so exuberant that I hugged the man I
was paired with—and Lee Trevino is no raving beauty.

Actually I was exuberant over the shot I had just pulled off
on number seventeen to save my par and my one-stroke lead
over Nicklaus, who was already off the course with a four-day
total of 68–69–73–73–283.

My approach shot on the seventeenth, the "Road Hole," had
landed in its pot bunker, a craterlike pit of sand at the left
front of the green. I had found the ball pressed against the
sheer face of that bunker. I had to make a sensitive lob stroke
—something a heart surgeon maybe does better—to make the

ball come out fast and fall like a feather, without backspin. The very real danger had been "over-escaping" and finishing off the narrow green on the cursed little road on the other side, from where a bogey or worse would surely have developed. The shot ended up less than two feet from the hole and I made the putt for a four.

I thought this was going to be talked of as *the shot* in the 1970 British Open. More than one British writer described it as one of the finest shots they'd ever witnessed on this historic hole. In fact it was a shot I had learned from watching Hogan play years before.

So I felt elated coming to eighteen. And now that the championship was in my pocket, so to speak, I began tinkering with the idea of being the only player to break par all four rounds. A birdie on the relatively easy eighteenth, I mused, would give me another one-under-par 71 and a total of 281— two strokes better than Nicklaus.

Trevino's caddie, who had worked for Tony Lema during the 1964 Open at St. Andrews, when Tony had won, suddenly thrust a white tee in my hand. "Use it on the last hole," he said. "It's one of Champagne Tony's."

I teed up my ball and took my stance.

"Hit it to the clock," I remember my own caddie saying.

The clock, a good aiming point for your tee shot on the 358-yard finishing hole at St. Andrews, is on the façade of the stolid gray three-story building located directly behind the first tee and the eighteenth green. This, the somber and dignified clubhouse of the Royal and Ancient Golf Club, is the fount of golf and the source of its rules and traditions. Here is where the game's soul rests if such a devilish endeavor as golf can be said to have a soul.

At this point, the R and A clubhouse appeared to be carried on the shoulders of the mass of spectators, huddled in their tweeds and plaids, waiting for the last twosome to finish. In spite of the early bad weather, the galleries this year had been the largest in Open history.

It crossed my mind that once again I was giving the press corps something to sink their teeth into. I sensed how dramatic it was all going to sound—

REFORMED PLAYBOY
ENDS THREE WINLESS YEARS
WITH FIRST MAJOR CHAMPIONSHIP
AT HOME OF GOLF.

I could not imagine what would make it more dramatic, short of a typhoon breaking out at that instant.

I hit my tee shot in the center of the broad double fairway, and adequate for what I needed to do next: pitch on and then negotiate the classic "two for the Championship."

I was not overconfident or jittery, I was just plain sure of myself. I believe that after they saw me hit safely off the eighteenth tee, many in the galleries were sure of me too. One photographer in the crowd tried to get my wife, Scotty, to look nervous—to pose biting her lip or crossing her fingers—and she couldn't give him a convincing performance. There was nothing to feel nervous about.

Scotty was standing with our friends Dave Thomas, the British professional, and his wife, Robbie. (There had been a lot of wives of pros in the gallery all week—the knitwear shops in town had done a record business.) After seeing my respectable drive, they hugged Scotty and said,

"Look, he's won it, wonderful, we'll call you tonight."

And they sped off in their car to beat the traffic.

Thomas, I knew, was especially pleased with the apparent result because together we had been runner-up to Nicklaus by one stroke in the 1966 Open at Muirfield. Misery had loved company and we became friends. Just last night, in fact, we had worked on Dave's short game for two hours.

In pitching to the eighteenth, my main concern was to get past the so-called "Valley of Sin," a huge depression fronting the green. It is simple, almost inevitable, to three-putt from this hollow. In fact Nicklaus had done so in finishing before me, after reaching the green with a tremendous tee shot. Today the spot was especially dangerous because of the wind. Putting uphill going downwind is like that old co-ordination trick of rubbing your belly and your head at the same time—which I can't do.

The ball jumped off my sand wedge a bit, and went thirty feet past the pin. As I walked onto the green, the applause sounding in my ears, I felt full of anticipation yet relaxed. My chance for birdie was slight, I realized, but at least I had stayed out of the valley. And I was warmed by the feeling of the crowd's support. The gallery, predominantly Scots (I felt like I was inside a giant argyle stocking) were packed around the green like subway riders, red-faced and wind-blown, and though they were not effusive, I sensed that they were with me, as prodigal son or underdog or whatever, in these last minutes of their championship.

My first putt was well struck and right on line and I thought it would drop. To my great surprise it stopped two and a half feet short. I had underestimated the effect of the wind on the ball and on my stroke.

I would have liked to putt out immediately but Trevino, I knew, had a chance to break a deadlock for third with Henning by making his twenty-footer, so I marked my ball and stepped away. Lee birdied and walked off to a big hand. Already—this was before he had won this title two years in a row himself—Trevino was eyed with affection and wonder in Britain.

There was a great hush, magnified somehow by the sound of the harsh wind blowing off the North Sea, as I replaced my ball and prepared for the final stroke. After I studied the line,

I stood up to the ball and actually began taking the putter back, when I suddenly spotted what appeared to be a piece of dirt on the path to the cup. I stopped in the stroke, stepped out with my left foot—keeping my right foot in my original stance—and brushed away the impediment, a tiny pebble that the wind had bowled across the green. Then I stepped back into my stance with my left foot and reviewed my line.

Later I learned that Ben Hogan—the real Hogan, not the "Hogan voice" in me—while watching the Open on television in the States, called out at this point:

"Walk away from that putt, Sanders!"

Unfortunately I was not among the millions of TV viewers myself or I might have noticed. Apparently I had slightly altered my stance when I stepped out of it and then back into it with my left foot.

At the same time, there were a few nervous titters or chuckles in the gallery in response to my strange gymnastics. I felt the crowd was behind me, as I said, but I could not defend myself against a fleeting sense that someone might be snickering.

It was a second good reason to start all over again.

But, of course, I did not, and as I reported to the press afterward, I would have missed that particular putt for a dollar as surely as I missed it for the championship. I stroked the putt just enough in the heel of the club to miss it off the right-hand side of the cup by an inch.

There was a stunned silence, then a collective moan.

I don't remember any of what happened immediately afterward, and I still can't comfortably look at the newspaper pictures of me staring helplessly down at my somewhat scraped Slazenger-*Plus*, the ball I played in Britain.

Back at the house, it was tears, silence, sighs, anguish, and more tears. The last time the Open had been held at St. Andrews, Tony Lema and I had been roommates in a similar rented house. After his notable victory that year (it was his first trip to Great Britain, and he played only two practice rounds on the Old Course before the tournament proper), I had bought up all the champagne stocked in town to handle the celebrants we had over that night. Now in 1970 it looked like I needed cases of Kleenex instead.

Actually only Scotty and the musician Buddy Greco, who was my guest for the week, remained after a while. But they didn't know what to say to me about what had happened, any more than I knew what to say to them.

Finally I grabbed a dish of sugar and started to leave.

"Where are you going?" Scotty said.

"I'm going to feed the goddam cows, that's what," I said. We were staying in an isolated old stone farmhouse about ten minutes' drive from town and, judging by how long it took our tub to fill up every evening, about ten hours from the nearest water reservoir. That was another thing I liked about my trips to the British Open. It gave me a chance to hole up with friends for a couple of weeks, far from the demands and the temptations of the telephone.

"But cows don't like sugar," she pointed out gently. "They like salt."

"Well, these cows are going to eat sugar," I replied stubbornly. I grew up among farmers and I knew perfectly well cows liked salt, not sugar.

She let me go without another word.

I crossed the road, tripped on something and fell headlong into a ditch. "Well," I thought as I picked myself up, "at least my luck is running true to form." Then I climbed over a fence and walked out into a green, sweet-smelling pasture full of cowslips and dandelions.

The few cows standing there scattered when I approached.

The local breed wanted nothing to do with a magenta-clad stranger bearing gifts.

So I picked out a clear spot and just lay down. I stared up at the bright gray sky—it would not begin to darken in this northerly region until after ten o'clock that night—and I realized how much I really did need to be alone for a while.

Of course the tournament was not over yet. Jack and I would meet in an eighteen-hole play-off round the next day. I had beaten him in a play-off before—in the 1965 Pensacola Open —and I was sure I could beat him again. In 1970, his skills had not yet been classified as superhuman and the whole tour had not yet caught a deadly psychological flu known as the inferiority complex. But it was irritating to realize how unnecessary all this additional punishment of mind and body really was.

I was embarrassed, too, for having three-putted the eighteenth. Maybe the single statistic that is most revealing about Hagen's greatness is this: In more than thirty years of topflight competition, he never *once* three-putted the home green.

As I lay there—in the manure of my missed putt, so to speak —I felt my grip loosen somewhat on an old secret desire. As only Hogan, Sarazen, Nicklaus, and Player had already done, I always wanted to achieve the lifetime slam—winning all four major titles at least once. I had never talked about it before because I knew it sounded unrealistic coming from a player who hadn't won *any* of the four. After winning this British Open, though, I could have mentioned it. More important, I saw how aiming at the other three in this context could have given fuller meaning to my remaining years on tour.

Vivid pictures of past disastrous flirtations with success also went through my mind.

In 1966, I believed for the first time that I could win the Masters Tournament. Normally I do not play well in the spring because I'm worn out from playing so hard during the first few months on tour, when in fact I have gained about half of my victories. But in 1966 my game still seemed to be rising to its peak at azalea time. I arrived in Augusta with three wins, including my play-off victory over Arnold Palmer in the Bob Hope Desert Classic early in the campaign and back-to-back victories in the Jacksonville and Greensboro Opens in the two weeks preceding the Masters.

My Waterloo was Augusta National's par-3 sixteenth hole. During the third round, I cut a shot over the pond to bring the ball close to the pin, which this day was set close on the left front of the green. I hit the ball exactly as I intended to, but a swirling wind came up—as often happens among the corridors of pine there—and blunted my shot. The ball landed short and trickled back into the water's edge. Instead of possibly making birdie and challenging the lead, I took five and slipped into dismay and discouragement.

Later that same year, I tied the British Open scoring record for Muirfield with rounds of 71–70–72–70—283. Unfortunately for me, Nicklaus broke the record with 282. On the final nine we were tied for the lead until Jack reached the long wind-blown par-5 seventeenth with two rifled iron shots, and there made the birdie that made the difference.

In 1961, the year I won five tournaments—more than I had ever won in a single season—I led the U.S. Open by a shot going into the final nine holes at Oakland Hills in Birmingham, Michigan. A butterfly crept into my stroke and I three-putted number seven, bogeyed number nine, three-putted number ten, and took four from the edge on number twelve. I played the remaining six holes in one under par, but that was not good enough to catch up with Gene Littler, who finished in front of me with a string of birdies. My birdie putt on number seventeen lipped out. My second shot on number eighteen, from a misplaced drive in the right rough, was one of the best shots I ever made, a power 2-iron that cut around a huge tree and finished just short of the green—which had been out of sight from my line. My chip shot, which I needed to make to tie, missed the cup by inches as it rolled past, and Gene was the winner.

In 1960, I led the PGA Championship after an unusual third round at Firestone Country Club, the big tire company's green fringe benefit for employees in Akron, Ohio. I birdied five of the first eight holes that day, including the par-5 second hole which I played from the wrong fairway on the second shot, and number eight, which I salvaged with a lucky seventy-foot putt. I hit the ball even more squarely in the final round, which occurred on my twenty-seventh birthday, but my putting failed again and I finished two strokes behind winner Jay Hebert. He birdied number seventeen and I bogeyed number eighteen. As a friendly bachelor, Hebert had joined me from time to time in search of diversions of an evening, but he wasn't about to make me a gift of the title, no matter how many telephone numbers I offered him.

That same year I played well in the U.S. Open. I was tied for the lead with Mike Souchak as we teed it up on number eighteen in the second round, played at Cherry Hills, Denver, Colorado. As I took my club back, a fish jumped in front of the tee. Stunned, I line-drived the shot straight into the water. People joked later that I had killed the fish. In fact the fish killed me. It ruined my score for the day and routed my morale for the last two days.

In 1959, for the first time in my then three-year-old touring career, I knocked a tee shot out of bounds, during the second round of the PGA Championship, played at Minneapolis Golf Club in St. Louis Park, Minnesota. It cost me two strokes in a week when I missed only six fairways in all and eventually finished only one stroke behind the winner, Bob Rosburg. In my attempt to tie Bob during the last round, I missed birdie putts on number fifteen and number sixteen, three-putted number seventeen, and birdied number eighteen. But it was that uncharacteristic OB drive that really stung me.

Later I found out I never had a chance in that tournament —Art Wall had dreamed Rosburg would win even before it began.

Seriously, a decade later, as I lay in the meadow contemplating these various near misses, I really did think I was spooked. What with sudden winds and flying fish and foiled birthdays and weird dreams, I needed supernatural aid to win a classic, it seemed. I needed to eat batwings for breakfast, maybe, or hire a witch for my caddie.

But then I realized how much easier it is to remember the bad shots that cause you to lose, than to recall the lucky ones that help you to win. And I knew I could not let myself get defeatist or bitter, or I would be useless the next day.

I cheered myself with the following observation: Who is the better golfer, the man who often comes close in major contests, and never wins, or the man who wins once, and never comes close again? Though few fans realize it, it is also possible to play well all year long and still not make a mark in the major events—it all depends on when you have your ups and downs. In any case, I was proud of the fact that I had been a man to win periodically over the long haul. And I said to myself that it was not that important to be introduced on the first tee every round in every tournament for the rest of your life as the such-and-such-a-year British, U.S., Masters, or PGA champion, instead of as the current Podunk Heights title-holder, or twelfth-ranked current money-winner. You can't trust those loudspeaker guys anyway. One year at the Los Angeles Open they announced Johnny Pott by saying, "Now on the pot, Johnny Tee."

By this time the cows had come back. Everything was back to normal in the pasture as far as they were concerned. The situation felt more normal to me, too, after having taken the time to drift over the ups and downs of my playing career, and having held back the rising tide of bitterness.

I got up and moved fast in the direction of the nearest cow. I climbed aboard the startled beast and kicked it in the ribs with my gleaming sixty-dollar-patent-leather loafers with the magenta tassels.

My ride was brief and bumpy—even as a kid in Cedartown I never really got the hang of cowpunching—but when I jumped off and started back to the house, I felt a lot better about everything.

Next day began in a creepy fashion even though my confidence was fairly well restored and I was prepared, even anxious, to do battle with Big Jack and nail down my elusive ticket to lasting fame.

After I hit practice balls, Scotty and I walked through the big tent that is set up every year at the British Open for exhibitors of golf equipment and apparel and related services. We had made the stroll a daily thing because it gave us a chance to chat and joke with the sales reps and company officers in the trade and the pretty girls minding the stalls.

This day there was no one in the tent. It was Sunday and in stern Presbyterian Scotland business is not conducted on the Sabbath. The Open had been scheduled to finish on Saturday as always, and the St. Andrews Old Course, although a public course, is never open on Sunday. Only the exceptional deadlock made it possible for the natives to tolerate our playing golf for money now.

Thus the merchandising center was a wasteland of dismantled exhibits, overturned chairs and tables, trampled grass, and discarded promotional signs. The wind ripped noisily through openings in the sides of the tent as we walked through on our way to the first tee, and there was no one to greet or joke with. I felt like Gary Cooper walking into town for the big gunfight in *High Noon*—alone.

The Sunday gallery got another good show, but they had to wait for it. I bogeyed numbers three and four, we played evenly through the turn, and then I bogeyed numbers eleven and thirteen. Spectators started home. The contest seemed over. Giving a player like Nicklaus four shots with seven holes to play is like playing Russian roulette with only one chamber empty.

I did not get discouraged. Now that I was out on the course, I felt carried along again by the feeling that had been with me all week, an impetus toward victory that nothing I felt would be able to stop. I was certain something would happen presently to change the course of the match.

Sure enough, it began to happen. I birdied numbers fourteen and fifteen and Jack bogeyed number sixteen when he overshot the green on his approach. We both parred the Road Hole. Thus I came to the eighteenth tee one stroke behind. Even so late in the day, I had no "negative inputs." I felt as sure I would win as I had felt yesterday standing on the same tee with Trevino.

For his tee shot, Nicklaus dramatically whipped off his bright yellow sweater. Jack, I had already noticed, was getting to be a clotheshorse—it looked like he was going to give me some heat in that department too.

In the following wind, he clouted his ball *over* the par-4 green.

My tee shot landed in the middle of the fairway, five yards short of the green. I made a good running chip with a 4-iron that finished four feet from the pin. In fact when I went up on the green I noticed I was in about the same line I had missed from on the previous day.

I marked my ball and stepped away. Jack's shot had finished in some tricky long grass on a bank behind the green. With his sand wedge he escaped to between twelve and fourteen feet of the pin. It was a superb finesse shot. Then, in that fiercely deliberate manner of his, he lined up the putt—he was still "away" and putting first—and stroked it in.

And I was dumbstruck. In jubilation Jack tossed his putter high in the air and I think it nearly hit me, which provided some comic relief for the galleries in the great tension that existed. But I was caught entirely in my own feelings of shock. Not until that moment did it finally get through to me that I was not destined to win the 1970 British Open.

In a daze I made the putt that was a slightly longer version of the one I missed yesterday. Then, before we all climbed the few stairs leading up to the R and A building for the ceremony of presenting the trophy and checks, I found myself locked in a four-way embrace with Jack, Jack's lovely wife, Barbara, and my Scotty. Jack was muttering something like, "I'm sorry, Doug," and Scotty was saying to Jack and Barbara both, "Don't be sorry, be *happy*, you should be *happy*."

There we were in the middle of all the cheering and shouting and buzzing around the eighteenth green, yet for a split second totally alone with each other as well, with moistened eyes and an unbearably intense feeling of comradeship.

Hagen used to say, "To miss by a stroke is to miss by a mile." But in those few moments at St. Andrews, the emotions of winning and losing seemed to merge completely.

3 / Famous Foursomes

The day after the British Open play-off, a tournament official brought a carton out to us at the farmhouse. It was full of cables and cards. I was still in a daze, and I flipped through the messages from all over the world, it seemed, without really absorbing what they said.

I wanted to go into hiding for a week, really, but I had agreed to appear in a golf series being filmed at Gleneagles, another fairy-tale golfing spot in Scotland.

There were many local well-wishers waiting for me at Gleneagles:

"Ah, Mr. Sanders, it must've been turrible."

"Yes, sir, it was."

"Now, Doog, tell me, was it really less than three feet, that little knock of yours?"

"Yes, sir, it was."

"Oh, Mr. Sanders, my heart goes out to ye."

"Yes m'am, it was."

I mean, it wasn't long before my responses got somewhat automatic.

On the flight back to America, it was the same.

Stewardess: "Mr. Sanders, we're so sorry."

"Thank you, darling."

Going through customs, one of the officials said,

"I don't play golf, sir, but I know what you've been through."

"Yes, sir, I know you do."

When we got home, the condolences kept coming. Friends and strangers alike felt obligated to say something, and of course I couldn't blame them. It's just that I got a little twitchy and gun-shy about it. Pretty soon I could recognize the I-saw-you-lose-the-British-Open approach at cocktail parties. It usually started with a kind of sideways gait, then a tentative smile, and a searching look with beagle eyes. Then there was a pat on the shoulder, a few philosophical remarks delivered in a hoarse voice if possible, and finally the Purple Heart was pinned on my chest.

By the end of summer the flow of questions and comments finally stopped, and I stopped having nightmares every time I lay down for a nap. But I felt wrung out emotionally. I don't believe a British Open *victory* would have lingered so long or so clearly in my life, as did the loss.

I had gotten a measure of how total and rich had been the sympathy from my supporters. No one had put me down for the defeat. In fact I no longer sensed, as I had sensed before the Open, that some people regarded me as a has-been. It felt good to be taken seriously again as a golfer.

I also saw in retrospect how the year had been one of enormous gain as well as loss, and that maybe I should begin to see my disappointments in a larger way. The big minus in

1970 was losing at St. Andrews. A big plus was the chance to make friends with the then Vice President Spiro T. Agnew. In some ways, this friendship showed to me anew that luck and personality can be almost as important to personal and professional development as skill and education. In a way, that was becoming the story of my own life in golf. It made me more aware of values that exist beyond titles and trophies.

I stepped in the way of the V.P.'s now famous misfire, which more or less christened our friendship, four months before the British Open, at the gala Bob Hope Desert Classic. It was the first of three consecutive years that I would play in this elaborate pro-amateur format tournament with him—and it took us about that long to get off the tee straight.

The Bob Hope Desert Classic in Palm Springs and the Bing Crosby National Pro-Am on Monterey Peninsula are the two most notable and storied events on the pro golf winter circuit. Along with the other celebrity events that take place in the early part of the year, they present a lot of distractions to a social animal like myself. If the major championships are the meat and potatoes of golf, then the celebrity tournaments are the cocktails and canapés. A lot of fine associations have come to me through extracurricular activities, so I never blame a poor score on the good time I had the night before. Anyway I like mingling with top athletes in other sports, the fantastic entertainers, and so many business and civic leaders. I would say my being able to meet a high ranking government official really epitomizes the kind of opportunity that pro golf uniquely seems to offer a young man, even a former cotton picker, who can smile once in a while.

The entertainers especially impress me with the energy and imagination and humor they bring to their golfing. I have never considered trying to sing like Andy Williams, even though I greatly admire his voice and own all his records. If I rehearsed constantly, I don't believe I could sing as well as

Andy Williams' fox terrier. But Andy has occasionally betrayed the desire to play golf like me, or like some of his other cronies on the tour. And he probably would be willing to rehearse every day to do it. And by night too: I have seen him at midnight involved in tense putting matches at his club—Riviera, outside Los Angeles—lining up ten-footers by flashlight.

I don't know whether it's show business, or California air, or some mysterious combination, that brings out the zaniness in these people, but something does. Theatrical agent Pierre Cosette, a friend of Williams, once paid $600 for a custom set of fourteen clubs—all wood clubs. He had lost confidence in his iron game, obviously. Anyway he spent a week carefully figuring out how to use his new clubs on his home course. He needed to do this because his all-wood set produced such unfamiliar shot results. He made a complicated chart that supposedly told him exactly what club to use from wherever he happened to be on the course, taking into account such factors as lie, wind, and pin position.

After all this he challenged Andy and two other friends to a friendly match—meaning Pierre was friendly to the idea of cleaning them out. The day of the match came, everyone teed off and Pierre arrived at his ball in the fairway. Now it was time to put his scientific program into motion.

"How far am I?" he asked his caddie.

"180 yards."

"What kind of lie is this?"

"I'd say tight."

"Wind?"

"Oh, looks to be coming at us five miles per."

"Okay, check the poop sheet and give me the club it says."

"What poop sheet?"

"That piece of paper I gave you in the clubhouse."

"Hell, I threw that out with my hot dog wrapper."

Improbable things happen, too, because the entertainers are

performing for each other on the course. Playing with Jan Murray one year, Buddy Hackett hit a shot deep into the woods. Betraying no emotion, he vanished into the trees in the wake of his ball.

A few minutes later he came out yelling, "Locusts! Locusts!"

The oddest part, Jan Murray later pointed out, was he was absolutely naked.

Once Jack Lemmon, trying to play a deliberate hook shot, rolled his hands so violently that his wristwatch flew off. He lost the watch and his ball in the weeds along the fairway. The only thing he saved on the hole was his club, which as he remarked probably was the only thing he should have thrown away.

Jackie Gleason, who at one time owned 150 putters and a golf cart equipped with a bar and telephone, was a great verbalizer of his difficulties, another trait that seems to be common among the showbiz golfers. "If I put the ball where I can see it, I can't reach it," Gleason used to say before he trimmed down. "If I put it where I can reach it, I can't see it."

Some of the comments that the entertainers make at each other's expense are withering. Once I played in a March of Dimes benefit in Miami with Hope, Gleason, and Demaret. On the first tee, Hope sized up Gleason and declared to the gallery, "This is the first time I've ever played with a blimp." Then he admonished him: "We're playing USGA rules today, Jackie. That means you've got to tee up your own ball and get it out of the cup yourself."

Phil Harris and Dean Martin were on the first tee one day after a night of partying. Phil whiffed his first attempt at a drive, then missed another. He picked up his ball in disgust and declared:

"I'm not playing today."

"Don't quit now," said Dean. "You've got a no-hitter going."

Once Andy Williams had a particularly trying round in Atlanta. On one hole he hit it in and out of the woods a half-dozen times. When he finally reached the green, he turned to his caddie and asked,

"What should I do with this putt?"

"Keep it as low as possible," replied the caddie.

Such remarks probably would be devastating to the ordinary golfer, yet the entertainers, used to adulation and success in their lives, somehow tolerate it with great good humor. At least usually. One year during the old Thunderbird in Palm Springs, comedian Don Adams was addressing his ball about three feet in front of the markers on a certain tee. A lady galleryite strolling by spotted that and poked a marshal.

"Tell that dummy to get behind the markers," she said loudly. "Doesn't he know the 'Rules of Golf'?"

Adams stepped away from his shot, glared at the woman, and told the marshal,

"Tell that ding-a-ling I am hitting my second shot."

Danny Thomas hit his tee shot on the tenth hole at Bermuda Dunes one year straight up when a loudspeaker blared forth in the middle of his downswing:

"TELEPHONE CALL FOR LOUIE HICKS."

"Who the hell is Louie Hicks?" Danny kept muttering during the remainder of his round that day.

Practical jokes are another feature of the entertainers' private lives, and Phil Harris is a master in that category. Once he had room service in a Hawaiian hotel deliver Jimmy Demaret and me a breakfast of banana sandwiches on rye, in honor of our memorable previous evening together when we had drunk, by actual count, seventy-six banana daiquiris, downstairs. My favorite practical joke is the one he perpetrated at Las Vegas one year. After a day of fishing out by Hoover Dam, he and some friends were riding back to town when they were hit by a taxicab driver. It was a minor accident, but the cabbie's insurance company got into the act promptly, sending out a limousine to bring Phil and friends back to the Frontier, where Harris was performing that week. An adjustor met the group and got Phil's friends to sign a no-injury statement and made a generous settlement of the mishap. But Phil hung back. In fact he went into another room and poured some ketchup into one of his socks. Then he returned, sat down with the adjustor, chatted some, and finally exclaimed in seeming pain, "Oh! Ooooh!"

"What's the matter?" said the adjustor, naturally a little concerned.

"Damn," said Phil Harris. "That foot *hurts*. Oooh. I got a little pain in that kid, all right!"

"What is it, Mr. Harris?" said the adjustor.

"Well, when we had the accident there was a real sharp pain when my foot jammed underneath the seat and now all of a sudden it's back."

"Maybe you better take a look at it," suggested a friend.

"I think I better," said Phil.

He bent over and carefully pulled off his shoe and rolled down the sock. "Goddam!" he called, holding up his ketchup-covered fingers. Then he pulled off the sock completely and stuck out his foot for the adjustor to see. "Goddam!" he exclaimed again. "Where is that kid? That kid was in there this morning when I got dressed!"

"Your toe, it's missing," stammered the adjustor. He checked Phil's cuff, glanced around the floor, blurted out, "Oh, don't anybody leave"—as though he suspected somebody had pocketed Phil's big toe.

In fact, as Phil Harris finally revealed to the poor man, the toe was lost years ago in a boyhood accident.

One year I was grouped in the Crosby tournament with Bing's son Lindsay, former PGA Champion Walter Burkemo, and George Gobel. Gobel and Burkemo were friends from high school days, when they had been amateur diplomats—the two

of them once tried to place an overseas call to Adolph Hitler
to talk him out of the war.

Anyway, this year Monterey Peninsula was awash with icy
rain and wind. I wore all the heavy gear I could find in the
trunk of my car. I looked like a paratrooper. George and Lindsay, though, were sparsely clad in light windbreakers.

"George," I suggested, "don't you have any towels to put
around your neck to keep the water from running down?"

"Yeah," he said. "But we can't use them around our necks."

"Why not?"

"Well, we need them to separate the bottles in the bag."

"Oh."

Right then I knew we were not going to make the cut.

It came George's turn to tee off. George is a natural trem-
bler. Once we were at a cocktail party and he singed a girl's
hair when he tried to light her cigarette for her. Today, with
the cold making things worse, he set his driver about six
inches behind the ball. He knew if he put it any closer he
would knock the ball off the peg.

"Walter," he cried out, "these damn Spalding clubs are nervous again."

"Well," shrugged Walter, who was not the steadiest hand
in golf himself, "give them something to drink."

The first tee is not the place for liquid refreshment, so
George bunted one down the fairway and we were on our way.
By the time we reached the big tree at the dogleg corner of
the first hole at Pebble Beach, George was lying six and
mightily discouraged. But he was near a patch of woods. He
slipped behind a tree, unzipped his bag, and pulled out a
bottle labeled "George Gobel Scotch." He poured himself and
his Spaldings a drink and then reappeared. If you recall how
Gobel used to levitate on stage after a coy remark during his
highly successful TV show in the 1950s, you will be able to
picture how he emerged from the woods. He sprang from be-

hind that cypress tree and went halfway across the first fairway before his feet touched ground again.

Later in the round, I stepped on Gobel's ball, near a green, transforming what had been an easy chip-on into a buried lie in sodden turf.

A little girl at the edge of the gallery screamed, "Mommie! That old man stepped on Mr. Gobel's ball!" She glared at me and spat, "I hate you! I hate you!"

Naturally Gobel with his dry sense of humor would not get me off the hook with this fan. He just stared at me as he stood over his miserable lie and shook his head somberly as though I had done it on purpose.

If Pebble Beach was where the pros took a bath in the elements every January, then Palm Springs is where we dried out in the desert sun and crystal air in February. Strongly identified with the town, appropriately enough, are two mainstream golfing heroes—Ike, who loved to relax here, and Arnold Palmer, who loved to win here. He won the Bob Hope Desert Classic (formerly known as the Palm Springs Desert Classic, and before that as the Thunderbird Classic) five times in fourteen tries!

Palm Springs is a wealthy town, with a couple of dozen golf courses and about one swimming pool for every six permanent residents. Few of its homes are more luxurious than the McCulloch residence, where touring pros Jimmy Demaret and Lloyd Mangrum used to stay and where I have been lucky enough to stay every year I've played in the Classic since 1958. In fact Bob and Basie McCulloch introduced me to many of my showbiz friends.

Besides having money, Bob McCulloch has an engineer's passion for contriving gadgets and solving mechanical problems. He oversaw the stone-by-stone transport of the old London Bridge from England to his land community in Lake Havasu, Arizona. His own house is a $2,000,000 Creative Plaything. Push a button and the curtains across the room adjust themselves automatically to the incoming sunlight. Push another button at bedtime and the next morning, when you turn off your alarm, faucets in your tub turn on and fill the bath to six inches from the top, at your favorite soaking temperature.

I have had a lot of fun there though I have not always taken advantage of the bedside appurtenances. One year I fell in *like* (smart men do not fall in *love*) with an attractive young lady, so instead of coming home every day after my round, I went into town with her. Each morning I staggered into the McCulloch house just in time for breakfast.

Each night the maid came in to turn down my bed, but on the fourth night, Art Wall, who was supposed to be my roommate, quietly declared, "Alice, there's no need to do that for Doug. Obviously he does not sleep here in the evening."

Another year I returned late one night and found two young pros, Ray Floyd and Al Johnston sitting around a table with their dates laughing and cutting up. The only thing wrong with this was that the table was in the middle of the swimming pool.

"What are you doing out there with your jacket on?" I called.

"What do you mean?" Al shouted back. "You ever see a man attend a board meeting without his jacket on?"

McCulloch himself was an occasional practical joker. Once he asked me for help on his short game.

"How do I get backspin on my shots?" he demanded after dinner one night, handing me his wedge.

"Well, you got to hit down on it," I said.

"Show me," he said, dropping a plastic practice ball on the thick carpet.

So I hit an easy quarter-length wedge to give him the general idea.

"Show me with a full wedge," he insisted, retrieving the plastic ball and setting it down again. "Put all the spin you can on it."

So I made a full downward swing. A two-foot-long divot of carpeting flew through the air in the wake of the ball.

"Oh God, Bob," I said, abashed. "I'm *sorry.*"

"Well, all I asked you to do was put a little backspin on the ball," Bob replied after a long silence. He was staring at the bare floor showing through. "I didn't ask you to tear up my goddam carpet."

"I'm sorry, I'll pay for it," I said.

"You can't replace this," he said sternly. "It's from India."

Basie broke out laughing at this point, and it was then revealed that Bob had carefully set the ball down where the carpet had been ripped some time ago by Basie's brother, Jack, with *his* wedge.

I think people in civic life have been drawn to golf as much as people in show business. Maybe this is because, as someone once observed, golf is the best game in the world at which to be bad, and politicians usually are too busy to practice to improve. The tradition goes back centuries in the British Isles, where after all kings and queens used to endorse (or condemn) the sport with great vigor. The bond between Walter Hagen and the Duke of Windsor—probably the most famous link between royalty and sportsman—was formed on a golf course. Billy Casper's friendship with the King of Morocco may be the closest modern equivalent.

A practically unbroken succession of presidents and prime ministers have played the game in this century. My favorite story about Churchill has him playing, as a younger man, in a group in front of another group that included Wilfred Reid, a prominent professional in his day. At one point Reid hit a shot that flew dangerously near Churchill's head. In fact it grazed his ear. Churchill turned and called down the fairway in his booming voice: "Willie, that was the finest drive I have ever heard! Play through!"

In America, Ike has been our most conspicuous golfing president, but not the only one. Presidents Nixon and Kennedy both enjoyed the game. F.D.R. designed his own nine-hole course on Campobello Island. Warren Harding was a dapper hacker, closely involved in organizational golf; he donated a trophy to the USGA Public Links Championship which still bears his name. At one period, Woodrow Wilson played every day for exercise. William Howard Taft was once quoted as saying, "I would rather be out putting than President"—which no doubt went over big with his Democratic opponents of the era.

But no politician or statesman in Britain or America has ever matched Mr. Agnew's feat. In fact not even Astronaut Alan Shepard's unearthly pitch with a sawed-off 6-iron on the moon a year later would evoke as much wonder as the V.P.'s pass at my cranium. Fellow hackers warmed to it, political columnists had fun with it, comedians fueled their routines with it. Somebody said it made me "the Nathan Hale of the cashmere cardigan set."

Mr. Agnew was the brave one, though, not me. He was brave just to show up that day at La Quinta Country Club, one of the five courses in and around Palm Springs where the Bob Hope Desert Classic is staged. He had not played a round of golf in over a month. He did not even have time to hit practice balls that morning. He knew he was putting himself on the spot and that in the eyes of the media he would emerge at best in a standoff. Really, it was only his great affection for the game, and of course his respect for Bob Hope's various charitable actions over the years, that got him out there in the first place.

He didn't look too relaxed when he came to the first tee, which was jammed with cameramen for the occasion and surrounded by a couple of thousand golf fans. Our foursome this first year consisted of Agnew, U. S. Senator George Murphy of California, Bob Hope, and me. Counting the Secret Service, it was actually a twelvesome, not a foursome. Every time a soda can popped open, one of the security men jumped.

"Well, sir," I said, trying to think of something that might relax him, "you're the first Vice President I've ever played with."

"Yes," he replied, eying the mob behind the ropes. "My predecessors were too smart to get involved in something like this."

Of course the reason the V.P. had come was to boost the Eisenhower Medical Center in nearby Palm Desert, the main beneficiary of the tournament, and not to exhibit his golf swing. Hope had talked him into making the appearance.

Little did the V.P. realize how nervous I was to be playing with *him*. I had been selected as the pro in this foursome because of my ability to tolerate distractions—and to create a few myself—while playing. No one knew I would also be anxious to make a good impression on Mr. Agnew. I'm not a close political observer. But I had come to admire him for what I considered his public speaking ability.

Words have never been my strong suit and to hear them used well has always impressed me deeply. Among the vocabulary I never studied in high school were *desk, book,* and *homework.* In college I needed a tutor to get me through any sentence that did not begin with an "I." In analyzing a sentence, I could never tell a subject from a predicament. I get my point across, but no one accuses me of eloquence. My language is strung with corkers and curiosities.

I have a tendency to confuse similar sounding words, like predicate and predicament, or trigonometry and tracheotomy—which can be a problem if you've got something stuck in your throat.

Once I broke into a dinner party conversation between two men discussing fine art. I made a miserable entry with, "I am thinking of buying a couple of De Gaulles soon myself."

The fine arts men blinked at me and soon slid away. That gave me the chance to find out from my wife that what we were really thinking of buying were Chagalls.

I said to her, "I knew I shouldn't have corrupted their conversation."

"*Interrupted,* dear," she corrected.

Another time I described a jogging nut as a "health degenerate" and almost got him arrested.

I used to have a lot of trouble just pronouncing the word aluminum. This was no big problem until it suddenly began popping up in my golf clinics a few years back. Somebody would ask me, "Is the new aluminum shaft better than the steel shaft?"

And I'd reply in a roundabout manner, like, "Steel has certain playing characteristics that the other material you have just mentioned does not possess. On the other hand, that other material you are talking about may be suitable . . ."

Finally I did learn to pronounce aluminum—by visualizing the word in my mind just as I visualize a golf shot.

Anyway I wanted to make a good impression on this man I admired so much, as badly as the V.P. wanted to get off the tee halfway decently.

Neither of us really got what we wanted. The V.P., playing to an eighteen handicap, hooked his drive way left and the ball finished on a cart path. Senator Murphy, a sixteen handicapper at the time, put his tee shot about 150 yards down the right side. Hope, who had an eleven or twelve handicap at the time, was straight down the middle, as he usually is, about 200 yards. My drive finished about 250, also down the right side.

I stopped about half way to my ball, to wait for the others to hit their second shots. I stood on the right side of the fairway, leaning on Hope's $15,000 golf cart—a custom creation fronted by a giant caricature of Bob's famous ski-slope nose. I was chatting with the tournament queen, Barbara Eden (star of the "I Dream of Jeannie" TV show), whom Hope had talked into driving the cart for him.

Anyway that's when the V.P. took his second stroke of the day, the one that would become so famous. His ball had finished on a paved cart path, but he did not move it to a grassy area as he was entitled to do under the rules. Both the V.P. and his caddie were too nervous to get involved in jurisdictional disputes so early on. He just let it fly with his trusty 3 wood, and caught it on the toe of the club, angling the ball right. It was not a shank, as was widely reported. A true shank is hit with the hosel, the portion of an iron club where the shaft meets the head. Wood clubs don't have hosels.

Next thing I knew there was a blur as big as a basketball arriving in my vicinity. I joked later that I ran all the way across the fairway to get in the way of the shot, for its publicity value, but of course I had no chance to react. The ball caught me in the back of the head on the left side and I went down on one knee.

Once, caddieing as a kid in Cedartown, I had been struck on the head by a golf ball. At that time I estimated that the odds in a match between ball and human skull were eight to five in favor of the ball. Now I was prepared to revise the odds upward. This really was a celebrity tournament—I was seeing stars.

"Are you all right?" the V.P. said, rushing up a few moments later. Now I was rubbing my head and grinning, still somewhat stunned. The blow had broken skin and there was a little blood. The V.P. looked upset. "Can I get you a doctor?" he asked. "What can I do?"

"Nothing, sir, I'm okay."

Meanwhile of course the gallery didn't know whether to

laugh, cry or run back to the clubhouse. Neither did I, to tell you the truth.

"Here we are," the V.P. groaned, "with you our only chance to do well today, and I've wiped you out on the first hole."

"Please don't worry, Mr. Vice President," I said, trying somehow to placate him as well as to get myself organized. "My head is pure knotty pine. Besides," I added, pointing to his ball sitting up nicely about twenty yards away, "we got you back in the fairway."

I knew how he felt. One year at Pebble Beach I hit a lady in the gallery with a booming hook on the seventh hole. I had been playing only two or three shots behind the leader at the time, but I was so shaken up by the incident (and by the elements on the finishing holes, I should add) that I played the last ten holes in eight over par. Luckily the lady was not hurt by the ball, any more than was the poor man I had hit years before with an errant drive. I say "poor" because this man had been recently discharged from a hospital and was helplessly standing on crutches watching the tournament when my shot flew toward him. He had had two chances to get out of the way—slim and none.

Anyway, after that the V.P. never really had a chance, psychologically, to get his game going. I finished the tournament near the bottom, collecting $200.

"That's barely enough to cover your medical expenses," the V.P. joked. He apologized for preventing me from trying to match my performance here in 1966, when he knew I had beaten Palmer in a play-off.

"But I was drinking orange juice that year, sir," I said. Back then I would go on the wagon every January 1 and stay on it (sometimes letting my foot drag along the ground) until I won a tournament. That worked fine so long as I won by February or March. But if it got to be June or July and I still had not won, I would renege on the deal on the grounds that going to bed with Minute Maid every night was ruining my image.

"Still, you would have done better without me."

"Don't worry about it. We'll both do better next year."

"You don't want to play with me again!"

"Sure I do! It's my privilege!"

"No, it's mine!"

"We'll just have to practice in the meantime."

We had a pretty good team feeling going by the time we parted.

A little later I ran into former U. S. Senator George Smathers of Florida shortly after he had been in a luncheon meeting at the White House, where the Agnew-Sanders combination apparently had been the subject of some idle conversation.

"You know, Doug," said Senator Smathers, "you've made Mr. Agnew famous."

"I made *him* famous?" I replied in astonishment. If anything I knew it was vice versa. I had made headlines on the sports pages before. But never on the front pages.

The senator argued that the incident had made Vice President Agnew seem a little more human in the view of the general public. Thinking of next year's Classic, I sent off a note urging Mr. Agnew to hit a bucket of balls next time there was a break in the press of national affairs. Of course I knew he could not take time away from his duties to sharpen his golf game. On the other hand, it never crossed my mind that the 1971 Bob Hope Desert Classic would be even more challenging for us than the 1970 event.

In 1971 our foursome changed slightly. Instead of Senator Murphy we had the baseball Hall of Famer Willie Mays. Also there were many more photographers around the first tee, and greater crowds lining both sides of the fairway.

It was not the V.P. I was worried about on the first tee,

actually. It was Mays. Once in a while, Willie hit a violent
hook, I knew. If he uncorked one on his tee shot, with all
his natural power behind it, the ball surely would go through
four or five people before it stopped.

But once again it was the V.P., subject to a case of the jitters
that millions of other Americans have had, who misfired. In
fact he did it twice. Two tee shots went bouncing into the
galleries on the right side.

"Oh gosh!" I said each time.

No one was really hurt. In all the V.P. had grazed three
spectators. He went over to each of them, apologized profusely, made arrangements in fact to get in touch with them
later to be sure no injury had resulted (and to arrange a golfing holiday for them, at his personal expense), and finally
walked down the fairway shaking his head.

"I can't tell you how bad I feel," he said as I joined him. He
sounded like he was ready to quit.

"Well," I said, trying to make light of the whole thing, "I'd
probably be nervous addressing Congress too." That was
ridiculous—I would have been thrown out before I picked up
the gavel. I shrugged. "Hell, don't worry about it," I said,
"we'll get them next year," and I told him a joke.

In preparation for the next time, we did meet for a couple
of private fun golf outings. I was impressed with the V.P.'s
great stamina—he would play a dozen sets of tennis, nine holes
of golf, entertain guests for dinner, and then shoot pool in the
evening and still not look tired. I also discovered how strong
a desire he had to be good at whatever he did, including sports.

Basically the V.P. had a good strong swing. We worked on
his alignment. He had a tendency to aim to the right when he
stood up to the ball, and then to come across the shot in com-
pensation during the swing. This swinging-across is an action
well suited for tennis, at which he excels, but not for golf.

I also tried to get him to make his swing more compact.

His long, supple swing was not a swing he would be able to master unless he had time to practice a great deal to develop his rhythm, and obviously he did not have time to spare. So I tried to get him to reduce his swing arc by holding onto the club more firmly with his left hand—so he would not lose control of the club at the top—and by keeping the ball of his left foot on the ground throughout the swing.

We made great progress, but even so we seemed to be jinxed. Once we met at Palm Springs for a few days. One evening after dinner, we decided to play tennis on a lighted court. The V.P. and I challenged Tom Shaw, the young touring pro, and Barbara Marx, a vivacious tennis addict who lived nearby, to a game of casual doubles. In making a return that in fact won the match for us, I tripped and fell on my knee. By next morning the knee had swollen to the size of a grapefruit. I dropped out of the next golf tournament in Florida and flew home to Houston to recuperate. I tried to conceal the problem from the press, but I had to get off the plane in a wheelchair and some skycap must have tipped the wire services, because not long afterward both the Associated Press and United Press International had me on the line.

"Did the Vice President trip you?" said one.

"How did it feel when he threw his racquet at you?" said the other.

"Why are you people so interested in my limbs?" I said, knowing that the publicity that would come of this, no matter what or how I answered, would only make the V.P. look even more dangerous on the fields of play than he already looked.

His reputation as an athlete was unfairly tarnished by now, but he got some mileage out of it. In speeches he would soften up audiences by saying, "I shot 92 yesterday, which isn't bad considering that only two of them were seriously injured," or, "It's hard to concentrate on a tee shot when you hear the sound of hundreds of knees knocking in the background." But it is

doubtful how much he really enjoyed this role as high handicapper. In fact once when I saw him in Washington I reminded him that in five months we were to play in the 1972
Bob Hope Desert Classic, and he exclaimed, "Oh no, is it that
soon?"

In the 1972 Classic, our foursome included the V.P., Hope,
myself, and a newcomer, Frank Sinatra. Sinatra is probably
the most celebrated citizen of Palm Springs. He drives a
gleaming Rolls Royce with the license plate, FAS–1, and he
lives in a largish bungalow on Frank Sinatra Drive.

In spite of the casual air that Hope, Sinatra, and I tried to
affect, our trip to the first tee this time was more nerve-racking
for the V.P. than in the previous two years. There were people
wearing Spiro T. Agnew golf helmets—hard hats with funny
faces printed on them. Other fans carried placards with
pointed messages like, HE ONLY HITS THE ONES HE LOVES. A fake
medical team—including his personal physician, Dr. Bill Voss
—made up of tournament volunteers appeared dressed as
doctors and nurses with Red Cross bands on their arms.

The first hole at Indian Wells is not an easy driving hole,
either. There's water on one side, trees on the other and, for
this occasion, about five thousand people on both sides.

"Seventy per cent of your power, sir," I said to the V.P.
coachingly. "That's what I do. Just take it back nice and
smooth. All tempo."

The V.P. was introduced and there was a big round of applause. His hands were shaking as he addressed his ball. Everyone fell silent. It was impossible to imagine his finding the
composure to take that club back easily. But somehow he did.
The swing looked good. In fact it looked very good.

Until it made contact with the ball—a trick sphere that Hope
had secretly exchanged with the V.P.'s ball. The ball disinte-
grated.

Everyone clapped and guffawed. "That is it," I said to

Sinatra. "He cannot possibly come up with two super swings in a row." But he did.

At the end of that day's round, an old-timer came up to me and shook my hand for my score of 69. He declared it to be one of the finest rounds of golf he had seen in thirty-odd years of steady spectating. He could not understand how I managed to play so well between the buffoonery on one hand and the elaborate security measures on the other.

I told him my score for the round did not please me nearly so much as seeing the V.P.'s drive off number one. For Mr. Agnew somehow did find a second super swing, and his tee shot sailed down the center of the first fairway about 220 yards, with a nice rolling hook action at the end.

As we walked off the tee, I said, "Mr. Vice President, I don't know how you feel, but I feel like I've just won the tournament."

4 / Pro Golf Is a Pain in the Neck and a Few Other Places

A vice-presidential beanball is just a trifle in the life of a touring pro, of course, especially if he is accident prone, as I am. As I have said before, if I wake up some morning feeling good—with no aches, pains, bumps, or bruises—I'll know I'm dead.

I'm not the only one. The Ben Hogan Award is given annually to the golfer who has recovered from a physical impairment or who continues to play or support the game in spite of the impairment. Every year I notice the list of nominees getting longer. I know why—because so many touring pros are becoming eligible. Wrenched sacroiliacs, floating spinal discs, twisted neck vertebrae, strained arm and leg joints, and internal wear and tear like ulcers are some of the strictly occupational maladies found on the modern pro tour.

Just to list them hurts me. Golfers may not be athletes, as some maverick columnist suggested a few years ago. But you've got to give us credit for getting banged up like athletes.

We're all making medical history out on tour and I am in the first chapter. Jim Hereford, who runs an insurance agency in Dallas and specializes in selling medical insurance for professional athletes, says I've collected more money on my policy over the years than any other client—I get $1,000 per week whenever I am off tour on account of injury or illness. Actually sometimes I skip filing a claim, I feel so bad about it.

I'm not bragging. My slogan is, "Neither a hero nor a hypochondriac be." It's just that I've had such a variety of mishaps. And after forty years I have developed a mildly effective attitude for dealing with the physical problems. One chilly morning at the Greensboro, North Carolina, Open, I needed a shot of Novocaine to relieve the pain in my wrist so I could grip the club. I sent for a doctor in town—the tour has no "team physician" though it could use a staff of them. He got to me on the fifth hole, after I had floundered through a couple of bogeys with a hand and a half. It was so cold the doctor's hands were shaking. He couldn't hold the needle still. "Watch out for my knee!" I cried during one of his frostbitten lunges. Finally I used one hand to hold his hands steady so he could zap me with his needle in my other hand.

Actually there are better reasons than this somewhat comical forbearance for why I get the game on even though I'm hurting.

One reason is I want to earn money, and this requires getting outside on the course and not locking myself up in a shell with my problems. Self-pity, I have discovered, is not compounded semiannually.

Another reason is the example of my family, and particularly my blind brother, Ernest. All my relatives have had tough luck with accidents and ailments, it seems, yet I have never heard any of them bitch about it.

Mine was one of many families down south that was dirt-poor even before the Depression got started. When I was growing up in the 1930s, my father walked five miles a day to a job that paid him $2.50 a week. Some nights my mother dallied until she was sure everyone else in our family of seven got enough to eat, before she sat down for supper herself.

The strain of putting up with, or getting through, went way back apparently. My mother's grandmother used to tell about the day she watched her mother killing chickens left and right and stuffing them into a mattress, in preparation for something the history books later called Sherman's march through Georgia. People talk about America never having lost a war, but in a way, half of us lost that one, and my early family among others felt it sharply.

Naturally I'm proud of the ability to endure that seems to have existed in my English-Irish-Indian forbears, and though I'm the least courageous of the lot, I try to copy it when I can.

I also agree with my friend Francis H. I. Brown, the man who took golf to Hawaii back about the time of the first pineapple. When he turned eighty recently, he shrugged, raised his glass, and said, "Well, if I'd known I was going to get to be this old, I would've taken better care of myself."

I want to give you a kind of medic's report on my career without getting gruesome about it. I think it will bring out some of the strains of competitive golf that may not be widely appreciated, as well as fill in a few more of the low spots and ludicrous junctions in my life.

Some of my ailments stemmed directly from the way I picked to play golf long ago, or rather, the way my style of play picked me. The nine-hole golf course in Cedartown where I began playing as a kid had a tight layout. The hole where I usually practiced, after I had gotten started in the game, had brambly honeysuckle vines running down one side and a creek running down another. Without thinking about it, I played for accuracy long before I played for distance. The same thing applied when I would sneak shots between holes as a caddie.

I owe the phrase "telephone booth swing" to a Detroit sportswriter who saw me win the Western Open in 1958 when I was in my second year on tour. The swing really came from my Cedartown days and for a while I tried to convince people that maybe "compact swing" was a fairer description of it. But like another product of Detroit called the Edsel, "telephone booth swing" was funnier and it stuck.

The point is, I learned to hit down hard on the ball with my short backswing in order to apply extra force to the shot, rather than to sweep through the ball as most touring players do. Dick Mayer used to say I hit the ball with nervous energy. In fact, if I hit it with any single thing, it was the Popeye knot of muscles that developed in my forearm over the years through repetition of that downward stroke that jarred into the ground like a back hoe.

Sam Snead's swing—a model of graceful and efficient golf —was long, loose, and lovely. Snead's whole body absorbed the shock of the action. My swing was short, tight, and homely. When I dug into the ball, the shock waves registered in my hands, arms, and shoulders. Over the years the shock waves had their effect. That's why I need roughly two dozen shots of cortisone or Novocaine in those joints every year to keep going now.

Yet I know the shorter swing would be easier for the weekend player because it is simpler and does not require finely developed control and timing. It is not injurious to the amateur player. I've suffered from the swing only because I've used it so often—playing about forty tournaments and fifteen exhibitions a year, plus devoting thousands of hours to practice.

Some other problems originated because of my particular

makeup. For example the skin on my hands is unusually sensitive and it took years for me to condition it to the violence of my swing. As a youngster I practiced every day, but not without going through a painful ritual. First I soaked my hands in hot water for about twenty minutes, to soften the calluses I had formed in the practice session the day before. Then I packed cotton between my fingers and slipped on two old golf gloves—gloves discarded by club members and picked out of the trash barrel. Then I would hit balls for another twenty minutes or so until the calluses and cracks would open up. The gloves would fill with blood and at last I would be able to make a full pass at the ball and begin to practice comfortably.

Even after I turned pro in 1957, I had problems with my extra-sensitive skin. During a tournament in Flint, Michigan, a callus split between the middle finger and forefinger on my right hand. It became infected and I had to leave the tour for a few weeks to let it heal. When I returned, I taped the two fingers together near the base whenever I played or practiced, to prevent a reopening of the wound, a habit I still follow. The white tape on the fingers along with the golf tee stuck behind my ear became my trademarks, though not everyone realized it. One year the Internal Revenue Service questioned my income tax return—they wanted to know since I was not a doctor why the hell I would deduct $650 on Johnson & Johnson adhesive tape.

I am also cursed with poor circulation. In the morning I need a steam bath and a massage before I'm limber enough to turn off the alarm. My blood moves as slowly as my mail. My extremities have a tendency to stay asleep long after the rest of me is ready to go.

If I turn my neck at just the right angle to one side or the other, I can totally shut down half my internal transportation system. I first noticed this problem in high school when I would doze off during class. (The reason I slept during the day back then was because I spent most of my nights working late at the golf club, as an errand boy and aide-de-camp for the pro and club manager.) I used to take off my shoes for these mid-lecture snoozes—to reduce the chance of my feet going numb on me—and once I woke up and walked to my next class before I noticed I was in my stocking feet. Under a picture of me in a yearbook, they printed:

"Doug even stayed awake for this picture."

My final natural ill is an unusually rigid frame. If I touch my toes without bending my knees it means I have fallen over. I stand up to the ball in a wide, stiff-legged stance and, to make matters worse, start my swing from a dead standstill, rather than from the waggling action of one kind or another that most golfers employ to set their swings in motion. The more tired or tense I feel, the longer I stand over the ball and the tighter my back muscles become.

Nowadays I regularly shoot cortisone into the scapular muscles in my back. My orthopedist in Houston said I developed "secretary's complaint"—something common to office workers who spend six or seven hours a day hunched over a typewriter or adding machine.

"Secretary's complaint?" I said when he first informed me. "Doc, I don't care how you treat it. Just please find a better name for the distress."

The game of golf itself, as it is played on tour today, puts enormous strain on the healthiest specimen. After all, were humans really meant to play a sport in which the participant competes against 1) himself, 2) the golf course, and 3) 150 players who are also competing against 1) themselves, 2) the golf course, and 3) 150 other players? In my first fifteen years on tour, purse money went up by eight times. Tension and fierceness of competition increased as much. Today if you mis-hit one shot during a tournament, a thundering herd of rivals rushes past you before the ball has landed. If the competition gets much tougher, we will carry handguns instead of putters.

That is one reason why, when I am playing well, I find it so hard to drop off tour to nurse some minor physical problem—I know that chances to score well or win are not as frequent as they used to be on tour. I don't want to quit when I'm playing poorly, because then I will have to sit home and think about my rotten game. So I wait until I'm playing well again before I decide to stop. And then, of course, I decide not to stop because I'm playing so well.

This sort of circle can be pretty vicious to the person roaming around inside it.

Then there are the unusual weather conditions. I mentioned the hostile climate on Monterey Peninsula in January. You could die of exposure out there almost as easy as three-putt. Extreme heat is more common on tour. One Fourth of July I played in Dallas when the temperature was 110 degrees in the shade. On the second to last hole of the final round, when I tried to tee up my ball, I fell to my knees with faintness. I was as white as Casper the ghost.

How about the freak accidents that strike at the hapless touring pro? One year a British pro named Guy Wolstenholme bumped into a tree along Cypress Point's famous sixteenth hole during the Crosby and shattered a bone in his elbow. "I knew this hole was tough," cracked Arnold Palmer, who was his playing partner, "but I didn't think it could break your arm."

A good physical conditioning program, which younger pros seem to adopt as a matter of course, would have protected me from some abuses, but I suppose it never seemed right for my living style.

Once during a social round of golf with Joe Louis, he was telling me how much he owed his success in the boxing ring to being in tiptop shape before each bout. Then he said, "Why don't you go into training for a year and see what happens?"

I looked at him with gaping mouth.

"Well, what about two months?" he said.

My expression changed but only slightly.

"Would you do it for two *weeks?*" he finally pleaded.

Not long after that, in fact, I did purchase a pair of shin-splint-proof track shoes and a dashing jogging suit. I think of Joe Louis every time I come across the items, still wrapped like new, in my suitcase or bureau drawer. I'm afraid I am too much like Porky Oliver, who once explained a good score by saying, "I turned over a new leaf. I went into serious training for a month and lost one pound, three ounces."

Frank Stranahan was the first real conditioning nut I met on tour. His father, Bob, who founded the Champion Spark Plug Company, had been an active amateur player for years, giving up competition, I think, when he shot an exasperating 85 during a storm in the Western Seniors one year. After that the elder Stranahan devoted his golf time to building son Frank, and other good local amateurs, into championship-caliber players. He was an impartial supporter—once he gave a plant worker a few days off to prepare for the district golf championship, and the guy ended up beating Frank in the final.

The younger Stranahan's interest in body-building and such never got much attention because interest in fitness was not so widespread those days. Frank was not much concerned about public opinion in any case, and would jog along Fifth Avenue in a sweat suit as soon as take a gimmee.

Once we occupied adjoining rooms in a Los Angeles motel. Rain had canceled the day's round and we were at loose ends.

"Let's go down to the gym," he suggested.

"What's a gym?" I said.

"Come on, we'll work out."

"Frank, I don't want to use all my strength lifting bars and bells or whatever you do down there," I said. At this time we were both single and ready to entertain the fair sex at any hour. "What if there arises the opportunity for an afternooner?"

He could not talk me into going with him. So finally he asked me to sit on his shoulders.

"At least I'll get *some* exercise," he said as he began doing knee bends with me on his shoulders. After eighty knee bends —he counted them out in an angry voice—I couldn't stand it any more.

"Let me down," I cried. "I'm exhausted!"

For all my indolence, I have never doubted the effectiveness of conditioning programs for any player willing to follow one properly. Anytime Gary Player and I are playing in a tournament that is on a hilly course, for instance, I know he has an advantage over me. The advantage is not just physical either—I feel sure that fitness produces greater mental alertness, and builds decisiveness, which is an especially important trait in competitive golf. Of course Gary was training himself vigorously right at the start of his career, because he felt he had to make up in developed strength what he lacked in natural stature and power. Like Stranahan in earlier years, Player doggedly chalked up his three or four miles of running every day no matter where he was or what he had to do to do it. One year in Japan he jogged up and down hotel hallways for an hour, and the next morning other guests spoke of the "clazy little Amelican (they thought he was a U.S. pro) in black pajamas."

I did not have an injury-free year on tour until 1961—when I won five events and finished third in total money earnings, as high as I've ever finished. My most bizarre misfortunes occurred before 1961. The first was that infection in the callus between my "trigger fingers." I had turned professional on

December 7, 1956, but the rules in those days made me ineligible to compete regularly on the U.S. tour for another six months. So I played on the Caribbean tour and did not start officially in the U.S. until the Carling Open in June of 1957. Ken Venturi, who was fated to run into greater inhibiting physical problems during his career, happened to be making his pro debut in the same event, and oddly we tied for fourth place. It was two months later that my callus split, forcing me out of play for a month.

The next February, I went to South America to play in the Caribbean tour events I had played in the previous winter. During the Colombian Open in Bogota, I made a shot from a bad lie in the roots of a tree. When I stretched around the tree to see where my ball went, I tore several ligaments in my right ankle. That put me on crutches for five weeks and on a cane for six more.

I rejoined the tour in mid-May, managed to win a tournament (the Western Open), and then developed a soreness in my left hip that made it hard for me to swing the club with any force. This time I dropped off the tour for three months, returning in late 1958.

Next problem came in January of 1959. During the second round of the Tijuana Open in Mexico, I got severe chest pains. On the fifteenth hole I had to withdraw. They rushed me to a specialist in La Jolla on the American side of the border.

The doctor examined me and said I had a slightly enlarged heart that occasionally skipped a beat.

"That skipping of beats sounds bad to me," I said gloomily.

"Do you smoke?" he asked.

At this time I smoked four packs a day. I offered to cut down to three and a half packs. The doctor shook his head.

"Cut it out altogether. Slow down fast. Get off tour."

At first I did not heed his instructions, but I changed my mind when I discovered something strange happening in my golf game. I started having trouble drawing the club back from the ball. At first glance this seemed almost laughable to me. It would be as though a professional hockey player suddenly started slipping every time he stepped on the ice. But it turned out to be quite serious, and was a fitting climax to the two and a half injury-plagued years I had spent on tour, and to the marriage that was coming to a skidding halt before it was time to get the third anniversary present.

Not having a waggle—a little preliminary move to set the body in motion—made the trouble worse. I would stand up to the ball and say to myself, "Pull the trigger, you rat son of a bitch, I don't care where it goes, just swing, go, go," and nothing would happen. The harder I tried, the tighter my muscles got. I'd squeeze on the grip with my left hand until my fingers became numb. My shoulder muscles tightened into cables lashed on my back. It got to the point where I would be totally exhausted after playing only four or five holes. And when I finally did swing, I immediately would start fretting about taking the club back on the next shot.

I noticed that it was only on wood shots and long iron shots that I had the problem. Later I surmised that it had to do with being indecisive and insecure about the target at the greater distances. My worry about being off-target became so intense that sometimes I actually stopped in the middle of the downswing, and that is not easy to do if you swing at a pro's rate of speed. Doing that, I actually snapped the shafts on my clubs twice.

A friend of mine who was a psychiatrist in Miami told me the story of some famous pianist who once had an analagous difficulty. He would sit down at his Steinway, throw his tails out behind him, raise his hands above the keyboard—and then freeze. He could play like hell once he hit the first note, but it was anguish to get that melody started.

Finally I faced the fact that my own melody wasn't going

to get started again unless I abandoned tour life for a while. In fact I felt sure the great scorekeeper in the sky was preparing to kick my ass off the course for good. I really believed I was jinxed—that if I bought a pumpkin farm, for example, they would call off Halloween.

I quit playing for four months. It was a boring and uncertain time for me. I forced myself to sleep more, to drink and smoke less, and to deliberately relax. Slowly but surely, I got the skip out of my heart, the bug out of my takeaway, and the man out of the marriage—by mutual consent, my first wife and I divorced.

But I was never one to learn from his own mistakes, at least not as quickly as others might. Just before the Masters Tournament in 1960, I got married again, and appropriately enough I wound up the year in agony. Shortly after Labor Day, my second wife's little daughter accidentally slammed a door on my hand. I dropped off tour for six weeks. Toward the end of this period, I was driving home from seeing the doctor who was taking care of my smashed fingers, when a car ran into my car from the rear and twisted my neck. I had to put my upper body in traction for two months. One thing good: the pain in the neck took my mind off the ache in the fingers.

Technically the next year of 1961 was a spotless one in my health records. I did spend a week in traction in Baylor Hospital in Dallas but I blamed it on the 1960 accident.

In 1962 I returned to accident-prone form though this time the mishaps did not prevent me from competing for a change.

I was sitting in my motel room two hours before I was supposed to tee off in the final round of the Pensacola Open— which I was leading—when I dropped an ash tray on the floor. The ash tray shattered and sent glass splinters into my bare foot. We raced to a doctor who X-rayed, probed, shot, and bandaged me in record time. I arrived at the course in an ambulance a few minutes before my tee-off time, leaped out, and slipped into my golf shoes. I shot 69 that day and won the tournament.

Later in the year, on the morning of the final round of the Oklahoma City Open, I jumped out of bed and pulled a muscle in my back so badly that I was virtually paralyzed. Off to another doctor, this time for whirlpool treatment, massage, and more shots. Then to Quail Creek Country Club where I shot 35-32—67, including a finishing eagle 3, to win again.

Next year began with another freak motel room accident. At this point I began to wonder why the National Safety Council spent so much time warning people about highway hazards when so much seemed to be going wrong indoors. I was in Hawaii, this time, and unpacking. I dropped a pair of socks on the floor, bent to pick up the socks, bumped against the table and chipped a bone in my little finger. I was out of action for five weeks.

That was the last of my curious domestic wounds. My later years featured duller but more persistent problems like bursitis, tenonitis, muscle spasms, stomach upset, and calcium deposits.

Periodically my takeaway slowed up again too, especially when I kept late hours. Once again I would check and double-check and triple-check my target and ponder and say to myself, "Hit it! Hit it, you dumb bastard!" But on the whole I managed to keep it in control.

I felt better finding out that other players had experienced variations on the same problem, and not just famous pianists. Toward the end of his career, I heard, Cary Middlecoff would become so hesitant that at times he froze in the middle of drawing on his golf glove. For a while Gene Littler had a tendency to freeze at the *top* of his backswing. In similar fashion, there was a top amateur player in Britain in the 1950s who experienced great hardship getting his driver back down to the ball after he had drawn it up, and sometimes would literally stagger out of his stance and replace his driver with the psychologically more manageable 3-wood. To be paired with him in a tournament was considered the kiss of death to your own game since, of course, his difficulties created so much anguish in onlookers too.

I could not have gotten through my string of illnesses and injuries, some ridiculous it seems in retrospect, and others still serious in my view, without the example of my family, as I mentioned. Of the five children in the family, only two of us, my sister Sara and I, reached maturity relatively unscathed. My sister Stella had a hemophiliac condition and both my brothers were victims of explosions. All three of them learned to handle their difficulties with dignity and good humor.

My oldest brother, Ernest, lost his eyesight when he was four years old. Playing in the Cedartown coalyard, he had found a dynamite cap and mistaken it for a firecracker. Caps were used to blow up pine stumps in the winter to make kindling. He lit this one and it blew up in his face.

Perhaps because he was so young when it happened to him, Ernest never treated his blindness as a handicap. In fact it seemed to prompt him to be especially decent to others.

Once when he was fourteen and I was nine, my father was driving us somewhere to shop for a guitar for Ernest. We picked up two hitchhikers—a mother and her son—in our old black Ford somewhere along Highway 27 outside town. While we rode along, Dad and the lady discussed her plans: she was going to California to find a new place to settle and a better way to make a living; her husband and another child had gone ahead.

I wasn't paying much attention to the conversation, but when the car stopped to let the travelers out, Ernest sat up straight and thrust his hand over the seat into the front. "You go on and take this, ma'am," he said, passing over his $13.50

originally marked for the guitar, a small fortune in those days in my eyes. "You need it more than we do."

My other brother, James, lost his right hand serving as a Marine in the Korean War. One night a grenade sailed into his foxhole. He grabbed it and sent it back where it came from, only it detonated before it got far. Nevertheless his action saved his fellow Marines, who were sleeping in the foxhole at the time, from serious injury or worse, and James was awarded the Bronze Star.

Of course the family had nothing but deep admiration and loving sympathy for James, but when Ernest went out to visit him in the California hospital to which James had been sent from the hospital in Seoul, it was to convey those emotions in Ernest's uniquely constructive way.

"I can't see you," he told James, when it seemed as if our brother was unusually downcast about his prospects as a one-handed man. "I can't see you," he said, "but I've got two good fists and I'll knock you on your ass with them."

James could not feel sorry for himself for long with Ernest in the room, obviously, so he chuckled and replied,

"Ernest, I believe I could handle you with one nub tied behind my back."

Ernest has many talents. He's an electronics wizard—he assembles and operates ham radios and such—a fair country and western guitarist, and an expert on U.S. geography. One recent Christmas I picked him up at the Atlanta airport and I relied on him to get me through the country roads back to Cedartown where we were having a family reunion.

But it is that way he has of seeing himself, though he has no eyesight, that makes Ernest so special in the Sanders album.

Late one night he went up on his rooftop to fix a television antenna. A little later a policeman drove by, noticed him, and naturally became suspicious.

"Hey, you," he called up. "What you doing up there in the dark?"

"I'm trying to fix this here aerial," replied Ernest.

"Don't you need a flashlight then?"

"Naw, can see just as well without one."

Another time he was visiting friends in Boston. One of the younger members of the family had a new motorcycle and invited Ernest out for a spin. Well, Ernest would ride the back of a buzzard if it sounded like fun.

Off they went into downtown Boston. They came to a red light at a particularly busy intersection. At this point Ernest thought he would light up a cigarette, so he stood and reached into his pocket for his pack. Just then the light changed and the motorcycle roared off.

That left Ernest straddling nothing but air, with cars whizzing by him on either side, and with no cane (he had left it home) to feel his way back to safety, if that would have been possible in the traffic.

The cyclist friend looked back in amazement from the middle of the intersection. He called, "I'll be right baaaaack, Ernest!"

And Ernest replied, "You goddam better beeeeeeee!"

Can you understand why we not only enjoy Ernest, but respect him a lot? Someone once said, "A quitter can't ever win, and a winner won't ever quit."

My brother has known that all along.

5 / *Mind Over Mutters*

Then there is the mental side. Three hundred years ago some medical tract printed in Amsterdam listed golf as a healthful exercise with the following qualification:

> Let the game be played without too much excitement, and above all, not for money or for the sake of winning . . .

No one followed that advice too closely, least of all modern touring pros. That's why Snead felt scared to death before every round in his prime, why Nelson would throw up his breakfast, and why Hogan moved around like a cat.

In the last chapter I mentioned without exaggeration (with very little, I should say) some of the physical problems that beset me on tour. The mental challenges have been greater, stranger, and even more persistent.

Let's face it, excitement, money, and the pride that comes in doing something better than anyone else can do—three no-nos according to those medieval Dutch physicians—are factors in almost every human activity, not just golf. How does someone succeed under the occasionally enormous pressure these factors place on you? Mainly, I think, a person develops habits or attitudes, mostly in youth, that carry him through the moments of greatest stress. A man does not think his way through crisis, as is popularly conveyed in adventure films: He sinks or swims on the basis of his natural or developed reflexes.

Two valuable mental habits were ingrained in me through incidents that happened when I was a youngster. The first one came when I was twelve and playing in my first real match against an adult. My partner was a soft-spoken accountant in town named J. A. Gammon, who had often hired me as a caddie. He had given me his old set of irons when he bought a new set, and otherwise helped me and advised me.

On this particular day he and I were paired against two other local merchants in a nine-hole match played for a quarter a hole. We were one up coming to the final hole, a par-5, and our opponents pressed, meaning the stakes were doubled. By the time we reached the green, Mr. Gammon and one of the other men had picked up. I was twelve feet from the hole in three. My remaining opponent was bunkered, likewise in three. To my shock, he promptly holed out the sand shot for a birdie. Now my twelve-foot putt looked much longer, of course. Only if I made it would Mr. Gammon and I win the quarter apiece.

Modest stakes of major import. I stood over the putt until tears came to my eyes and blood flooded my cheeks: I was choking so bad I couldn't swallow, or breathe. The whole world seemed to be collapsing around me. Finally I scuffed at the ball some way and it rolled half the distance to the cup. We had lost. Mr. Gammon patted me on the shoulder as we walked off the green, but I felt too bitter and ashamed to speak. I vowed to myself right then that I would never let a putt scare me again. I've missed a lot of putts since that day, of course, but not for choking.

My second lesson came a couple of years later when I signed up for a strongly fielded summer tournament in nearby La Grange, where Maurice Hudson, the pro at Cedartown for some years, had recently transferred. For my first match I faced the current captain of the University of Georgia golf team. A tough draw for a high school sophomore, but I held him even through eighteen holes. Then I stepped up to the tee on the first extra hole. I knew something was wrong because all at once I noticed how narrow the fairways were. Without realizing why, I just bunted my tee shot down the fairway.

As I walked off the tee, Maurice Hudson, a mild-mannered man with kindly eyes and glowing cheeks, came next to me. During his few years at Cedartown, Hudson had helped me quite a bit and I greatly respected him. Mainly he had inspired me to take golf and self-improvement seriously. When I had become good enough to play a friendly nine holes with him of an evening, he would always finish by saying something like, "You're not getting to your left foot fast enough, it needs work." His easy but firm, almost fatherly declarations made it possible for me—pleasurable even—to go hit balls for three or four hours to try to fix the problem. In those days few teen-agers played golf in Cedartown. I recruited the first high school golf team, and without the encouragement of men like Hudson and Gammon, and also E. J. Dugan, another local benefactor, I never would have devoted myself so fully to the game.

Anyway, after that bad tee shot on the nineteenth, Maurice

put his arm around my shoulder and said quietly, "Now, Doug, listen. More tournaments are lost than won by retreating on shots, which is what you just did. Don't play for second any more. When you're in a position to win, don't let up on your game. Holding back will get your swing in a mess of trouble."

Somehow I managed to beat the golf team captain in spite of the puny tee shot. Next day I drew another tough match— the tournament's defending champion. But once again I held my opponent even through eighteen holes. When I stepped up on the first extra hole, I knew how to feel and what to do. My drive flew far down the fairway, straight as frozen rope. I winked at Maurice Hudson, standing nearby. I went on to win the match and the tournament. But overcoming runner-up-itis with that tee shot was the sweetest moment in the week.

Choking and holding back are two familiar methods for fighting yourself mentally on the golf course. Indecision is another. I believe that was at the root of the slowness in takeaway I have experienced from time to time, which was always worsened by fatigue.

I mentioned luck earlier too. Bad luck seems to get to some golfers faster than others. The biggest egotists—the ones who believe the sun does not start moving through the heavens until they get up in the morning—are the most vulnerable. They're the ones who get torn up when something unpleasant unexpectedly befalls them.

I try to treat unfair fate as though it were passing through, like an unwanted in-law—and I never take it out to dinner. Bad luck falls as well as good, I say to myself, and sooner or later everything balances out. This formula never works clearly or in extreme cases. The man pinned under a tractor-trailer one week seldom wins the lottery the next week. Nor when I find my ball lying against a beer can, do I smile and reflect that a stock I recently purchased is now going to go up four points. But as an everyday proposition, the formula works: It helps you shrug things off instead of getting sullen.

Thus I recall my lucky shots if I find myself simmering in the juices of an unfortunate break. One such lucky shot I made in the 1968 Los Angeles Open. Aiming at the wrong green for the hole I was playing, I hooked a 4 iron and sent it flying way left. Moments later the air shattered with applause as, two hundred yards away, my ball came to rest on the correct green for the hole I was playing, six feet from the pin. "Man, that was a great hook you played," someone called from the side lines. "It was nothing," I replied, "I mean I had nothing to do with it."

Once on a dogleg par-5 at Silverado Country Club in California, I hooked my tee shot too close to the corner of the hole and the ball rolled into the edge of a shallow pond. When I reached the ball, I decided to play it out of the two or three inches of water in which it lay. I took off my shoes and socks, stepped into the water and began wiggling into a firm stance. As I wiggled, the muck under the ball started to rise, and pretty soon the ball was teed up high and dry.

Bad breaks in weather have to be taken philosophically by the golfer or else even tiny clouds on the horizon will begin to persecute him. The way I handle bad weather is to joke about it, which gets the problem out in the open where it often does less harm than locked up in your mind.

One year at the Masters, the Canadian player Moe Norman reacted to bad weather quite unexpectedly. But then he reacted in an antic spirit to a lot of things: He used to shock purists by auctioning off any trophy he won as soon as the presentation ceremonies were over.

This year it was blustery at Augusta when the tournament began. Moe played near par through six holes, and his tee shot on number seven split the fairway. Then, to the astonishment of the galleries and also his playing partner, Vic Ghezzi, Moe picked up his ball off the fairway.

"Too much wind for Moe," he declared, "too much wind for Moe."

That was the way he usually spoke, repeating things for emphasis.

A spectator called out, "Hey, you can't leave Vic out here playing by himself!"

"Why not? Why not?" said Moe. "Vic's a big man, a big man. See you later, see you later."

And he walked in.

If imagined problems don't eat at a golfer, he is likely to find fault with real ones—other people. No one on tour is ideal to play with, because no one dresses, talks, walks, swings, or putts exactly as one would like. Different playing tempos have created much hidden tension on tour. Some players don't need much time to hit—Trevino walks up to his ball and swings at it as though he's doing nothing more challenging than buying a tamale. But Nicklaus has a painstakingly deliberate procedure that he has to follow every time. With my grueling target orientation and takeaway I've often been conscious of seeming slow to galleries and especially of causing delay for my partners. That's why I always walk fast between shots, to make up for it. Sometimes I've told my playing partner in advance that I'm taking a little longer to get the club back. This kind of communication defuses a potentially explosive situation, I think.

Incidentally, I don't believe the touring pros are as much responsible for the slow play crisis in the U.S. golf as we are often made out to be. Many of the newer tournament courses, with their tremendous length and huge greens, are simply impossible to negotiate quickly, especially when you are playing for money. Modern golf course architects must shoulder some of the responsibility for slow play, too, and perhaps scale down some of those parking-lot greens on their drawing boards today.

One of the classic mismatches in playing tempo occurred in the final match of the 1955 PGA Championship at Meadowbrook Country Club near Detroit, which pitted Cary Middlecoff against Doug Ford. About Middlecoff they used to report jokingly, "two shots and twenty years later, . . ." while Ford liked to hustle all the time. He would be on the green checking his putting line before other players in his group had hit their approaches.

Ford won the match four and three, partly because he refused to let his opponent's different playing tempo rattle him or annoy him. In a similar situation, it was said that Ford once took a book and portable seat along and read a page or two whenever he felt the pace of the match had slowed up too much for him to bear.

Of course that little action—bringing along reading material—borders on needling. Needling is the deliberate effort to annoy your opponent so he can't concentrate, or undermine his confidence or self-esteem. True needling is an art; it is done so subtly that no one can ever say for sure that any needling has occurred. On the pro tour there are enough problems without having to face problems of needling and counter-needling, I suppose, but it does go on.

Needling uses the power of negative thinking a lot. Take a certain player who had a tendency to shank the ball. You could get him started shanking as easily as turning on a water tap, just by mentioning the word. Late in one round, an opponent said, "Well, looks like we'll be finishing in the shank of the evening," and blam, blam, blam, the other guy started shanking every shot.

Ask a player whether he inhales or exhales in his downswing, or make a remark like, "What kind of putter you got there with all that loft?" That brings his mind to rest on a technicality that has nothing to do with his game, and that will probably misdirect his concentration powers. Or say, "How can you play a shot with a grip like that and not hook it?" "I don't hook my shots." "With that grip you *got* to hook it, are you kidding me?" Pretty soon he'll start hooking every shot, or he'll knock every shot off to the right in an unconscious effort to be sure he doesn't hook.

Smiley Quick, a great needler on the tour in the 1940s, once played against a fellow who was absolutely impervious to Smiley's lances and arrows. All during the round, Smiley made pointed remarks about his opponent's swing, his taste in clothes, even his physical appearance. He finally lost the match and offered some half-hearted congratulatory remark.

"I'm sorry, you're going to have to shout," said the other at last. "I'm hard of hearing."

Maybe golfers are unusually thin-skinned among athletes because the game forces them to develop such extreme sensitivity. A golfer sometimes can visualize a shot so clearly that it practically burns through the sky toward its target in his mind. That's confidence. I've also been sure another player's shot was going to work too, or a long putt was going to drop. It is a kind of intuition that comes out of long experience in a certain field, I think, though I would never set up an off-course betting window on the basis of it.

The only protection a golfer has against the negative devils inside him, and the bad luck and adversity and needling and all the other crap outside him, is concentration. It also helps a player to draw on his experience more effectively. In the right frame of mind, a player can come to a tournament with a clear memory of every putt he made or missed and every dogleg he mis-played for that course.

I used to be able to lie in bed in the morning and mentally hit practice balls. I could actually find and correct an error in my swing that way.

Concentration is total absorption of the self in the act, and probably no one ever did it better than Hogan. He seldom talked during a round for that reason.

"Ben only said three words to me on the greens," Sam Snead always insisted.

"What was that?"

" 'You're away, Sam.' "

Once Hogan and Demaret were playing in a team event. They were five up after eleven holes in the match and Jimmy started to sing and quip with the galleries.

"Come on now, settle down," Hogan told him.

"About what?" said a startled Demaret. "They can't catch us in eight holes no way."

"If we keep fighting," Hogan said, amazing even Jimmy, who knew him well, with his determination, "we just may pull it out."

More recently, a younger pro named Babe Hiskey showed me the value of focusing on objectives. During the 1972 Danny Thomas Memphis Classic, Hiskey shot 80 in the third round. Realizing he had no chance to win much money in the fourth and final round tomorrow, he decided to practice with his 3-iron for an hour and see if he could win a new car the next day. On one par-3, a sponsor was offering an automobile to the player who put his ball closest to the pin during the tournament. It was a 3-iron shot for Babe, so he worked on it for the rest of the afternoon—and next day won the car.

I learned a lot about the power of concentration from my wife, Scotty. Once before we were married, in an argument with a friend, Scotty declared, "You can do anything you want if you set your mind to it."

"Not true," said her friend, who happened to be in the music business. "Say you wanted to be a singer? You have no experience, no proven talent. You couldn't do it just because you set your mind to it."

"I bet I could."

And suddenly it was a bet. For the next two months, Scotty studied almost daily with a voice coach, continuing in her job at the American Airlines office in Los Angeles all the while. Then she auditioned for a singing job along with hundreds of other applicants.

Without pulling strings, she got the job—a three-week singing engagement in Las Vegas with Eddie Fisher.

Nothing destroys your concentration faster than a bad temper. In the 1930s and 1940s, Clayton Heafner, Ky Laffoon, Bobby Cruickshank, and Bill Melhorn all had bad tempers and half the stories about them probably are true.

Heafner was a keg of dynamite who could go off at any time. One year he finished a tournament with a six when he had needed a four or five to win or place high. After holing out, he walked over to a nearby sapling and shook it furiously in his hands. At next week's tournament an announcer who had seen this display jokingly introduced Heafner on the first tee as "Clayton 'Tarzan' Heafner."

"You're getting paid to announce, not be a comedian," Heafner snarled. "Besides, you're not very goddam funny anyway."

Heafner proceeded to hit his drive off the toe and it flew low and straight into some rough-looking woods. He found the ball lying against a big rock. Normally his best tactic would have been to take a penalty and go back for another tee shot. But he wasn't about to return to the first tee. Finally he said to his caddie, "Pick that ball up, caddie. We're going in."

At about this time a woman burst through the underbrush and said, "Oh, Mr. Heafner, Mr. Heafner, please don't pick your ball up. I paid $1,200 for you in a calcutta!"

Heafner looked from the lady to his ball, and said, "Okay, caddie, just leave the sonofabitch there." Then he marched off.

In my time Tommy Bolt became most famous for furiousness. One year I played with him when he broke a club in two tournaments in a row, the first in Brookline, Massachusetts, when one of his tee shots dared to finish in the rough, the second in Cleveland when he four-putted a par-3 green after a spectator moved and distracted him during his birdie putt attempt. He finally stomped off the green and smashed his putter against the post of a television tower and the putter head went flying up in the air.

"What was that, a rock?" a cameraman called down.

"No," replied a spectator loudly, "that was Mr. Bolt breaking his putter."

"Goddam right it was Mr. Bolt," Tommy said, on his way to the next tee. "And I'll tell you goddam Yankees one thing, I will never play the game of golf north of the Mason-Dixon line again."

Of course if Tommy had been south of the Mason-Dixon line at the time, he probably would have said "goddam Southerners" instead. And he did return to play in the north again and again. To see his swing and his superb shot-making was worth the occasional outburst to most galleries. Many pros only wondered how many more tournaments a more placid Tommy Bolt might have won.

As Bobby Locke pointed out, "Temper never got anyone anywhere in golf." But it is probably an inevitable consequence of tour life and tensions. At the start of each new season, the pros are rested and amiable. We walk around during the first tournament like it's old home week. "Good to see you again!" "Enjoy your Christmas?" "How's the family?" "Good luck this year, I hope you tear 'em up!" A month later we're swearing under our breaths, rejoicing in each other's bogeys and glaring toe-to-toe in the locker room.

One year Doug Ford almost took a swing at me in the locker room, but I cooled him down somehow. Another time

Doug showed his fist to George Bayer which was a different story. George, bigger and stronger than both Dougs put together, picked up Ford by the collar and placed him in a nearby open locker, at which point Doug decided to resume the battle on verbal terrain.

Temper tantrums and other emotional displays became less common on tour because a stricter code of behavior evolved as the game got larger and as television transformed it into an even more publicity-conscious spectacle. When rules against throwing clubs began to be enforced, there were some catches made on tour during that period that rivaled Willie Mays in his prime.

Billy Casper once escaped penalty when he smashed his putter on a bench, by explaining, "I didn't break it, the putter just crystallized."

All the next week, pros kept warning each other facetiously, "Careful now, you might crystallize that club of yours!"

Personally I don't see anything wrong with breaking your putter now and then. If you hate it, why not break it? Usually you're better off without it anyway. During the first round of the 1973 Jacksonville Open, I bent my putter in two (there is no rule against bending) after missing a short putt on the sixth hole, then proceeded to make birdies on seven of the last twelve holes using a kind of raking stroke on the greens with my 2-iron.

Some rules, like some putters, really are made to be broken. I've been fined only twice in my career, once for actually busting a putter—during the 1964 Texas Open—and once for publicly criticizing the PGA. I was put on probation once too. That occurred during the 1967 Carling World in Toronto. It arose out of a disagreement about whether or not I was entitled to a free drop on a certain hole. Steve Shabala, a PGA tournament official, examined my lie and ruled I was not entitled to a free drop. As a caddie-yard type of golfer, I am used to playing out of bad lies and I could have gone ahead and played the shot easily enough. But on a previous hole I had happened to see a ruling made in favor of a free drop for another player, and I felt the conditions were identical, so after I finished the round I asked to go look at the other player's lie.

As the three of us—Shabala, Bob Rosburg, and I—rode over in the golf cart, Steve said, "When are you going to grow up and learn to accept the rules?"

"Aw, Steve," I replied half jokingly, "why don't you . . ."

I don't know what was worse, Steve's sanctimonious remark or my locker-room English. But I thought nothing more of it—I figured it was just another mildly exasperating run-in with the highways and bylaws of tournament procedures. That night another official called to tell me I had been disqualified for conduct unbecoming to a professional golfer and placed on probation as a PGA member.

Goddam! GODDAM!!! I was stunned, numb. I didn't know what to do. I sat and stewed in my hotel room. Here I was, an established golf professional, one of the game's leading money winners, involved in all sorts of serious business ventures, a responsible parent—summarily dismissed from the only thing that gave my life meaning, by someone whom I felt had acted somewhat beyond the bounds of his position anyway. Not that I didn't respect and genuinely like most of the PGA field staff, whose unheralded work in smoothly running so many tournaments a year, involving so many detail decisions and so much coping with individual personalities, was nothing short of amazing. But at this time the encounter was too rough to shrug off. In fact it was such a violent shock to my sense of myself that I started to stutter every time I opened my mouth. I holed up in my room for a few days, joined by a friend, Bobby Freedman, who flew in from Los

Angeles after talking to me on the phone and realizing how badly shaken up I was.

It took a few weeks for me to get rolling again. The stuttering ended and I went back on tour, but the harsh memories of the shock lasted for many months afterward.

That was the run-in with the rules that hit me in the gut the hardest. The most famous one came in 1966 when I was disqualified from the Pensacola Open for failing to sign my score card. It was the first time in modern PGA history that a tournament leader was sent packing.

I was playing as well as I ever played the week that it happened. I shot 64 in a practice round on the tournament course at Pensacola Country Club. I shot 30 on the front nine the next day. In the pro-am event on Wednesday I shot 67. Next day in the opening round I shot 63. Friday it rained too hard to play. Then on Saturday I shot 67 for a two-round total of 130. This gave me a four-stroke lead over Gay Brewer and at least a seven-stroke lead over any other contender. In modern professional golf this is an unusually strong position—an almost insurmountable lead over everyone in the field except one player, and a pretty good lead over him. If I wanted to lose this tournament, I would have had to practice to do it.

On Saturday, though, I putted out on the ninth green, which was the eighteenth hole in my round since we had started play on the back nine. The fact is of passing significance since the official scorer's tent was set up near the eighteenth green. At the ninth green, though half the field would finish here, there was no place set up for a golfer to sit down and go through the routine business of verifying his and his partner's scores.

Anyway, I was soon surrounded by autograph seekers, mostly youngsters, and I began putting my signature down on the scraps and torn pages and tablet sheets extended to me. I used to stock autographed photos in my golf bag to pass out to kids when I would finish a round, when the demand was really high, because otherwise my fingers would get worn out.

I've signed autographs on hands ("I'll never wash again!"), clothes, shoes, plaster casts, and panty girdles. Once I was standing in a bar in Miami when an unknown woman came up to me, yanked the front of her dress down, and asked me to sign my name around her nipple. She gave me a felt-tip pen to do it with, and I was preparing to write my name and maybe a few long sentences down too, but her boy friend appeared and made me get it over with. Another lady made a similar request once. I knew she was fickle by the number of other signatures across her bosom.

Anyway, at Pensacola, an elderly woman now appeared among the youngsters, whom I had pretty much finished with, and said, "Oh, Mr. Sanders, I've been trying to get your signature for three years now." She handed me a sheet of paper and I put it on top of my score card, which I had just checked hole by hole for the third time. Unconsciously, I must have thought that when I signed my name for the woman, I had signed my score card. Because after I handed her the autograph, I gave my card to a runner to take over to the official scorer's tent.

Shortly after, Doc Giffin, PGA press secretary and later an aide to Arnold Palmer, sped up in a golf cart.

"Come on," he said, "they're waiting for you in the press tent." There was a special urgency, he explained on the way over, because West Coast writers were trying to make early deadlines for their Sunday columns.

In the press room, for the standard post-round leader's interview, I was saying something like, "I think I could be four shots *behind* and win the tournament, the way I'm feeling right now," when another official showed up with the bad news: I had been disqualified for violating Rule 38, Section Two, which states:

> The competitor shall check his score for each hole, settle any doubtful points with the Committee, ensure that the marker has signed the card, countersign the card himself, and return it to the Committee as soon as possible. The competitor is solely responsible for the correctness of the score recorded for each hole.

When I got back to my motel room, deflated and enraged and miserable and annoyed all at once, I immediately got a phone call from Bear Bryant, the legendary hard-driving Alabama football coach ("That's all right, fellas," he used to say at half time if his team was behind, "if we don't win today, we'll win in practice on Monday."). We had played together in the pro-am at Pensacola three days earlier.

"Doug, this is Coach," he growled. "I just heard the goddurn news. What's first place?"

"It's $10,000," I told him.

"You got it," he barked. He wanted me, then and there, to write the figure, his name and my name on any old piece of paper, and send it to his bank in the morning.

"It's very kind of you, sir."

"Just sign that goddurn piece of paper and they'll give you the $10,000."

There were other notable expressions of support. Jacksonville mayor, later Florida governor, Hayden Burns called my disqualification "embarrassing" and urged the PGA to update its regulations. First Flight, my equipment company affiliation at the time, sent me a check for $1,000, the amount it had agreed to give me as a bonus for each tournament victory I achieved (I cashed that check but not Bear's).

I felt wronged and I managed to get that feeling across to reporters who came around to see me on Sunday. I called the rule "asinine" and I said that if Arnold Palmer had failed to sign his score card, officials would have been willing to run halfway across the country to keep Arnie in the tournament. Here I was, defending champion at Pensacola (I had beaten Nicklaus in a play-off in the 1965 tournament) with no convincing evidence that anyone in officialdom really cared if I kept playing.

They cared in some ways. For my public complaining that day, the PGA fined me $100.

Actually the incident came at an awkward time. Previously PGA tournament supervisor Jack Tuthill had declared that the score-card rule was going to be strictly enforced. Prior to that, if a player had not signed his card, someone would chase him down in the locker room or parking lot. Once an unsigned score card caught up with Dave Marr in his hotel room, and he was as low as twentieth place for the tournament.

But six weeks before Pensacola, Tuthill had gone on record about strictly interpreting the rule. And the week before, he had disqualified Howie Johnson for not signing his card. With a score of 79, Johnson had not been in contention and in fact had been glad to get out of the tournament. Later, on tour, as strict enforcement of the rule continued, it became standard practice to deliberately fail to sign a score card, or to deliberately enter a wrong score for a hole, in order to get out of an event where one had no chance to win or no desire to keep playing for personal reasons. Thus the PGA's policy of enforcing this rule eventually made liars, not honest men or good bookkeepers, out of the touring pros. Since then the PGA decided to permit withdrawal without penalty after completion of any round.

It also seemed clear to me, at least at the time of my disqualification, that I was never going to get the special consideration from officials and functionaries and clerks and middle-level exec types, that players of "sounder" character and "safer" personality obtained. Once as an amateur I had been harshly questioned on my amateur status by a panel of U. S. Golf Association officials, and I felt then, perhaps mistakenly, that my particular style of life was also being judged by these sober well-meaning gentlemen. Now I seemed to have inspired distrust or perhaps envy among the established powers in professional golf too. I don't know whether it was because of my partying and girl-chasing, odd hours and zany friends and endless celebrating, or whether it was because I did all of this openly, that created the aloofness. It was a feeling I never bothered to substantiate, or troubled to overcome, and I knew in the long run it would be better left unexpressed anyway.

After the Pensacola tournament (which Gay Brewer went on to win), I got thousands of letters from fans. But nothing amused me and touched me more deeply than a poem written by a youngster named Peter Fleming, a student at a Pensacola high school. His civics teacher had asked the class to write essays on some "current and controversial subject." I still know by heart the poem that Peter submitted:

> Saturday was a crucial day
> When Sanders lost his right to play.
>
> Deadly with wood, iron and putter,
> But unable to write, we now discover.
>
> There he was, ahead by four,
> When officials said, 'Can't play no more.
>
> 'No more practice at your game
> 'Until you learn to write your name.'

Rule 38, Section Two,
Now has Sanders oh so blue.

Oh so blue is human error they say,
But what a drastic cut in pay.

6 / The Wheelchair Gambit and Other Curious Matches

Gamesmanship and hustling are not treated in the "Rules of Golf" but they have shaped and flavored the sport some. Titanic Thompson, one of the greatest hustlers in American sporting annals, put his finger on what it is all about when he said not long ago, "To be a winner a man has to feel good about himself and know he has some kind of skillful advantage going in."

I grew up feeling good about myself as a golfer and didn't need to or care to make some of the arrangements the professional hustlers made to win. Confidence was a big enough edge as far as I was concerned.

When I was thirteen I went to Augusta to play in the Georgia State Junior. I was a rough-looking boy with long black hair and blue jeans. I had no money and carried my own clubs. In my first match I faced a local city boy who had his own caddie and a weekly allowance. I teed up my ball and said, "I'm Sanders from Cedartown, I'll play you five, five and five."

My proposition ($5.00 on the front nine, $5.00 on the back and $5.00 total) unnerved the other boy so badly his hands started shaking. He couldn't get his tee into the ground.

But betting and bootlegging (Georgia still leads the nation in the production of moonshine) were important diversions in Cedartown when I was growing up and they started to influence the kind of golf I played at the town's nine-hole course. If it had not been for some stern outside opinions on my activities, and my own increasing desire to achieve some kind of legitimate success, I might have turned into a full-time hustler myself.

In seven years at grammer school I never missed a single day of school. But in high school my attendance record was almost as bad as my scholastic. First I just took off an occasional half-day to play or practice by myself. I would fake written excuses from my mother to get out of afternoon classes. The one time I really did get my mother to send an excuse for me, the teacher studied the unfamiliar hand, looked up at me severely and said, "You wrote this, didn't you?"

Then I began skipping school for matches that older men in town arranged for me. Sometimes they would drive me two hundred miles to a match. When my game really came into its own, the men started bringing golfers in by airplane to play me. They paid me $50 to play each match, with a bonus of $10 for each birdie I made, and a penalty of $5.00 for each bogey. For a time I had more money than I knew what to do with. At school I once had to borrow 25¢ to buy my lunch in the cafeteria because I knew the cashier wouldn't have change for a $100 bill.

One of the men who occasionally set up a match for me was

an amiable and colorful character named Red Greenway, whose nephew, James R. Greenway, later became my side-kick and close friend on tour for some years. Red ran to extremes in his standard of living. One day he'd show up at the club in a snazzy green convertible with a wad of bills in his pocket. Next day he'd be walking and not have a quarter to his name. That was the way luck treated him.

Red had developed various "skillful advantages" besides betting on me. He regularly outshot the top pool hustlers who came through town every year looking for action. He could fashion a bet out of any circumstance—what parts of Cedartown would get rained on during an approaching summer storm, for instance, or whether the next car to drive into town from the west at dusk would have its lights on. He also had trained an old bulldog to urinate on command and to jump off bridges, and that brought in some cash. He would use the dog in what are called proposition bets.

Red would station the dog on top of a bridge, then find some way to walk along the bridge in the company of a sucker. Upon nearing the animal, Red would say, "Gawdam, that little bulldog is going to *swim* for it."

"Are you kidding? Dogs don't jump off bridges."

"I can tell by the look in that bitch's eye, and I got $50 that says I'm right."

"Well I got $50 that says you're full of grits."

At which point Red would whistle once and the old dog would promptly jump into the river.

I was cocky and naive and did not realize I was something like that trained bulldog myself in those days, or what might be the consequences if I kept it up. I liked Red and the other gamblers a lot, but I also respected E. J. Dugan, J. A. Gammon, and most of all, Maurice Hudson. The week after I won the National Junior Jaycee Championship in Durham, North Carolina, Mr. Hudson took me aside and said, "Now you got yourself a chance to get a scholarship to college, Doug. But not unless you stop messing around with gamblers."

I didn't really quit playing for the gamblers, though, until the day I overheard the terms of a match I was involved in. Standing on the first tee, I heard my opponent's backer say to my backer, "What if you lose, where you going to get the money?"

"Shoot, I'll put up my house," said my backer. "I'll pay you with my mortgage."

I played that round under more pressure than I had ever felt before. I kept thinking that somebody's house—the home of a man and *family*—was riding on my skill. I didn't like the sweat at all. Nor did I care for the kind of caution that was suddenly creeping into my game. I found myself making overly safe decisions about club selection and taking too long on key putts.

All in all, I finally decided it would be better in the long run if I followed my older friends' advice, and I did.

But hustling and gambling, I soon discovered, were not confined to Cedartown, Georgia. I got an athletic scholarship to college, as the men had predicted. During my three years at the University of Florida—I "quituated" in 1955—I had a chance to play golf all over the country and I found out how widespread the betting instinct was. In those days betting was taking place at a lot of calcutta tournaments. Sometimes the bets totaled over $300,000. But those larger calcuttas attracted a breed of ringers and con artists to rival the most flamboyant creations of Damon Runyon.

The most common subterfuge was for a player to enter a calcutta with an inflated handicap. Before the calcutta season began, he might run his actual handicap of four, say, up to eleven or twelve, by losing match after match to friends and paying off his losses by check. If the calcutta chairman questioned his handicap, the man pulled out his check stubs and said, "You think I'm losing all this money for my health?" Actually his friends would have returned all the "lost" money to him in cash, in return for a piece of the larger winnings later on.

After the player was accepted, he would buy himself or his own team for $10,000. In the bigger calcuttas, first place was worth as much as $50,000. Even if he came in second or third —with his inflated handicap, his chances to come in first were excellent—he would make out financially. And he'd have five or six more calcuttas to play that summer.

Of course one man's idea of luck may be another fellow's definition of cheating. Ray Ryan, who used to be a member at LaGorce in Miami, once played a round with a man known as The Count. On an early hole, The Count hit a shot into a jungle of bushes and water. He plodded in after it and shortly called out, "Hey, Ray! Look how lucky I am. My ball ended up on a bird's nest."

And The Count proceeded to play out.

A few holes later, when Ryan hit into the woods, it was time for a kind of revenge. Ray disappeared among the trees and a few moments later came back and announced, "Hey, Count! Come on over here and look. You won't believe how lucky I am. My ball rolled up on a big wooden tee!"

The most unscrupulous act I ever witnessed on the golf course occurred early one evening on the eighteenth green at the old Tam O'Shanter Country Club in Niles, Illinois. I had finished playing a practice round earlier in the day and was on my way to the parking lot. I stopped under a big tree to watch a foursome coming up the final hole. Later I heard the players in this particular foursome were prominent Chicago underworld figures and that about $20,000 was riding on the match. (In those days, the average first prize on tour was only $3,000.)

There was a ball sitting up nicely in the bunker on the right side, near where I was standing. The golfers came up in their carts and got out. Three of them went toward the left side of the green and one toward my side.

This near golfer did not see me, or if he did, he didn't care, because he walked directly into the bunker, put his foot on the ball and ground it firmly into the loose sand. I was amazed. I could understand his creating a buried lie for the other side —there is no honor among thieves—but I couldn't understand why he would do it to his own ball.

The other golfers on the far side played their shots onto the green. Then my friend addressed his now completely buried ball. It was a deep bunker and the golfers on the green could not see him as clearly as I could. He held the club with his left hand and reached into his pocket with his right hand. He swung back and down with his left hand and tossed with his right hand—tossed a ball he had just pulled out of his pocket. The ball flew through the spray of fine white sand and finished two feet from the pin—an easy putt for $20,000.

I knew instinctively this was not a situation, and these were not players, for me to interfere with. I turned on my heels and hastened to the parking lot and my car.

Speaking of easy putts, the TV actor Forrest Tucker made an amazing one not long ago. In fact it had been such a short putt —less than two feet—that he felt it was a gimmee. His playing partners did not agree.

"Why, I could knock that in with 'The Chief,'" Tuck observed. "The Chief" being what he and his pals have named Tucker's sizeable male member.

No sooner had Tucker made that remark than money appeared to bet that "The Chief" could not make such a putt. But Tucker promptly dropped to his knees, undid his trousers, and stroked the ball into the cup with his penis.

"What they didn't know," he told me afterward, "was as

soon as I said it, I stuck my hand in my pocket to kind of get 'The Chief' ready."

It was at Tam O'Shanter that I made my first national impact as a golfer in 1955, when I won the All-American and World Amateur tournaments in successive weeks. Dutch Harrison happened to be in town for the World Pro Tournament, which offered an incredible $50,000 first prize, and watched me play and had lunch with me a couple of times. He was always shopping around for strong young golfers he could use to surprise opponents in future matches, but he was also naturally friendly to youngsters coming up too.

Anyway, later that summer, I called Dutch to tell him about getting beat in the U. S. Amateur in Richmond.

"By the way, boy," he drawled after cursing me out for losing, "you care to come play with me down here in Odessa?"

"I'm a little short of funds, Pops, I'm sorry."

"How far you live from Western Union?"

"A few blocks," I said, getting the message, "I walk fast."

"Well, I'll send you $200 for your ticket to Dallas and pick you up at the airport."

I arrived the day before the pro-am. On the way out to the course, Dutch explained the situation.

"Lookie here," he said, "we got to win the pari-mutuel tomorrow because I am going to make a generous bet on ourselves. But that means when you're out there practicing today, you got to look fair to bad, so as we can draw some odds."

Later, on the practice tee in front of a sizeable gallery, including the local bettors, I guessed, Dutch walked past me and whispered, "Slice a couple!" A little later he hissed at me, "Shank one!" I started scattering balls around like confetti.

"You done a fine job, boy," he said that night in my room, contemplating our approaching windfall.

I held up a pair of lavender slacks. "Thinking of wearing these tomorrow," I said.

"Real purty," Dutch said, without really noticing.

"I had them on when I lost in the National Amateur," I re-marked.

Dutch leaped out of his chair. "Whoa now!" he said. "Don't wear 'em. No, no. Burn 'em, get rid of 'em. Don't even let 'em close to your other garments, it might rub off!"

Dutch would not be satisfied until I hung the trousers in a closet all by themselves.

Next day, wearing luckier slacks, I birdied six of the first eight holes, at which point Dutch beamed.

"You can sit back now, Dougie. Big Daddy is going to take over."

We ended up low team that day and won far more in the pari-mutuel than the winner of the tournament in prize money.

One of Harrison's greatest assets in head-to-head matches was his ability to hit clubs to an unorthodox distance. He had a big looping outside-in swing arc and it was hard to tell ex-actly how much force he actually applied to a shot with his hands. He would foxily take a 5-iron and put his hands into it so much that the shot would come out as long and low as the conventional 2-iron shot, or he could make it pop and fall like a 9-iron shot.

Once I was partnered with him when he played a 1-iron into a par-3 green encircled by a fair-sized gallery. There was a big round of applause from the crowd when his shot landed, obviously near the hole.

"Man, I really crushed that one," Dutch declared, walking back and forth on the tee, holding his 1-iron conspicuously in front of our opponent, who had just pressed us for $100.

"Doesn't really look that far," the other player said to his partner, biting his lip tentatively as he pulled out a 2-iron.

Then he hit and we watched for the gallery reaction: Everyone's eyes lifted skyward as the shot sailed over the

green and out of bounds into a cornfield. He was at least two
clubs too strong.

The ability to make finesse shots is a matter of great pride
as well as convenience to a touring pro. It is an ability more
characteristic of the older players, who by and large learned
how to play by improvisation and feel, than of the younger
ones who are the products of more standardized instructional
methods and more uniform playing conditions.

In fact it used to surprise people to find that an emerging
postwar player like myself was able to execute off-beat shots.
Years ago I annoyed Paul Hahn, the trick shot entertainer,
when I bragged about this knack.

I knew Paul only casually at the time. Once, Dave Ragan
and I, college golf teammates at the University of Florida,
had played Paul and his brother in a friendly match in Orlando.
We made three birdies and two eagles on the front nine and
beat them for $8. At this juncture Paul decided to give us a
lesson in humility. He dragged his bag of trick clubs out to the
tenth tee. He challenged me to play out of it with him, shot
for shot, and soon won his money back. I gave up when I
cracked myself in the ribs with a club that had a rubber hose
for a shaft. "Mr. Hahn," I declared, "you have made your
point. I will go no further in this embarrassment."

A couple of years later I overheard Hahn talking about an
exhibition given by Ben Hogan and Sam Snead. We were
sitting at different tables in the dining room at a golf club. He
was expressing surprise that two of the greatest players in
golfing history had been unable to deliberately shank a ball
for the exhibition.

"Hell," I called over, "I can shank a ball any time I want."

"Oh really?" said Hahn. "And when are we going to see
this display of talent?"

"Why, soon as I finish this here sandwich," I said.

After lunch I walked down to the practice range and found

that Hahn had assembled a small gallery. Apparently he thought he was going to continue the lesson in humility he had started to give me in Orlando years before. This time, however, I had him, because unlike Snead and Hogan, I had a short swing that enabled me to lead enough with my left hand to hit it in the hosel. As a hands and arms player, I move the club in and out of grooves as a matter of course.

Hahn threw some balls down on the practice tee and said, "Would the young amateur care to wager on his talent?"

"No, sir," I said. "I really don't think it would be fair just to take your money like that."

That really made Paul angry. "You are free to take my money, young man. You may bust me, if you like."

"No, sir," I said. "Just let me show you here now." And I proceeded to shank three balls with a wedge, then three with a 7-iron, then a couple with a 5-iron. I went through my whole bag.

At the end of it Paul grinned and said, "You really could have busted me if you wanted to." Then he handed me a cigar. And we've been friends ever since.

Once I used my ability to shank in ignoble circumstances. I was playing in a tournament in Philadelphia but I had also promised to play an exhibition in Miami that weekend with Jimmy Demaret, Bob Hope, and Jackie Gleason. To make the weekend exhibition necessitated not making the tournament cut on Friday. But here it was Friday and I could not do anything wrong. Putts were dropping in from all over the greens. I came to the sixteenth hole needing a high score badly, or I would surely qualify for the last two rounds of the tournament. I did not want to embarrass the sponsors, and I did not want to let my friends in Miami down just because I had foolishly double-scheduled myself.

I half closed my eyes on the tee shot on number sixteen and still it went straight down the middle. Now I knew extreme measures were called for. I pulled out my 2-iron and shanked my second shot out of bounds. I dropped another ball and shanked it out of bounds.

Jay Hebert, my playing partner, looked at me in astonishment.

"I have never seen you shank a ball in my life, Doug!"

"I don't know what happened, Jay," I said scratching my head. I couldn't tell him then I had shanked the shots on purpose. "The lie must have been bad and I didn't know it."

But my caddie sensed what was going on, I think, because after he recovered the balls he said, "Those were two identical swings, Mr. Sanders. I found the balls ten inches apart out in the weeds."

Dutch Harrison also showed a lot of finesse in the way he set up matches, which is probably just as important to a hustler as being able to execute the skill involved. The most devastatingly successful one that he told me about involved Herman Keiser, long before he won the Masters in 1946.

Dutch had told his original partner in a certain match to stay home that day. Then he made Herman put on overalls and go sit in the caddie pen.

When tee-off time arrived and Dutch was without a partner for the match, he shrugged and said, "I believe I could beat you two jokers with just a caddie for my partner."

"Well, take your choice," said one of his opponents acidly.

Dutch went over to the caddie enclosure and pretended to analyze the available talent for a while. Finally he said, "Hey, you, the lanky one with overalls, you play any kind of golf?"

"I play some," Herman replied.

"Come on now, then, you're my partner."

At the end of the round, during which Herman shot 67, one of Dutch's opponents said, as he handed over his money, "That's the best goddam caddie I've seen play in my life!"

Not all Dutch's matches turned out the way he had arranged

them, however. Once a match he set up for George Low went awry. Low was one of the top touring pros in the 1930s and 1940s, with a deserved reputation for great stroking ability around the greens. Later he became a successful putter manufacturer and was often seen at tournament sites. He also became famous as "America's Number One Guest" because of his great knack for not picking up a tab, and for seemingly always being among millionaires. In fact the main reason Dutch arranged this match for George was to keep Low from freeloading at Dutch's expense.

In this particular match, Dutch equipped George with a Detroit bankroll—that's a roll of singles with a $10, $20, or $50 bill on the outside—and pitted him against a dentist lusting for action. After beating the dentist three days in a row, George made the mistake of becoming involved in an argument with the dentist at the club bar. The argument centered on who was the greatest player of his era—Hogan, Snead, or Nelson.

"No one measures up to Hogan," declared George.

"No one matches Nelson," the dentist retorted.

"Hogan," insisted George.

"Nelson won eleven tournaments in a row. Hogan never did that."

"Well you know who ended your Nelson's string?" George replied in a fury. "Me! Me!"

Actually it was Freddie Haas who won the tournament that broke Nelson's record winning streak of 1945. But Haas was an amateur at that time—the top finisher among the pros had been George Low.

This new information changed the direction of the discussion slightly.

"How could an 80-shooter beat the great Byron Nelson?" demanded the dentist.

"I'll tell you as soon as I return from the bathroom," replied

George, rising as soon as he realized his indiscretion. He skipped out the back door of the clubhouse.

Once Low beat a man for a handsome sum by borrowing a red umbrella from a pro shop display, subtly rebuilding it, and returning it to the rack. A few days later he found himself in the shop with the man he was after, and he said, "I believe I could play against you putting with the wrong end of the stick, or a goddam umbrella."

George pulled a blue umbrella out of the rack, dropped a ball on the carpet and putted a couple of times. Then he handed the umbrella to the other man. He tried putting with it as well and noted that results were very erratic because of the vibrating lightweight wooden shaft.

"You're making a mistake, George," warned the other man.

"Why then let's play and find out," retorted George. He added casually that blue was not his favorite color, and he would just as soon exchange it for an identical style umbrella in red, if the other man didn't mind. The guy was so anxious to take George's money that he unhesitatingly agreed. At which point George took down the red umbrella—the one whose wood shaft he had bored out and filled with lead to make a remarkably good weapon on the greens—and the match, which George won handily, was on.

When there was no action on a golf course, the hustlers could always find it at the nearest track.

Many years ago, Dutch and a friend were at a track without a dime, wandering through the grounds expertly flipping discarded tickets with their shoes to locate winning horses that might have been cast away in error. They stopped directly behind two elderly ladies to watch the end of the second race, the Daily Double. When the horses crossed the finish line, one of the ladies held up her ticket and squealed, "I got him! I got him!"

Plucking the ticket from the poor woman's fingers and dancing into the crowd, Dutch's friend said, "You had him, you had him."

"Don't worry, ma'am, I'll get the thief," Dutch cried, and high-tailed after his pal, not stopping until he had caught up with him—at the WINNERS' window.

Al Besselink also betrayed a great fondness for the track, and like many gamblers, he was personally generous even when the ponies were not running according to plan. One morning at breakfast he asked to borrow $100 and I naturally handed it over; money moved between us as between Wells Fargo clerks. Five minutes later, one of Bessie's friends stopped at the table and started telling his troubles.

"Do you need some money?" Bessie said at last.

"I could use a pittance," admitted the friend.

"Take $100 for now," Al said, handing over my money. "When you need more, let me know."

There were very few golfers on tour who could play as well for their own money as Bessie. He and I made a strong team in the old days because it was then customary, after a private match in the day, to continue testing your opponents in gin rummy at night—and we were both good in both leagues.

Our best official finish as golf team came in the 1966 PGA National Team Championship at the former PGA National Golf Club in Palm Beach Gardens, Florida, where we played seventy-two holes without making a single bogey. We finished second to Palmer and Nicklaus. During four rounds, we put a ball in the water eight times—in team play you can attempt shortcuts over water and other risk shots more often—and seven times still made birdie on the hole. On one such occasion, Bessie tried to play his shot out of the hazard. He took off his shoes and socks, stepped into the pond, and wiggled into a stance with his six-foot-four, 240-pound frame. I stood on the bank watching him get shorter and shorter as he sunk more and more into the muck. Finally I said, "Al, get out of there before you disappear! I can't play them alone!"

"Well, help me," Bessie cried, "I am sinking still."

Finally I pulled him out with a club, but it got to the point where it looked like he was going to pull me in on top of him instead. I considered giving his head a few light taps with my club so I could be assured of staying dry, which surely would have ended a beautiful friendship.

There's an extra sense of satisfaction in winning a private bet, whether for money or not, from a fellow professional whom you respect. One year, after Arnie beat me for $50 in an exhibition match we played together, I noticed him watching me practice bunker shots—sand play was always the weakest part of Palmer's game.

"I'll take two to one I can blast out of here with a putter and get it up and down," I called.

"I'll take $25 of that," he replied, no doubt observing the big lip on the bunker and deciding that I really would have to blast out—something he could not conceive of my doing with a putter.

I laid the putter as flat back as I could, to maximize the spin on the ball, and blasted to within two feet of the cup. I had got my $50 back with an old Cedartown shot.

I never set up a player for a hustle unless the situation cried out for such a thing, as it did one year during the Desert Classic.

I had come in from a date just in time for breakfast. Frank Stranahan was also staying at the McCulloch house for the week. When I arrived and saw him sitting there nursing his orange juice, I knew he was ripe.

I sat down next to him, necktie loosened and hair disheveled, and sighed, "What a night!"

"Where you been?" said Frank, eying me carefully. He had

already done his roadwork and calisthenics and looked fit enough to pick up the refrigerator.

"Frank, you wouldn't believe it," I replied. "I have been at the most exhausting party in my life."

"And you're just getting in?"

"Hell, yes," I said.

"What were you doing?"

"Drinking, messing around. I'm beat." Actually I had slept soundly—in my girl friend's bed.

At this point Basie McCulloch set a cup of coffee in front of me and I picked it up. My hands trembled so much I nearly spilled some.

Whereupon Frank said, "What are we going to play for today?"

"I can't play you the way I feel."

"You've been beating me all week. Give me a chance to win some of my money back."

"Hell, no. You probably want to bet something like a thousand. No thanks."

"Let's just make it $500."

Usually I couldn't *get* Frank to bet as high as $500.

"Aw hell," I said, setting the coffee cup down so shakily it chattered in the saucer. "What's the difference! The game's on."

A few minutes later Frank left, pleased with himself and with his prospects for the day's match.

I asked Basie for a refill on coffee, and held the cup out for her with my hands as steady as rock.

"Oh, Doug," she said in disgust. "How could you!"

Once an amateur at the Dallas Athletic Club C.C. tried to hustle me. I knew he was nearly a scratch player but he claimed to have a nine handicap. So I challenged him to play a round in 100 or under, providing that he played two balls on each shot and that I picked which ball would count each time.

He failed to see the implications of this challenge, and it turned out to be a long, tiring, and ultimately losing effort for him. He came to the last hole needing a four to make 100. Both his tee shots were good, but one of his second shots landed in the bunker. His two recoveries from the bunker left him fifteen and thirty feet from the hole. I picked up the fifteen-footer and watched him try unsuccessfully to make the thirty-footer —twice.

Ky Laffoon once ended a match with a shock too. He had bet he would not take 72 strokes during the round. His seventy-first stroke was his approach to the eighteenth green. But he picked up the ball and said, "All I told you was I wouldn't take 72 strokes."

No one is ever likely to match Titanic Thompson's exploits. Titanic, who once said at least $1,000,000 passed through his hands every year since he began hustling in earnest around 1910, was first of all an incredibly fine athlete. In golf, he once shot 29 on the back side to beat Byron Nelson in a match, and with Ky Laffoon as a partner he was virtually unbeatable in team play for many years. He was ambidextrous and drove opponents crazy because he used both left-handed and right-handed clubs during a single round and no one ever knew where to stand when he hit.

He could have excelled in formal tour competition, but there was more glory than money in pro golf in his prime. Furthermore his nature pushed him to win not just by being more skillful than another man. He wanted to win by proving he was smarter too.

Of course he didn't always win, and wasn't always right. Not too many years ago he tried to interest me in a match against a young Texas player who was said to be strong. Ti was prepared to back me against him, but I couldn't make it. Finally he recruited young Ray Floyd to come down.

When the day came and Ray showed up at the course, a

young fellow took his clubs out of the trunk for him and brought them over to the first tee.

"Say, where's this guy I'm supposed to play?" Ray asked.

"I'm the guy," said the same fellow.

"Who are you?"

"I'm the caddiemaster here."

Floyd shook his head at the thought he had come all this way just to play a caddiemaster. But as it turned out, Ray had all he could do to break even that day. And at the end of fifty-four holes, Ti had dropped a bundle betting against Ray's opponent. The match would have continued except the caddiemaster had to stop to take care of the golf cart fleet for the night.

Subsequently Ray told me how good the caddiemaster was, but it wasn't until a couple of years later that I had the pleasure of seeing him—Lee Trevino was his name—play myself.

No one knew more about hustling psychology than Ti. He knew how to get a person mad enough to enter into a bet with him in the first place. In the early days he would drive up to some unsuspecting pro, a total stranger, step out of his sixteen-cylinder roadster and say, "I don't believe you can play this here course of yours worth a damn."

Once Ti phoned Morgan Baker, now the professional at Sharpstown Country Club in Houston, who helped me with my game a few years ago, and said, "Your name Morgan Baker?"

"Yes, sir," said Morgan, who had never heard of Mr. A. C. Thomas—Titanic's real name—at the time.

"Well, you've got a reputation for being the best young player in Houston. I just came down here 180 miles from Tyler to show you you ain't."

Later Morgan was dazzled by Titanic's facility with his hands, not just in his golf. Once he saw him flip a deck of cards over a forty-foot oak tree, one card at a time, while sitting in a chair propped up against a pro shop building. Another time he "chipped" a ball into the middle of a green fifteen feet away by skinning it with two expert pistol shots that only smudged the ball cover. Morgan lost $40 another time when Titanic threw five golf balls into a cup from exactly twelve feet away and not one of them bounced out. Morgan would say, "It is impossible to tell all the things that Ti has done and still have people believe you are not insane."

My favorite feat, and one that must surely rank as the greatest golf hustle of all time, is the series of matches that Titanic perpetrated one winter during the Depression years in Miami. He had trained a Kansas City man to play golf from a wheelchair, then took him down to Florida. There they sniffed out a group of wealthy textile merchants from New York. Titanic revealed to the action-minded vacationers that his friend, whose two legs were in plaster casts (which came off at night so he could rest properly) and whose wheelchair was pushed about by a burly dark-suited attendant—had been in a bad car accident on the way down to Florida. His holiday was ruined, but Ti casually opined that he was still a good enough player to get around Miami Country Club in his wheelchair in 98 or less.

The textile merchants jumped on that proposition and the game was on. In fact the game lasted for three months as the "cripple" slowly but surely worked his way down to shooting 78—the score he had made sure he could shoot from a wheelchair in Kansas City before they left—and Titanic worked his way up to pots of $200,000.

There have been many varied and colorful figures in golf such as Dutch, Titanic, George Low, and Bessie, who have achieved national fame of a kind, and many others of purely and permanently local distinction. In fact I don't think any game at its grass roots has more "characters" and more genuinely dramatic or funny competitive moments. That is why I think golf really does provide a universal experience, much more rich and complex in human personality and motivation than it is usually given credit for.

That's also why I enjoy playing with some of the hackers as much, and in some cases more than the celebrities or touring pros. It's fun and even educational to meet the rogues and basket cases and hustlers and emotional hurricanes who exist in golf at the club level just as surely as they exist at the top.

One of my favorite hackers over the years has been Harold Wiesenthal, owner and operator of Harold's Men's Shop in Houston and member at Champions Golf Club. Champions co-owner Jimmy Demaret once called him the worst golfer in Harris County—the north Houston surroundings—so Harold's supporters decided to find the worst golfer in neighboring Montgomery County and arrange a match. The Montgomery County golfer turned out to be a farmer who knew so little about golf that whenever he hit into a group in front of him, he yelled, "Excuse me!" instead of "Fore!" The match was played in front of a modest but enthusiastic gallery at Conroe Country Club. It didn't end until the last hole, a tough par-5 laced with fairway bunkers. The farmer shot fifteen and Harold nailed him with a fourteen.

Harold is the type of golfer who constantly improves and never gets better. Once, after mentally reviewing a round he had played two days before, he declared to me, "I shot 112 and still don't remember a bad shot."

He was always after free advice from Demaret or any other pro he could collar. After some cajoling, Harold finally did get Demaret to walk over to the practice tee one day to see his swing in action. Harold worked himself into a sweat hitting some beetling low iron shots and then turned to Demaret and asked, "What do you think I should do?"

Demaret reflected a moment and then said, "Groove what you got, Harold. Just groove what you got."

7 / The Caddie Who
Walked on Water Hazards

A black caddie named Ernest worked for me in 1960 fairly regularly. I didn't know his last name. Some of the caddies on tour did not give out their last names and others could not remember them.

Anyway, Ernest was working for me during the Pensacola Open and I was playing for the title. I was tied for the lead with Arnold Palmer going into the seventy-second hole of the tournament, and Arnold was two holes behind me. So I felt a lot of tension.

I hit a good drive off the final tee and we walked up to my ball. It looked like I needed one of the middle irons to get to the finishing green, which was packed with galleries.

"Ernest," I said, "what should I hit?"

"Don't ax me, Mista Doug."

"What's that?" I said, somewhat surprised. I was intensely involved in the shot at hand, determined to finish strongly. "What do you think I should hit?" I repeated.

"Please don't ax me nothing, Mista Doug. I don't know what club you should use."

"What the hell's the matter, Ernest?" I said sharply. I was paying him pretty well and we were in a position to win, which would have meant a bonus for the caddie, so I couldn't understand his sudden indifference.

"I'm choking bad, Mista Doug!" he finally declared. I looked at him. His arms were rigid and his eyes were all watery. "I don't know whether you got a 2-wood or a 9-iron to get up there," he groaned. "I cain't see the flag, I cain't even see the green. I cain't see nothing!"

Well, I doubled over right there in the fairway, laughing.

"Ernest!" I cried. "I'm the one who's supposed to be choking, not you!"

"Oh, Mista Doug," poor Ernest said, "I jes know you got to get it up there!"

Finally I picked myself up. I took out a 5-iron, whaled my second shot to eighteen feet of the pin, and finished with a birdie. I figured I had the tournament sewed up, in spite of my quivering caddie. But Arnie birdied the last two holes to win by one stroke.

The main reason I tell this story on Ernest is because I think it shows how intense a good caddie gets about his job and about the golfer he is working for. I think it is something that outsiders particularly would not appreciate. Newcomers to golf would assume the caddie is little more than a carrier for the golf clubs, and would wonder why the golf cart didn't catch on sooner. In fact to some players, the caddie has minimal duties and is invisible as a person. Other players, including myself, involve the caddie in the emotional struggle of the game, perhaps because we need the feeling of support more. The caddie becomes a kind of social refuge from the lonely demands of golf too.

You can learn a little about what a man is like by studying how he relates to his caddie. I get to know mine and tend to depend on them. I have had all kinds of caddies, from well-to-do sons of country club members to Skid Row dropouts. I've gotten along better than average with most of them—maybe because I am a caddie at heart myself.

When I was seven, my family moved into a house not far from the nine-hole golf course in Cedartown. At that time I had never heard of golf or saw it played. That first summer in the new house I was picking cotton for spending money. We—my brother James and some neighborhood kids—would get up at five in the morning and troop out to one of the cotton farms outside town. It was important to pick the cotton before it got too hot and while the morning dew was still on the plants. The dew added weight to your bag and when you get paid at the rate of $2.00 per 100 pounds, you think of weight. I also packed rocks and melons into my bag when I could get away with it. Sometimes we picked for strangers, sometimes for relatives, but I cheated equally on all of them.

Cotton-picking was hot, hard work and we frequently stopped for breaks to eat fresh tomatoes or crack open melons or drink from the clear water of a stream—Cedartown is famous in the region for ice cold clean spring waters. One day we walked home past the golf course and I saw some boy not much bigger than I pulling a cart along in front of men with sticks in their hands. I asked one of the older children in our group what that boy was doing. When I found out he was being paid for walking, I knew I was in the wrong business, and I never picked cotton again.

Directly I began to hang out around the clubhouse. I was too small to carry a golf bag on my shoulder but in time I got to pull a cart along as that other boy had done. A foursome would store their few clubs collectively in the one bag, and pay a boy 25¢ to pull it around on a cart for them. I began to do this regularly. I also collected lost balls for resale. I filled any cuts and nicks with soap and covered them over with white shoe polish and sold the balls for more than they were worth to out-of-towners. We fetched balls from the water hazards by night. One night we cleaned out a lake of two hundred balls and I cleaned out the raiding party by flipping coins for golf balls. I had two coins in my pocket at the time, one with two heads, the other with two tails.

Pretty soon I began to sneak shots in the course of a round. I would pull the cart down the fairway to watch where my group's tee shots landed. Whenever I got over a hill or around a bend, I dropped one of my balls and hit at it quickly. The main thing I wanted to do was hit it fast and keep it straight. That's how my swing got started so short, as I mentioned earlier.

I also squeezed in a few shots whenever the pro went home for lunch on weekdays, more or less leaving the course in the charge of the caddies. Eight or ten of us would play nine holes in forty-five minutes, using the four clubs we owned among ourselves—a 2-iron, a 5-iron with no grip, a brassie with part of its wood head broken off, and an old putter recovered from the water pond. As soon as one boy hit a ball, he would toss the club to someone else and start after his own ball. You played your shot with whatever club you had in your hand, no matter if you were putting with a chipped brassie or driving with a rusty putter.

As I got older I spent more and more time at the course. I would get there before dawn with my lunch, a bottle of buttermilk, and my pillow, a towel I bundled up under my head whenever I got a chance to take a nap. I tried to get in eighteen holes before regular play started, and another eighteen in the evening before going home. Some nights I woke up with cramps from all the walking and my mother would have to rub my legs with alcohol.

I began to spend more time playing and practicing than I did caddieing. I also worked on the greens in the absence of a full-time caretaker for the course. Atop an old Ford tractor, I would sand greens to keep down the weed growth and smooth out the putting surface. I moved the cups mornings, practicing my putting as I did so until I knew every possible break and angle for every conceivable pin position.

During the war years many of the regular caddies at the course were drafted and black caddies began showing up for the first time to carry bags. I tried using some of them to retrieve my practice balls but they didn't like working for another caddie. Lazy, unfriendly ones I punished with certain practice techniques. Late in an afternoon I would send a boy down range about 130 yards so that the slanting sun made it hard for him to see my shots. Then I would take my 6-iron or 7-iron and start playing shots, from right to left or from left to right, into the fellow's ankles. He'd be out there dancing around on his bare feet and hollering at me, "Hey, man, you almost got me there!" or "Hey, man, don't hit that goddam ball so close!"

Pretty soon no one would work for me, so I bought a small motor bike, a fish net, and a basket and started retrieving my own balls.

My only real caddie-yard battle involved one of the newcomer blacks. We were having a putting contest and a dispute arose as to who won the nickel. He called me "a rebel son of a bitch" and I knocked him down. Then he picked up a board with a nail in it and came at me screaming like a samurai. I threw my arm up, which saved my face, but didn't do much for the arm. The sight of an eight-inch-long gash gave me unexpected courage and I got my arm around his neck and forced him downward while I brought my knee up to introduce it to his head. I broke off two of his teeth and hurt my knee so badly I limped for a week.

That was the last of my fighting experiments—I knew right away that testing myself with my fists was never going to do much for my golf game. I saw plenty of fights thereafter however. When I won the La Grange Tournament for the second time, my own caddie got punched on the chin and sent sprawling down a thirty-foot embankment next to the finishing green. It was the second year in a row that the caddie of the player I had beaten, had reached the final match only to lose, and he let my caddie have it along with all the money. In those days, on a side-bet basis, the winning caddie in a match collected a certain amount from the losing caddie, and this went on throughout the tournament until the final, when both caddies to the finalists would be carrying sizeable amounts on them. It was hard to blame the losing caddie, that particular year, for losing control of his emotions. The previous year he had caddied for the tournament's defending champion and this year he had caddied for the captain of the University of Georgia golf team. Each time he thought he was a shoo-in for the big caddie purse, and each time he emerged without a cent.

Anyway my background in caddieing plus my friendly nature automatically made me interested in the caddies I ran into on tour. When I first started playing professionally, there was no such thing as a full-time touring caddie. Purses were not big enough to justify guaranteeing someone a weekly sum. It was in California where I first began to hire a caddie for a string of tournaments because there seemed to be a pool of caddieing talent out there, older men, mostly white, who made their living carrying bags and seemed to know the tournament courses well enough, at least when they were sober.

My first steady caddie was a man named Earl German, a self-confessed former problem drinker who worked for me in a half-dozen events a year on the West Coast, and was with

me when I won the 1966 Bob Hope Desert Classic. Earl
conveyed the kind of emotional support that, as I mentioned
earlier, some golfers want and need from their caddies. The
real test of a caddie probably comes when the golfer is in a
position to win. The good caddie, without considering the
financial consequences of taking too much of a risk on a certain shot, for instance, is always the caddie who wants you to
win, and doesn't care about second. Earl had a way of bolster-
ing my spirit in this way. If I expressed doubt or worry about
a certain club selection, or how I was reading a certain putt,
he would say, "You got the wrong seeds planted, young man.
Dig those seeds up and plant some brand-new ones!"

Some of Earl's positive philosophy came out of his own
life experience. As he told me the story, he had once been married to a handsome, wealthy woman who worked in real estate, but he had become an alcoholic. He used to go to sleep
with a bottle of whiskey on each side of the bed—so that if
he woke up in the night he would not have far to reach to
quench his thirst. One unsteady day he pushed one of his wife's
customers through a picture window in her real estate office
and she said, "Dust." That's when he began drifting and
caddieing.

By the time I met Earl he had gone dry and religious. He
spent a lot of his spare time trying to reform some of his fellow caddies who were raffish and drunken wayfarers with no
families, roots, or prospects. I'm sure some of those types,
who never had anything and never seemed to miss it, were
impervious to Earl's suggestions, but I respected the quiet and
dignified manner in which he would go about trying to make
himself useful to others.

About the only thing some of the old-time caddies possessed
was their nicknames. "Scorpy" Doyle was named after the
scorpion because every time you turned around, he was putting the bite on you—$2.00 here, $5.00 there. There was another

fellow named "Stinky" who drank four ounces of some form of formaldehyde each day, cutting it with a gallon of economy-priced California red. The combination made him sweat profusely and give off the odor of a winding sheet, hence his nickname. When Stinky died, one of the show business people for whom he had caddied in the Palm Springs area took care of the details and the expenses of his burial—there was no one else to do it. Actually, many of these characters were treated generously by the entertainers, who seem to tolerate human failings and even appreciate eccentric behavior better than most people do. Some of the caddies in earlier times added personality and plain talk to tour life. Others, admittedly, got drunk too much, ran out on motel bills, fought among themselves, abused the public, and generally annoyed the establishment. I always had a problem with the caddies I hired, as I did with anyone working for me, in that I became too involved and trusting with them. I did not keep a "guarded employer-employee relationship" as they might say in a business psychology course. I gave my caddies clothes, found them free lodgings, picked up some of their eating expenses and did other favors for them. Sometimes I was taken advantage of, I guess, but it never bothered me much. Once I had a caddie working for me, who also served as my chauffeur. On an off-day I decided we would drive out to a golf course so I could hit balls.

"I'm sorry, you can't do that," my caddie-chauffeur informed me. "I've got a date this afternoon and I need the car."

The black caddies especially had a sense of humor that I always liked, though I'm not sure why—I think I realized that beyond the apparent simplicity of some of their funny remarks, there was a crafty awareness at work. One day during the week of the 1961 Los Angeles Open, I had lunch at the home of my friends Tony Martin and his wife Cyd Charisse.

I didn't have a car, so Tony offered me the use of his Rolls-Royce, which I gladly accepted.

My arrival in a Rolls-Royce created a sensation. One caddie ran alongside stroking the fender and exclaimed, eyes popping with excitement,

"Mista Doug! Goddam, I know you has some smart lawyer now (I had just signed to be represented in my business dealings by Mark McCormack) and I know you is doing good, but I didn't know you is doing *this* good!"

Another time I overheard Al Besselink's caddie talking to young Raymond Floyd's caddie.

"Tha' Mista Ray," Raymond's caddie was saying, "he gonna be a great player, ain't he?"

"He be all right," Al's caddie replied, "if he stay away from Mista Doug and Mista Bessie."

At the Masters one year, a caddie named Poe was assigned to Cary Middlecoff. On the first tee, Cary said to him, "'Poe'? Is that like the 'Poe' in Edgar Allan Poe?"

"Sheet, Mista 'coff," replied the caddie, "I *is* Edgar Allan Poe."

Some of the caddies liked to bet on their golfers—or on the golfers they thought were going to win. Porky Oliver's regular caddie on the West Coast used to store his winnings in one of his shoes. You could always tell when he was doing well because his gait changed. And when he hit a jackpot, he would limp along as though he had a peg leg.

After using Earl German for some years, I hired a young man freshly out of the Navy named Sonny Austin, originally of Kansas City, on the recommendation of his cousin Del Taylor, Billy Casper's regular caddie. Not long after Sonny began caddieing for me, I realized that he was smart enough and loyal enough to do much more than carry my bag for me. I gave him a lot of duties as a kind of personal secretary, and eventually I hired him and his wife, Pauline, to manage my household in Houston.

After that I often used Walter Pritchett, known as Cricket, as a caddie, particularly in tournaments in the southeast, when I could get him. He had been a bus driver by profession in Atlanta but he liked to get away from time to time for the sunshine and the chance to dispense his pungent commentary. At the end of a round when I putted badly in 1968, Cricket remarked dryly, "Nice work, you turned a perfect 64 into a 72."

Sometimes I might play nearly an entire tournament before Cricket would congratulate me on a shot, and if I then remarked on his absence of enthusiasm, he was likely to say, "Up to now, Doug, you ain't deserved no comment."

Cricket's only weakness was a tendency to outspend his income, but I could hardly criticize him for that since I often did the same thing. He was not averse to cabling friends on tour for travel money from time to time. Once he said he billed George Plimpton for $50 when he discovered that writer had quoted him in his book *The Bogey Man.*

A caddie who costs you strokes is the one who costs you the most money in the long run, though. The pros could cite dozens of examples of when a caddie, through inadvertence or natural stupidity, has spoiled a golfer's score. Julius Boros was penalized two strokes once when a caddie picked up his ball and tossed it at him, after thinking Julie's opponent, and not someone in the gallery, had said "That's good" about the putt he had.

Of course caddies have their own foibles and fears. In Jacksonville, Florida, one year, Bob Rosburg's caddie unexpectedly came upon a small alligator in the long grass near a water hazard. He happened to be afraid of alligators, which was understandable. He dropped Bob's bag and ran down the fairway like a quarter-miler.

Superstitious caddies abound. Many believe in "lucky balls," for example. As a rule, a pro goes through a package of three new golf balls a side during competition, and more if he has to play any sand shots, which tend to score the surface of a ball. But if you happen to be making a lot of birdies, you're not likely to get a new ball from your caddie every few holes. He is likely to keep sneaking that original ball back to you. One year I won the Florida State Amateur by 18 shots, shooting rounds of 65-66-67-73. I was playing so well my caddie wouldn't let me alter a single thing in my daily routine. I used the same ball for the entire tournament.

Caddies also believe in unlucky balls, naturally. If you are getting a lot of "lippers"—putts that just rim the cup and stay out—it's very possible your caddie will dump out your entire supply of new golf balls and start you fresh. Also, a good caddie will never hand his player a ball imprinted with a "4" or "5" (all brands of balls are imprinted with numerals for identification purposes) on a par-3 hole. That would be an intolerable form of negative suggestion (bogey or double bogey) for most players—who of course are just as superstitious as the caddies.

There has never been a surplus of decent caddies to my knowledge. Unknown or young pros have an especially hard time getting caddies they can depend on. Years ago Bobby Brue slipped $10 to a caddiemaster to see if that would do any good. He ended up with a young man who resembled a caddie in manner and appearance, but who after the tee shot on the first hole revealed himself to be practically a newcomer to the occupation.

Standing by his ball in preparation for his second shot, Bobby asked the caddie how far it was to the green.

The boy deliberated for a while and replied, "I'd say about three blocks."

Bobby did not think that was inspiring or even funny but

he let it pass. When he finally reached the green, he asked the caddie to help him line up the putt. After the two of them had surveyed the putting line for a while, Bobby said,

"How much do you think it'll break?"

"Six inches," the caddie promptly answered.

"Which way?" said Bobby.

"Just a minute, let me look again."

At that, Brue sent the boy back to the caddie pen.

I found myself with a novice once, during the Masters. After my tee shot on the eighth hole at Augusta, I asked him, "How far is it home from here?" I knew I was in trouble when the caddie replied, "I'm sorry, Mr. Doug, I don't even know where you live."

In San Diego one year, I hired a smooth-talking fellow with a brightly striped shirt, neat goatee, and a nice easy way about him. I figured I had picked out the Mr. Confidence of the caddie pen and he would give my game a much needed (at the time) lift for the tournament.

"Yes, sir, I'm your man this week," he declared.

"Get my bag and let's go down to the tee."

"Yes, sir!" he said, snapping his fingers. "Yes, sir, I'm right with you." He chuckled a bit. "We're together all week, yes, yes." More chuckles.

I shrugged off his hilarity and walked down to the practice grounds.

"Now, dump out my practice balls," I said, "and get down range about 100 yards to start with."

He dumped the balls out, but he didn't get down range. Instead, he turned to a ten-year-old boy who had suddenly appeared and said, "Get on out there, hear?"

"Who's that?" I said.

"Man, that's my *runner*. He gonna pick up your balls while I dig that cool little swing you got."

"I think you better dig it back to the caddie pen."

"Hey, man, what's wrong?" he said. "Don't you dig me? I dig you!"

"I dig you," I said. "But I might have dug you more if you didn't drink that pint or smoke that joint or whatever you're flying on."

Looking genuinely crushed, he took his runner and left.

A good caddie thinks like you, not for you, and provides information about yardage or club selection or green contour in a firm, decisive tone. Orville Moody once had a caddie who walked through water hazards with the golf bag held above his head, to be sure he got distances just right. That was a little extreme. Besides, machine-like attention to yardage does not assure sound advice in the heat of a tournament round. I've had caddies get confused about which water sprinkler-head they originally stepped off their yardage from, who will swear up and down that it is 150 yards to the green when common sense would tell them it is not. Former Masters champion George Archer used to avoid this problem by carrying three cans of different-colored spray paint around with him. He would actually color-code the key sprinkler heads until the PGA made him stop.

I once had a caddie in Britain who, in stepping off the yardage for me on the tournament course, attempted to match my own pace by taking unnaturally long steps. But he was an older man and when he began to get tired, his steps got shorter. By the end of the practice round, he was at least ten yards off the measure he had established at the beginning, which created havoc in the first couple of rounds of play for me.

The caddies in Britain, particularly those in Scotland, have a tendency to underclub the player, while American caddies are inclined to give the player exactly the club he needs. If the shot finishes short of target, the British caddie can always blame the player for not hitting the shot hard enough. In the first round of golf I ever played in Britain, I encountered a 250-yard downwind shot from the edge of some rough. My caddie handed me a 6-iron. I argued about the selection some, but finally used it. I hit the shot well and the ball ran and ran. As we walked up to the green, I realized I was still twenty or thirty yards short.

"That just wasn't enough club," I declared.

"Mr. Dougie," replied the caddie, "you did not hit it exactly as I planned for you to hit it."

George Buss, a gardener by trade whose nickname "Buzzard," derives from the profile offered by his nose, had been my regular caddie in Britain for several years. I had always had trouble understanding what he said in his thick Scots accent, but I had become attached to him and on the whole Buzzard had played a decisive and strongly supportive role in my play abroad. On the third day of the 1970 British Open, I had a two-stroke lead going into the Road Hole at St. Andrews. My tee shot was in the fairway all right but I was unsure about the distance to the green for my second shot. I said, "George, what club do you think I should use, a 3- or 4-iron?"

"Well, the win' is comin' from right to left," he observed.

"George, I realize that."

"Well we don't wanta go over the green because we make an eight if we go into the road."

"George, just tell me, is it a 3-iron or a 4-iron?"

"Only thin' we want to do on this hole is make our par four, and we'll try to birdie at number eighteen." Each time he spoke, his voice got higher pitched and more flustered.

"George, I realize that," I said, "but is it a three or a four?"

In the meantime, a BBC sound man had approached with his remote microphone to get some candid repartee. So George's near desperate reply to my last question reached the ears of millions of avid golf fans in Great Britain.

"Well then hit a fuckin' 4-iron," he finally declared, "anythin's better'n being in the fuckin' road."

It turned out to be the wrong advice, unfortunately: my 4-iron approach landed short of the green, I chipped into a bunker, and made six on the hole. But at least Buzzard had made up his mind—for all to hear.

The very first time I went overseas, to play in the British Amateur at Troon in 1956, I was surprised to be met by a man named Steele at Prestwick airport.

"I'll be your man this week, Mr. Sanders," he informed me in the terminal, and then presented me with a brown paper bag in which were two rolls of soft toilet paper—exactly the amenity he thought the traveling American would miss most outside his country. Especially since, as I discovered later, the native brand was like sandpaper.

"Thank you, Mr. Steele," I said, dumfounded. After all, no one had ever given me toilet paper before. "Thank you very much."

During my first wind-blasted practice round at Troon, I wore thermal underwear, two sweaters, a windbreaker, and even a kind of overcoat. Steele had on a thin long-sleeved shirt and a porous sweater. After a few holes I dispensed with my overcoat and Steele remarked, "Aye, Mr. Dougie, it looks like it's gonna be a scorcher."

Wind conditions confounded me utterly in my early outings abroad. So did using the small ball which I kept hitting over my target. Steele kept saying to me, "Nice shot, Mr. Dougie, but it's through the green." I heard that "through the green" all during the qualifying, and I was not surprised to get beat in my first match.

When I was still unschooled in handling the men of ginger temperaments, who are caddies abroad, I made a terrible mistake. Thinking back to my own greens-keeping experience in Cedartown as a boy, I suggested to one caddie that he not set his bag down on the green, or it might damage the putting surface. The old Scot glared at me and said, "I been caddieing over here for twenty-eight bloody years and I'm not going to have any bloody American coming over to tell me where to set my bag." And he went on and on, berating me loudly in front of a gallery, until I raised my hands in surrender and apologized profusely.

Frank Stranahan, playing in the same tournament, also ran head-on into that thickest of brick walls, a Scottish caddie's pride. When Frank refused to accept his caddie's club suggestion on a certain shot, the old-timer dropped the bag off his shoulder, declared, "If you're not gonna use what I tell ya, carry the bloomin' bag yourself," and marched off the course.

Whenever I go back to Cedartown, as I do at least once a year, I always stop at the golf course, where my fate was sealed, after all, when I gave up cotton-picking for caddieing. I play a fast round with old friends, or I ramble over the grounds by myself and let my mind flood with pictures from my caddie past. The second hole is where I used to practice a lot. I like the third hole because that's where I fed off wild strawberries when they grew in abundance along the edge of the fairway. Number four reminds me of the time a fellow shanked a wedge off the tee and, to our great delight, made a hole in one on the wrong green. The eighth hole runs next to the railroad tracks and brings back the time a visiting pro deliberately caromed his second shot off a passing freight train and onto the green. Now that was ball control!

The bench on the first tee reminds me of the day I became a scratch golfer. Older teen-agers used to give me a couple of shots when I played against them, though never enough to win. It annoyed me always to lose, and I used to warn them that someday they would be afraid to play me at all. As I improved, they reduced my handicap but never enough to lose their edge. They started by giving me three strokes a side, then two, then one, and then finally half a stroke.

One day I went down to the first tee for a game with them and ran into an argument. Suddenly the other players wanted shots from me. They wouldn't even consider playing me even. I sat on the old pine bench on the first tee for nearly an hour, trying to get favorable terms for the match. Inside I didn't really care. I was delighted, dimly aware I had reached a new level in my golfing. I was thirteen years old. I wouldn't play that day. It was the day I stopped being a caddie and started being a player.

8 / "We Don't Care What Sanders Shot, Just What Is He Wearing Tomorrow?"

You could say I acquired my first wardrobe in a card game. This was in 1951 when I went to Durham, North Carolina, to play in the National Junior Jaycee Championship. The Cedartown Jaycees had given me ten $10 bills to cover my expenses for the week of the tournament, but during my first night in Durham—we were staying in a dormitory at Duke University —somebody stole my wallet.

Next day I reported the loss to the police and to tournament officials, one of whom gave me $10 to tide me over. That night I found an investment for it—a card game in the dorm among students enrolled in the summer school program. There were fellows from all over the country but I felt pretty certain I could hold my own. I knew a lot about poker and gin rummy from working nights at the golf club at home and studying the way men played cards there.

We played until 5:00 A.M. that night and I ended up a winner. Next night we played again for bigger stakes and I was even luckier. By the end of the game, some of the big losers were fetching clothes from their rooms to throw into the pot. I won a couple of sweaters, some shirts, a suit, even a tuxedo. Finally I played for two suitcases so I'd have something to take all my winnings home in.

Besides the assortment of clothes, I won $800 in cash and the championship itself. I would not have won the title, either, if I had not used my gambler's adrenalin to get me playing sharp early in the week. In my first match, I was two holes down after nine, so I proposed a $10 side bet to my opponent who foolishly accepted. I won seventeen and eighteen, tied nineteen and twenty, and beat him for the match and the $10 on the twenty-first hole. In my match the next day, I was again two down after nine holes, so I made another bet. My opponent in the first match, who was watching us play, told my present opponent, "That's a mistake, he plays harder for his own money." Sure enough, I was one down on seventeen and I beat him on seventeen and eighteen to win the match.

A few months later I was crouched in the back seat of a car in an outdoor drive-in theater in Rome, Georgia, when a short subject came on entitled, *The Boy Next Door.* Usually these short subjects took you on an African safari or a walk through the Tivoli Gardens. But this time the film was about me winning the Jaycee tournament—I had not even been aware of a movie-making crew in Durham. I untangled myself from the girl in the back seat and stared in amazement at my image on the screen, where another girl, Miss North Carolina, was kissing me while I held the Jaycee trophy.

The same short subject reached the Cedartown movie a few weeks later just as the fall school term started. The publicity embarrassed me a lot. Already I was regarded by some of the more conventionally tough boys in school as a little odd for playing golf, a sport not then widely recognized in Cedartown as a major athletic endeavor. To annoy me they sometimes called me "golf ball." When *The Boy Next Door* film came to town, I knew it would give my taunters more juicy material. Every time I walked by a group in the hallway, it seemed, I would hear someone whistle or hum mockingly.

I bore with the taunts—which stopped in a couple of weeks —because I was still so happy about winning my first national title, not to mention all that money and the wardrobe and an official "Doug Sanders' Day" complete with parade and band and banquet.

Actually most of those clothes didn't fit, I discovered, and I never wore them. Even as a young teen-ager I had been a conscientious dresser. I would not be seen in ill-fitting clothes. I used to have my blue jeans dry-cleaned. When I was fourteen, I paid $32.50 for a pair of shoes. I paid $35—top price in those days at Glen's Men's Shop—for a new jacket and ripped it apart sneaking under a fence into a football game that would have cost 50¢ admission. That showed where I placed my values. In fact my interest in personal appearance was at least as deep-rooted as my short swing. I have always taken care of my cover better than my core.

There was never anything artificial about my liking clothes, or commercially motivated. Still it was inevitable that I would end up playing some kind of role in the golf fashion industry. As it turned out, I believe what I did was carry on a distinguished tradition in golf that Walter Hagen and Johnny Farrell, the 1928 U.S. Open champion, started.

Outfits in golf over the years have been almost as distinctive as the playing styles. Once Hagen played an exhibition match against the great British professional Harry Vardon. While they were on the course, some curiosity seekers persuaded a clubhouse attendant to open up the players' lockers for them to see inside. Hagen was found to have two lockers both stuffed with carefully pressed and hung suits and shirts and knickers. Vardon's single locker contained only two items: a pair of black street shoes and a necktie.

Vardon was the epitome of sedate Victorian men's dress in golf. He and fellow Briton Ted Ray would play entire matches under broiling midsummer sun when on tour in Florida or Texas without removing or even tugging at their stiff collars and ties and heavy English jackets. American professionals in their era and succeeding years adopted the same severe style, only they made it a great deal more casual.

Hagen and Farrell brought elegance and color to the golf course. Hagen wore silk shirts, florid cravats, alpaca sweaters, and screaming argyles. His custom-made black and white shoes were always gleaming. He probably invented the sports monograph which today exists in such abundance on shirts and sweaters in a veritable zoo of such symbols as the penguin and the alligator. This came about when Hagen noticed that his friend the Duke of Windsor often appeared in white flannel knickers with the Royal Crown embroidered on the side of the pant leg at knee level. Hagen started embroidering HAIG into his knickers in the same place.

Farrell, who was somewhat flashier than Hagen and just as neat, had dozens of outfits that he carted to tournament sites in trunks—he was said to be the first golf pro ever paid by a manufacturer to wear a particular line of apparel. Between them, the two players offered the galleries of those days something to look at besides fine golf shots, and by their example pricked some colleagues into putting on clothes with more care. Wives helped in the tour redecoration program by knitting the argyle socks that their less successful husbands could not afford to order from Scotland as Hagen and Farrell did. Morgan Baker later claimed that his wife, besides knitting socks for him, also knitted the first head cover in golf history, a sock-like bag she made for him to protect a driver he had just refinished.

The next real clotheshorse in golf was Jimmy Demaret who played on tour both before and after World War II. As a kid, Jimmy used to help his father, a carpenter and house painter by trade, mix new colors in their garage. He claimed that experience got him started being color-conscious.

Demaret made one of his greatest inpacts as a fashion plate at a tournament at Riviera near Los Angeles in 1947, shortly after getting out of the Navy. Each day he appeared in a completely different, fully co-ordinated outfit that had been designed and made expressly for him by Neiman-Marcus, a top department store chain. He wore pastel colors like rose, delicate green, and ivory, and had on shoes specially provided by Foot-Joy to match. The galleries, among them each day the actor Clark Gable, were delighted by Jimmy's bold dressy act.

Demaret's bright new looks always got publicity in the newspapers and magazines of the day. His flamboyance paved the way for a brand-new leisure wear market and an era when the advantages of color co-ordination and action-fitting design would become available to masses of hobbyists and sports nuts. In his day everything he himself wore had to be fastidiously acquired, though. He used to have his slacks made, for example, out of bolts of the bright materials then being sold mainly for ladies' clothing.

Demaret believed that the more gaily he dressed, the better he played and the more good-spirited he felt, but of course he was ribbed and razzed by his colleagues, particularly by his good friend Hogan, who would not have been caught dead in one of Jimmy's ensembles. Hogan was neat, even impeccable in his dress, but he avoided color totally—as did Nelson, who usually came out in one of several shades of gray. Hogan believed bright colors distracted a man from the main job, which was trying to hit a golf ball perfectly.

Clothes are largely a personal matter, a belief that excuses colorless but not sloppy dressing, in my opinion. I could never play golf well unless I dressed well. And I dress just as carefully for activities off the course, as a matter of fact. If I walk into a business meeting with a well-fitting suit, polished shoes, gleaming cuff links and a watch that keeps the right time, I can deal with the situation even though inside I may be depressed, disappointed, anxious, or plain sick. If I have a spot on my tie, however, even if I'm feeling great inside, I know I'm not going to be able to handle myself effectively. All I'll be able to think of is the stain on the tie.

There is nothing romantic about soup stains or out-of-style shoes, either. If a man fancies himself a lover, he should look the part. If clothes make the man, they can make the lady too.

The main reason I came to favor color-blended outfits, both on and off the course, for golf, business, or romance, was because they had a quieting effect on my emotional makeup which tends to be jumpy, high-strung, and full of turmoil. I never liked all-black outfits—such as the ones Gary Player made famous—because they reminded me of funerals. All-white outfits reminded me of weddings and their logical conclusion—in my case, anyway—alimony payments, so I never liked them either. Black-and-white outfits seemed like a jarring combination to me, while the "what-not" combination—a little blue, some black, some red, and green—would have put me in a loony bin.

It was not much easier for me to get the colors I wanted in the early 1960s than it was for Johnny Farrell to get his in the 1920s and 1930s and Jimmy Demaret to get his in the 1940s and 1950s, but I tried.

I would get ideas for new colors or color combinations from what I saw on women, who are better dressers than men any-

way, or in strange places like drugstores. I would go behind
the counter at a pharmacy and spend fifteen minutes looking
over the bright colored pills and tablets in the bottles. Clerks
thought I was a junkie. I'd get the pharmacist to give me a
sample of any capsule that had a distinctive color, or combination of colors, and send it to my tailor or to the apparel firm I
was connected with at the time, and try to get some clothing
made up in that tone.

In the various endorsement contracts I signed with apparel
or shoe firms over the years, there was always a clause giving
me freedom to wear whatever I wanted to wear. I was always
happy to help develop or promote a line, whether it was in
shirts, sweaters, slacks, or shoes—but I never wanted to be
obligated to wear something that might not fit in with my
current tastes. It was a problem of mass vs. class, in a way—I
always felt I was ahead of the kind of market the bigger firms
—the only ones who have the budget for endorsement fees—
were trying to reach. Magenta went out for me as a color, for
example, about two years before it came on the market for
the bulk of golfers.

If I found a shirt or sweater I liked, I would carry it around
with me until I had pieced together an outfit in which it
worked aesthetically. Sometimes that meant dragging the item
into a dozen stores throughout the country, not something
many persons would trouble to do. The typical outfit you see
on America's golf courses, in fact, is assembled much differ-
ently. A blue sweater received as a birthday present is first
combined with a pair of checked slacks on sale at the local
discount department store. The slacks turn out to be not that
bad a match for a blue shirt the golfer happens to find in his
drawer from last summer. To top it off, or rather to bottom it
off, there's the pair of yellow golf shoes. Thus our typically
dressed hacker is ready not just for a round of golf but for a
performance in the circus.

I don't mean to be overly critical of men who claim they don't have the time or the talent to dress well. It doesn't invariably impede you in your career or other goals. Peter Falk has been a great success in the TV role of "Colombo" and in many other roles, and he's famous for indifference to apparel. In fact not long after he joined Riviera, he went out to the club to play. The caddiemaster spotted him in his lackluster outfit and called, "Stand over here, you can get the next two bags that go out."

"I'm not a caddie," replied Falk. "I'm a member."

"You're a *what?*" said the caddiemaster incredulously.

It is true that a lively, contemporary fashion look is not easy to achieve, and not cheap either. With all the clothing available to me gratis, I still spend about $10,000 replenishing and updating my wardrobe each year. I pay $125 to $150 for a pair of slacks, $350 for a one-button business suit with a wild lining, $450 for a tuxedo. I know a lot of men are not willing or able to pay these prices for clothes.

But I'm inclined to agree with a New York menswear specialist named Jacques Bellini, who maintains that badly dressed men not only do themselves a disservice, they spoil the beauty of life for others. "A man who wears baggy slacks does not care about other people," he once charged. In that spirit I would suggest that the pros who wear nothing but the clothes they can get for nothing, and the club golfers like them who look as though they got dressed in the dark, all be penalized two strokes each for offending the public eye.

Here are ten do's and don'ts for becoming a better dresser:

1. Never wear hand-me-downs, freebies, borrowed togs, or Christmas presents.

2. Treat your shoes as part of your suit.

3. Never buy anything just because it's a bargain.

4. Buy quality. Buy one good shirt instead of three cheap ones, for instance.

5. Buy feeling. Originality in clothing is something that is neither too safe nor too daring for you. It is what gives you a feeling of pride in your own distinctiveness.

6. Check your closet and write down the various complete outfits (including shirt, tie, shoes, etc.) in which you customarily appear. Then write down the types of social and business functions you attend. Now compare the two lists and find the gaps and mismatches.

Mainly, the checking process makes you better aware of your clothing in terms of the outfits it provides you. Outfits—the total of what you put on—are what create the effect, not the odd lavish item like your $100 ruby stick pin or the socks from Saks.

7. Find a men's store clerk or tailor whom you like and trust. Tell him the gaps and mismatches in your wardrobe (See number 6). Then ask him what to do about them.

8. Check out the clerk's suggestions with a woman friend whose own appearance you admire, before you spend any money.

9. Pick out the friends and culture heroes whose appearance gives you feelings of envy, and then copy them.

10. Figure out how much you spend on clothing each year, then spend it in equal sums twice a year instead of in dribbles. Once a year thereafter, thin out your wardrobe, giving away what you don't want to younger brothers or friends from the country who are not aware of number 1, above.

I was paired with a young amateur in a pro-am once who was quite proud of his golf shoes, which he had just painted blue. Yes, he actually had colored them with Pittsburgh paint.

"I look like another Doug Sanders!" he declared.

"Yeah," I said, thinking of all the time and effort it used to take me to get patent leather dyed certain colors at the shoe factory. "Let's just hope it doesn't rain."

Men have also been too sensitive about their masculine

images when it comes to responding to things like color and
design and fabric, though this seems to be less true of today's
younger generation of males. It never worried me that I cared
a lot about clothes and about my personal appearance generally. I didn't need Tommy Bolt or any of the other he-man-
looking athletes who appeared in that series of funny Brut
commercials on TV a few years back, to tell me it was all
right to sprinkle myself with cologne now.

Bolt and I had an amusing run-in on the subject of clothes
a couple of years ago. It started when Tommy was quoted as
saying that I wasn't built the right way to wear good clothes.
I replied I spent more on my buttons than he spent on entire
outfits. In fact I had just outfitted all my sport jackets with five
$50 14-carat gold buttons each, so I was telling the truth. Bolt,
insulted, challenged me to compete with him in dress on any
fashion runway. I told him that no matter how hard he tried,
he would still finish like Avis—number 2.

I was having my hair styled, as many younger men do today,
in an era when most barbers attacked your head with machete
and bowl. In the summer I would shave the hair under my
arms so I felt more comfortable playing in hot weather and so
that by the fifteenth hole I did not smell like a muskrat in heat.
I always had my nails manicured and polished too. Years ago
when I was in Sweden for the Shell show, I lit a cigarette for
a date. When she saw my fingernails, she iced over instantly.

"What's the matter?" I said.

"I didn't know you were that way."

"What way?"

"You know . . . queer."

"Queer? Goddam, I've been called a lot of things by women
in my time, but never queer."

Then she explained that in her circles in Sweden, only
homosexuals cut and polished their nails. I told her there were
only two goddam ways I could escape from that charge, one

being to un-manicure my nails. She pondered and picked the other way.

Mainly I've had a good press and warm gallery reaction to my fashion consciousness over the years. I've gotten a variety of honors, such as being ranked among *Esquire* magazine's "Ten Best Dressed Jocks" in 1973. Newspapers often covered my appearances in town on the society page as well as on the sports page. In fact I felt the balance in my press treatment had finally tipped when I saw in a Florida newspaper one year the headline: WE DON'T CARE WHAT SANDERS SHOT—JUST WHAT IS HE WEARING TOMORROW? For a while after that, I sometimes wondered if people realized that, beneath the layers of pinks and roses and yellows and lavenders and pastel shades of brown and blue, I was still, and first and foremost, a professional golfer.

But that wasn't a serious concern. I liked knowing the public took an interest in my dress. Scotty started dyeing underwear shorts (also, long before men's underwear began appearing in colors and patterns in stores) when I got a letter giving me the idea from a boy who had seen me play in the Masters. It read as follows:

> Dear Mr. Sanders:
>
> I enjoyed watching you play at Augusta and I really liked your beautiful maroon slacks, shirt, and sweater. But on one hole you bent over to putt and your shirt came out and I saw your white shorts. Ugh. How uncouth can you get?
>
> > Signed,
> >
> > 007

(It was when the James Bond novels and films were at the height of their popularity, hence, I suppose, the signature.)

There were also many personally gratifying reactions. A woman in Oklahoma claimed that my colorful appearance on television during tournaments prompted her to take up golf as a sport, which led to her overcoming a lifelong allergy—to grass!

Some curious and amusing burdens fell to me simply because my shoe size (9½ C) and my shirt and sweater size (medium) are just about all-American average. That made me vulnerable to all sorts of free-loading.

One year I played in the Crosby with Ken Schnitzer, my friend and sometime business adviser in Houston. Each day he came out in a different sweater, and each sweater, I noticed, was bright and blended well with his pants. At the end of our indifferent performance in the event, I said, "Well, at least you looked good out there every day. Where'd you get all the nice clothes?"

"In your closet," he replied.

After another tournament, I was walking to the locker room when an older man, otherwise very mild in appearance, approached me and said gruffly, "I'd like to have that red shirt you got on."

"Yes, sir," I said, "I'll send you one just like it."

"You don't understand," he said. "I want that one."

"Well, all right, let me *send* you a fresh shirt."

"No," he insisted, "I want the one you got on, the one you played in."

"All right," I said finally. I was next to my car in front of the clubhouse, so I pulled the shirt over my head, handed it to him, and hopped in the car. Having given him the shirt off my back, I left quickly, noticing he had his eye on my slacks.

When I was in Britain one year, a chap offered me twenty-five pounds sterling for my red patent leather shoes of which he had never seen the like, he claimed, in his country.

"No, sir," I said lightly. "Not for sale."

"I'm going to make you a proposition you cannot reject, young fellow, I'll give you *fifty* pounds."

"No, sir, they're the only pair like them I got."

"All right," he said, thinking I was bargaining with him. "Make it a hundred."

Now he had offered me the equivalent of $280 for a pair of $60 shoes. I shook my head no, but later reflected that the man's passion for my shoes must have been indeed special. I resolved to give them to him as a present but unfortunately I never saw him again.

I voluntarily sought to improve the appearances of my friends and of people working for me, like caddies or drivers, if I thought their appearances needed work. James R., the fellow Cedartowner who was my sidekick on tour for some years, fell in love with a $300 white linen jacket I gave him once after winning a tournament. But the gift was ruined for him shortly after. He was wearing it the night I asked him to bring up two dinners for me and my date in my hospital room in Dallas, where my sore neck was getting treated. He picked up the medium-rare steaks and the wine and all the rest at a restaurant in town, then returned to the hospital with his package.

On the elevator, though, a nurse bumped into him, jarring his package and causing warm red steak juice to stream down the front of his jacket. The nurse added insult to injury by saying, "What have you got in the box, sonny?"

James R. would rather be dead than called "sonny" so he replied, "This is my friend's head right here," he said, steam rising from his eyebrows.

"I beg your pardon?"

"I said I got a friend of mine's goddam head in hyuh!"

At that moment the elevator door glided open and the frightened nurse flew out.

Another time James R. and I were driving along Wabash Avenue in Chicago in a pelting rainstorm. I was lecturing James about the need for some economy in the way we were

1. School picture of me at age ten in overalls, uniform of the day in Cedartown, Georgia, when I was growing up.

2. I am sporting a bikini-clad beauty on my shirt at the site of the National Jaycee Junior Championship in 1951, which I won at age eighteen for my first national success.

3. I was captain of the University of Florida golf team for three years before I "quituated."

4. At age twenty-two I became the first amateur to win the Canadian Open, whose Seagram Trophy I proudly hold. It was my most significant amateur win and it still remains one of the highlights of my competitive career.

5. Spiro T. Agnew examines the back of my head where his errant second shot during the 1970 Bob Hope Desert Classic conked me and got me off the sports pages and onto the front pages.

6. During the 1972 Classic, Mr. Agnew's personal physician, Dr. Bill Voss, and a fake "medical team" joined us and Bob Hope near the first tee.

7. I feel anguish and disbelief, and the spectators at the edge of the eighteenth green at St. Andrews, Scotland, appear truly stunned moments after my three-foot putt to win the 1970 British Open slides right of the cup by an inch.

8. In the gallery musician Buddy Greco and my wife, Scotty, share my shock.

9. I have to concentrate in order not to enjoy myself during a golf tournament, especially when I am paired with Joe Namath and Jackie Gleason in a pro-am.

10. When Gary Player and I run into each other on the practice putting green or range, we sometimes shake feet instead of hands.

11. Kaye Stevens tried to liberate me of my putter another year.

12. Tony Martin greets us at the table where I am feting my secon
wife, Joan, and Maurice Hudson and his wife. Maurice was the pro :
Cedartown who inspired me to practice and who kept me out of th
clutches of local hustlers.

13. One of my most satisfying wins was my sudden-death victory over Arnold Palmer in the 1966 Desert Classic. Former President Eisenhower and Bob Hope are with us at the presentation ceremonies.

14. Among the stars appearing in a show at Atlanta in 1969 to raise money for my college scholarship fund were my big-hearted friends Danny Thomas, Andy Williams, Chuck Connors, and Phil Harris.

15. My lovely wife, Scotty, and two of the game's finest gentlemen, Francis H. I. Brown, Hawaii's golfing paterfamilias, and Fred Corcoran, Walter Hagen's close colleague and now promoter of the World Cup and other golfing interests.

16. Our 1972 Desert Classic foursome was Bob Hope, Frank Sinatra, Spiro T. Agnew, and me.

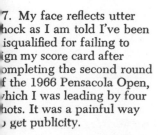

17. My face reflects utter shock as I am told I've been disqualified for failing to sign my score card after completing the second round of the 1966 Pensacola Open, which I was leading by four shots. It was a painful way to get publicity.

18. Big Chris Blocker gives me a bear hug after I defeated him in a play-off for the 1970 Bahama Islands Open. It was my first victory in over three years — the longest winless period in my career.

19. I travel by air about 400,000 miles a year. With Gene Kelly I display a huge Nile perch we caught in Kenya, East Africa, for ABC-TV's "The American Sportsman" program in 1970.

20. Jimmy Demaret and I give "The Squire," Gene Sarazen, a ride in a lounge chair between takes for "Shell's Wonderful World of Golf" program, now defunct, in 1967 in Faro, Portugal.

21. More recently, I try out the local transportation system in Morocco.

22. Before he was of school age I loved to have my son, Brad, on tour with me. I usually played better when he was with me because I tended to go to bed earlier in the evenings.

23. I played with a rose clenched between my teeth for a lady in the gallery, a variation on Walter Hagen's "Stop to smell the flowers" philosophy of life.

24. An older photo but still one of my favorite shots of Scotty and me walking along a fairway, our reflection caught in the water of a creek.

living—he handled a good deal of my personal finances as we went from one trouble spot to the next on tour. James R. kept shaking his head and groaning—I was the one piling up all the expenses, not him.

Finally the rain got so hard James R. pulled over and stopped. I peered through the window and saw we were in front of a well-known men's tailor in Chicago, frequented by top entertainers.

"We might as well go inside until it stops," I said.

"All right, let's just go inside with this new fiscal policy of yours," James R. snapped at me.

We got out of the store in forty minutes at a cost of a little under $5,000. I felt a little abashed as we drove away. I knew I should not resume my speech on economy, but after a while I did say, "James R., aren't you at least going to point out how much money I have wasted?"

"No," he said after a pause. "You have forgotten one detail that makes it easy to forgive you."

"What is that?"

"I am your size in shirt, shoe, sock, and slack."

9 / Trans Sanders Airways

I made my first plane trip, a hop from Atlanta to Augusta to play in a state high school tournament, at age thirteen. I wouldn't let the stewardess serve me lunch because I was afraid she would make me pay for it.

I'm less innocent about the customs of on-board meals and all the other aspects of travel now that I fly four hundred thousand miles or so a year. But in some ways I am still the thirteen-year-old from the country when it comes to seeing strange places and meeting new people. I need to keep moving and I always am fascinated by what I find when I get there.

My early experience in foreign lands in particular was so favorable that I never even thought of having serious complaints about the odd customs and languages, trying procedures, and occasionally ticklish political situations one stumbles against abroad. In my first trip outside the country—in 1955—I won the Mexican Amateur. In my second trip—in 1956—I won the Canadian Open as an amateur. In my third trip—1957—I won the Colombian Open on the Caribbean Tour, which I played while waiting to become eligible to play in the United States. How could I not believe travel yielded wonderful surprises? Only one thing—sex with a beautiful woman—has ever compared favorably in my mind with the experience of running head-on into the mystery and originality of a new sight such as mountainous Japan, or the lakes in Scotland, or African plains flooded with life.

Travel is inconvenient of course, not to mention expensive, and riskier than staying home. As often as I walk on a plane, and as trusting as I am of the equipment and the staff, I say a prayer every time I step on board. During the spate of hijackings a couple of years ago, I figured the odds against me were getting so high that I might as well go in a pine box via Air Freight. (The hijacker plays with lives in ways he does not fully appreciate. One time a San Diego businessman left his office to fly to Los Angeles for an afternoon's rendezvous with a girl friend. The plane was hijacked to Cuba, however, and the businessman had an awful time making sense of that to his wife.)

I don't see how anything interesting or valuable can come without suffering a little inconvenience and risk from time to time, however, no matter what your pursuit or interest. We are all from small towns, mentally if not actually, and though it is good to have the familiar sights and securities of our neighborhood, it's also important to meet the new persons and see the new sights even if getting there seems a struggle. The stimulation is worth the challenge, and it keeps the mental small town from getting smaller.

Flying has always been my favorite means of travel and it is the most characteristic form of travel for the touring pro-

fessionals of the "gilded age" I mentioned earlier. Some of
the older pros never really cottoned to it. Fred Hawkins flew
only on certain conditions that he had established out of prior
experience. Once he had been on a commercial flight that
actually grazed the top of some cactus while flying through
some low-visibility weather out west. After the plane landed,
he could see pieces of cactus sticking out of the fuselage.
Thereafter whenever Fred flew he insisted on a seat in the
back, reasoning that it was unlikely any plane would ever
back into the ground.

I've had a few close calls, some more imagined than real.
Once, I landed in a DC-3 by night in Dallas. I was sitting in
a jump seat behind the pilots, who were golfers I had made
friends with upon boarding. They had given me a set of ear-
phones to listen in on the communication between control
tower and plane. As the jabbering in my ears increased, and
the hands of pilot and copilot fluttered across the console, and
the fast approaching runway exploded with twinkling lights, I
got nervous. Just as we touched down, the pilot reached over
and threw open a window, stuck out a large hand light and
I got *real* nervous. In fact I thought we were about to crash,
but I couldn't figure out how any of us would be able to escape
through that tiny window. It turned out that the pilot merely
wanted to locate the terminal exit from the runway markings
—he had never landed in Dallas before.

Arnold Palmer took my son and me up in the Jet Com-
mander he had just acquired one year after an exhibition we
played together in Florida. When we landed in Winter Haven
we bounced on the runway like a golf ball—the first hop must
have exceeded a hundred feet. Afterward Arnie told me he
had never landed over water before and had come in a bit too
firmly. I was still shaking when Brad said, "Gee, Dad, what a
neat flight! Can we get Mr. Palmer to go do that again?"

Once I thought I was expertly flying a 707 on a trip back

from South America. Watching me closely, the pilot had let me handle the controls for a few minutes. I felt my hands were directing the plane through the air about as smoothly as they would stroke a putt on lightning greens. Then a stewardess walked in asking, "What's happened, Captain, are we running into bad weather? It's awful bumpy in the back."

I was crushed. Obviously I wasn't quite the flying pro I thought I was.

I was never airsick. The closest call was on a flight one year into West Virginia to play in the Sam Snead Festival. To avoid a tremendous head wind, which would have delayed the flight, the pilot kept the plane under five thousand feet where there was a storm in progress. During the next half hour we went through more pitches and rolls than the Air Force Academy. We were trying to play cards but since we had to keep bending and lifting with the plane, we weren't getting in too many hands. Finally the turbulence got to Al Besselink. His deep sun-tanned face turned pale as soap. He lay down in the aisle and groaned.

"Bess," cried Porky Oliver, standing astride the fallen giant with his dinner tray in one hand and an apple in the other, "Want a piece of some good greasy chicken? Come on pro, have a wing!"

Finally I staggered to the bathroom myself, which is where they found me when we landed. I didn't get sick in there, but I didn't get any better, either. They found me on the floor, holding onto the toilet bowl for dear life, so weak they had to lead me out.

I was sitting next to Gary Player on another rough flight a few years later when I noticed he was getting a little white in the face. I thought of how Porky had teased Besselink and said, "I have an idea, laddie, when we land—why don't we stop for some cold spaghetti and meatballs with the grease still sticking out on top?"

Periodically I made similar references to food and drink and finally Gary grabbed his airsickness bag and whooped into it. Then he got up and excused himself to go to the bathroom and, as he squeezed past me, he dropped the bag.

"Aaaagh!" I cried, practically snapping my back in two as I lunged sideways into the aisle trying to escape the spilled airsickness bag.

But Player had had the last laugh—the bag was empty.

My blind brother, Ernest, was on a flight with his wife one year when he happened to have a bad, running-nose cold. He groped around in the bathroom on board until he came upon some tissue paper he thought he could use to blow his nose from time to time. He stuffed a few packages into his pockets and went back to his seat. After a while he handed one to his wife and said, "Would you open this up for me, honey?"

She looked at the package and said, "What do you want with Kotex, Ernest?"

The one time I was on an airplane that didn't have a toilet turned out to be an intestinal comedy if there is such a thing. The entertainer Gene Kelly and I were going to be fishing partners on a show in ABC's "American Sportsman" television series. We were flying into Kenya to do the filming.

High over the jungles of central Africa, Kelly was seized with diarrhea.

"Stop the plane!" he said in desperation after looking unsuccessfully for some place on board to go.

"Why don't you just stick your ass out the window?" I suggested.

"Don't make me laugh, it hurts to laugh."

"Well, then go in your hand and toss it out the window."

"You dirty bastard," he said, laughing and swearing at the same time.

I knew what he was going through but I wasn't going to reveal any sympathy. I had the same problem once for four days during my first Caribbean tour. I lost so much weight I had to grab my pants after every swing to keep them from falling down.

Finally Kelly threw himself at the mercy of the pilot, a Nairobian, who to my great surprise immediately began to take the plane down. He had spotted a small airstrip next to a government outpost building and we went in.

Meanwhile Kelly was clawing at the door. He gave off the hustle and bustle of a huge crowd. His face darkened when the plane touched down.

"Oh my God!" he said. "What am I going to do for paper. I don't have any paper!"

"Why don't you use some of your $10 bills?"

"You bastard!" he repeated.

"Did I ever tell you about the caddie who met me at Prestwick Airport with two rolls of toilet paper under his arm?" I started to relate.

When the plane stopped, the pilot ripped off some of his navigation chart and gave the pieces to Kelly. Gene opened the door, jumped out, and disappeared into the dense brush at the edge of the runway.

"Hey, don't get too far away!" I called, jumping out after him along with the pilot. I really was concerned now—we were in lion and tiger country. Shortly we heard Kelly moan with relief. He declared, "It's green! It's green! Look at it!"

"I don't want to look at your shit," I cried.

The pilot sucked in his breath, elbowed me and pointed down the runway. Coming toward us at a high rate of speed were two Jeeps. When they were within better eye range, I noticed both Jeeps were stuffed with armed natives in khaki uniforms.

"Gene, we are going to be killed," I cried. "Let's get back on the plane."

"I can't move!"

"You got to!"

The Jeeps screeched to a halt and the soldiers poured out and pointed rifles and pistols straight at us.

"Explain to these guys," I whispered to the pilot nervously.

"Tell them my problem!" Kelly called. He must have gotten a glimpse of the troops through the bushes.

"I don't know the word for shit," I called back.

"Show it to them."

"If it's green they won't recognize it. They'll think it's a native flower."

Meanwhile the pilot apologized in broken Swahili, which sounds harder to understand than broken English, for not radioing his landing intentions in advance, and gave some kind of explanation for our impromptu visit. Kelly came out of the bush, pulling up his pants, and the native soldiers stared at him with suspicion and wonder.

"Let's get out of here before Gene has another attack," I suggested.

For many people, the pain of making travel arrangements whether for a round-the-world voyage or a Sunday drive in the country, exceeds the pleasure of making the trip, so they just stay home and forget about it. I believe you have to step over the routine problems, in a bullheaded fashion if necessary, in order to get where you want to go. We are too often awed by cheeky clerks and intricate paperwork, and too much impressed by our inability to handle them.

In traveling, I have often gotten into trouble for overlooking details, but somehow always have managed to get where I'm going, or leave where I'm escaping, anyway.

Once I got a call from the U. S. Health Service in New Orleans, shortly after getting off a flight from Hong Kong.

"According to papers checked at the airport, you have never had a cholera shot," said the health official. "Have you by any chance lost any weight?"

"As a matter of fact, a few pounds, yes."

"Oh dear," said the official, who promptly came to my hotel room with a doctor and had me vaccinated. Thereafter the health department followed me around the country for three weeks to be really sure I didn't have the disease.

One year I had to renew my passport while I was in Portugal, where I had flown to do a show for "Shell's Wonderful World of Golf." Before leaving New York, I had been told I would be able to do this at the U.S. consulate in Lisbon. But when I arrived at the consulate on the afternoon of the day my passport was due to expire, I was asked for three copies of a current photograph of myself. That was the problem. I hopped in a cab and hired the driver for the day. He took me to twenty shops all over Lisbon before we finally located a photographer who was willing to do the work within an hour.

He took my picture, developed the film on the spot, and made the required three prints. I was so grateful I tried to pay him $50 but he would not accept the money. In sign language he indicated that the job was only worth $5 and that was all he would accept. I am always impressed—I should say stunned—when I meet someone unaffected by greed, so without the old photographer knowing it, I slipped the $50 bill into his jacket before we got out of there.

My most complex travel adventure took place one year when I went to play in the Colombian Open in South America. It started in Las Vegas where my second wife, Joanie, and I had been staying for a few days. During our marriage there was an unwritten law that I would never stay in Vegas without her, but at this time I wanted to get in a few days of gambling and high life before flying to South America. Accordingly, I had a friend drive me and my baggage out to the airport, supposedly to catch a plane to San Francisco on the first leg of my trip to Barranquilla, Colombia. Joanie was with us. She was going to catch a flight the next morning to North Carolina to visit her brother.

I pretended to check my baggage (asking the girl to just store them behind the counter for a while), then boarded the plane, waving good-by to Joanie. Then my friend and Joanie left to return to town where they were going to attend a show. As soon as they left, I got off the plane again, recovered my baggage, and went with another friend, who had been waiting for me, to a place across town where I then stayed for three days.

After the three days I flew to San Francisco. I went to the Pan American ticket counter to arrange passage to Barranquilla. There I discovered I didn't have my passport or birth certificate. I had left both in one of Joanie's suitcases. I couldn't very easily call Joanie at this point, since I was supposed to have been in South America for the past three days. All I had on me was $480 in cash and a Georgia driver's license that had expired.

I explained my plight to the ticket agent but he said he could not permit me to get on the plane. I tried to reach California Governor Pat Brown, whom I had played golf with, and then the President of Colombia, but neither phone call got through. At least I impressed the ticket agent with my seriousness. Just before the midnight flight was to depart, he sold me a ticket as far as Guatemala, from where he figured I could at least phone home with a convincing story of some kind.

In Guatemala, I made a phone call to Barranquilla Country Club and after three or four hours, finally got through to someone who spoke a mixture of three languages, none of them English as far as I could tell. Anyway I left a message that I was a tournament contestant who needed credentials from Colombia in order to be able to board a KLM flight leaving the next day at 10:00 A.M. I spent the night in a hotel across from the KLM office. Bright and early next morning, I went to the U. S. Embassy to try to obtain some kind of documentation, in case my message to Colombia did not get through. All the man there could suggest was that I sue Pan American for letting me arrive in a foreign country without proper credentials, but I certainly wasn't interested in doing that.

I went back and forth between the Embassy and the KLM office for a while. Finally I walked slowly back to the hotel, having completely given up on getting to the tournament. It was about ten minutes before ten o'clock—the scheduled departure time—when as I neared my hotel the clerk came running out of the KLM office.

"Mr. Sanders!" he cried. "How long will it take you to get ready? I just got a wire from the president of KLM! It is all right for you to get on the plane!"

I rushed into the hotel, grabbed my bags and ran, leaving dirty clothes and what-not in my wake. We sped to the airport. The plane delayed its departure forty-five minutes for me. Finally I was on my way again. There was a stop in Panama for refueling, but I refused to get off the plane, feigning sickness to one of the stewardesses.

Finally we arrived in Colombia. I felt a sinking sensation as we went through customs. I suddenly remembered I was traveling with a snub-nosed .38, the gift of a detective friend of mine. It was inside a sock in one of my suitcases. Fortunately the woman did not feel it as she groped through the contents. Then she asked me for my papers.

"I don't have any," I said.

"You mean you lost them?"

"No, I don't have them. All I have is my ticket."

"But you've been through three countries," she declared. "I've been working here twenty-seven years and never heard anything like it."

At this point two men appeared to escort me through customs and to the golf course. They had special credentials

for me that permitted me to stay in the country for seven days
as a guest of the President.

All I really wanted to do now was to call up Joanie and
establish my location. As soon as we got to the golf course I
ordered a drink. Before they could bring it to me, I got a message there was a phone call for me. It was from Joanie!

Joanie chewed me out for not calling.

"The telephone service down here is rotten," I said. "I've
been trying for three days."

But if I had gotten to the course just two minutes later,
the explanation to Joanie would have been:

"Sorry. Mr. Sanders has not yet arrived from the United
States."

My travel mishaps have not been confined to the airways.
Once I nearly drowned off a small boat in Miami. Early one
morning we were motoring out to the Quarterback Club, a
building on stilts in the bay not far from Ocean Ranch Motel
where I lived at the time. This was during one of my extrava-
gant bachelor periods and I had seen the sun rise every morning for two months. My daily routine had been roughly as
follows:

3:00 P.M. – 6:00 P.M.	Play gin rummy
6:00 P.M. – 9:00 P.M.	Drink martinis and make love
9:00 P.M. – 9:30 P.M.	Get rid of date and change clothes
9:30 P.M. – 1:30 A.M.	Raid kitchen at Ocean Ranch for roast beef sandwich and glass of milk, then drink scotch at bar
1:30 A.M. – 3:00 A.M.	Dinner
3:00 A.M. – 5:00 A.M.	Make love and sleep
5:00 A.M. – 7:00 A.M.	Play gin rummy again

7:30 A.M. – 11:00 A.M.	Play golf
12 noon – 3:00 P.M.	Sleep
3:00 P.M. – 6:00 P.M.	Start all over again with gin rummy

Anyway this particular morning we had finished the gin rummy game and there was no golf scheduled, so we decided to go out to the Quarterback Club and have a drink. On the way out the boat hit a sandbar and a few of us got out to try to push it free. At one point I turned around to admire the sunrise. Only moments later, it seemed, I turned back and discovered the boat had shifted and I was now about seventy yards away. My swimming range is more like seven yards, not seventy, but I knew the boat could not come back for me without risking getting stuck again.

So I set out clumsily stroking through the waves, my clothes dragging me under with their sodden weight. It seemed like hours, but I finally reached the boat. I was so exhausted, I could barely hold onto the chrome strip alongside the boat with my fingers.

"Somebody pull," I gasped.

A friend of mine reached over to pull me in and toppled in himself, knocking me adrift again. Now both of us were floundering—he swam like an anvil—elbowing each other, spitting water, on the verge of panic.

"Goddam it," I said at one point as he continued pushing against me, "you have the whole ocean to drown in, why are you in my arms?"

At last the other passengers pulled us aboard, saving me, literally, for sure, because I know I did not have another full minute of buoyancy left in me.

My luck in automobile travel has varied. Once James R. and I made a belated start on a six-hundred-mile overnight drive from Miami to Atlanta for a non-deductible appointment with the Internal Revenue Service in the morning. We were both exhausted from partying and started off by alternating the chore of driving every hour. Each time the driver got sleepy and started running up on the shoulder, the other guy would come awake and take over. By the time we got onto some narrow backwoods roads in Georgia, we were switching the chore every ten minutes, and to make matters worse, it began to get rainy and foggy.

At one intersection James R. drew up to a blinking red light and waited for a truck to cross. He decided to rest his eyes for a second. Two hours later we both woke up, fresh as daisies, when another truck came up behind us blowing its horn.

James R. and I once drove from Dallas to Los Angeles on a similar share-and-share-alike basis. Without telling James R., however, I loaded up on sleeping pills and Statler Hilton pillows before we started. I handled the first one hundred-mile stint, getting us past Fort Worth, and then conked out among the pillows in the back seat.

James R. drove the rest of the day and well into the night. When I finally woke up, we were in the Rocky Mountains. "I'm feeling pretty alert," I said.

"You should," he said. "You've been sleeping twelve hours straight."

"How are you?"

"I'm jumpy enough to win the hurdles in the Olympics," James R. said. His eyes drooped about to his chest.

I looked out the window. "How high are we anyway?"

"If we drove off the road, we could say the Lord's Prayer about ten times before hitting bottom."

"Then maybe you better drive a little farther," I suggested.

"You're damn right," said James R., who had no respect for my skill behind the wheel.

One year I had a narrow escape trying to make a plane in

Seattle. Bob Rosburg and I were delayed in leaving for the airport because another pro, Phil Rodgers, was throwing a champagne party with some of the $10,000 he had won for making a hole-in-one in the tournament that week. Finally we got going. We should have realized something bad was in store for us when a black cat ran in front of my car after we had gotten only two blocks from the site of the party.

It was on the highway to the airport that the problem occurred. While going about eighty miles an hour, I was chatting on my car phone with a friend in Chicago. All of a sudden the car swung up on a concrete divider. "Hold on!" I said to my friend in Chicago and dropped the phone. At such high speed I knew I could not jerk the steering wheel much, so I let the car's tires sort of ride against the curb of the divider for what must have been nearly the length of a football field. Finally I was able to ease it off the divider. We lurched across the highway, into a shallow ditch and finally swung back on the road.

"Goddam that cat!" said Rosburg after a long silence. We were both a bit shaken.

Another skeptic about my driving is Basie McCulloch, my Palm Springs friend and hostess. Once I took her to Ojai, the resort I formerly represented on tour (now I represent Devil's Nest in Nebraska), for a round of golf and a few rounds of drinks. In the evening, as we started home, she offered to drive for me—Basie drove trucks for the Allied cause during World War II—but I claimed I was okay.

"You're steering it like it's a canoe," she pointed out a little later.

"Don't worry about a thing."

Pretty soon I started having double vision. Instead of one truck coming around the bend at us, suddenly there were two. Instead of one set of lines down the center of the highway, now there were two sets of lines.

"Nothing wrong with the canoe," I said. "It's the damn river."

Finally I figured out how to get rid of my double vision. And for the last half hour of the drive, I covered one eye with my hand. Basie still makes me drive that way if she finds herself in a car with me. In fact, she says that the way I drive, it might be safer if I covered both eyes.

On tour the pros lose their cars to thieves almost as often as they win them in "closest-to-the-pin" contests during tournaments. Miller Barber had his car stolen two years in a row in Akron. Another pro left his car running in front of a motel office once. He went in, checked out, returned, and found the car gone. Bob Smith lost his car with all his credit cards in the glove compartment to his caddie one year. The caddie signed "Bob Smith" for the next few weeks and had a good time judging by the places he went and the amounts he spent.

Touring pros, like convention-goers in a strange town, are prime targets for thieves and other low-life characters and no-accounts. One year I went abroad to play in the British Open and left my car with the young man working as my chauffeur-valet on the West Coast at the time. In my absence, he was supposed to get the car tuned up, but when I got back I found that the car had been impounded by the Los Angeles Police Department. The cops explained that one day three young women shoplifters had been chased out of a fancy women's shop in Hollywood, and one of them had taken refuge in the back seat of my car. Now they realized obviously I had nothing to do with any shoplifting operation, and were happy to give me back my car.

I drove straight from the police station to the course where I was playing that week. When I got there I opened my trunk to get some golf balls. There before my eyes were furs and fancy evening wear to dress a roomful of socialites—thousands of dollars' worth, I learned later. I slammed that trunk down like I'd seen a corpse and shot back to the police station with the stolen goods.

I've been robbed a number of times and for some reason have had especially bad luck during the Crosby, where my room was burglarized three times in four years. The last time we were taken with some class, which made it slightly more tolerable.

Here is what happened. One evening we had been celebrating the wedding anniversary of my playing partner, Ken Schnitzer, and his wife, Joan. Scotty complained of a headache, so we decided to cut the festivities short and go back to our rooms. When we got there—we had adjoining suites—we discovered both doors were locked from the inside.

We surmised later that the thief was still inside our rooms when we returned. But by the time we got help from the management in getting inside, he had left by a rear window, taking with him two fur coats, a camera, two antique rings of Scotty's, a wristwatch that Joan had planned to give to Ken for their anniversary, and a pair of cuff links that Vice President Agnew had given to me.

We were sitting in a daze, a few minutes later, when room service arrived with six bottles of iced champagne. We figured the manager had sent them down to try to calm our nerves when the police came. Later we found the thief had ordered the champagne, no doubt to celebrate his success, and charged it to me.

Next day we were having a somewhat subdued meal together downstairs in the hotel, when Ken suddenly remembered he was supposed to return an important business call. He called over the maître d' and asked for a telephone to be brought to the table.

"Of course, of course," said the maître d', particularly anxious to be nice to us in view of our misfortune the night before.

A few minutes later he returned empty-handed.

"I am sorry," he said, blushing grimly, "it appears that our dining room phone has been stolen."

Once I checked into a Manchester, England, hotel after a tiring transatlantic flight. I unpacked a couple of suitcases and then set myself to throw the weightiest suitcase of all—the one with all my sweaters and slacks—up on the bed. I threw it all the way across the room and fell into bed after it—the suitcase was completely empty. Somebody in Dublin, where the plane had made a stop, or in England, had cleaned me out good. I was angered and impressed and bemused—I wondered how the thief would explain to his customers the "D.S." monogrammed on all those pink and purple sweaters.

Another common problem when you travel is snags in reservations, like when you and your family show up at a fancy resort hotel for your first vacation in two years and the room clerk stares at you coldly, as though you had said "typhoid fever" when you gave your name.

Once the musician Al Hirt made reservations for me at a hotel in New Orleans when I took a week off from the tour to relax with him on a fishing trip. I got into town late and arrived at the hotel just before midnight.

I announced my presence. The girl at the desk looked at me, looked at some papers, walked away and came back in five minutes with a hurt look in her eyes. When something goes wrong with their system, clerks take it hard.

"You *are* the Mr. Doug Sanders who Mr. Hirt made reservations for?"

"That's right."

"I'm afraid there's been a mistake. Would you take the elevator to the twelfth floor and meet our manager? He will take care of it."

I met the manager on the twelfth floor and he explained that on instructions from Mr. Hirt, he had prepared the hotel's finest suite of rooms for me, and had set out bowls of fruit and nuts, personalized matches, vases of flowers, and a bottle of champagne for my arrival.

Unfortunately, he added, a Mr. *Bill* Sanders had checked into the hotel first, and happened to be carrying a bag of golf clubs when he walked into the lobby. The girl innocently assumed he was Mr. Hirt's famous golfer friend.

After explaining all this, the greatly offended manager then marched into my original suite of rooms and stripped it of every complimentary nut and matchbook in the place.

Another mix-up happened once when I dropped out of a tournament and flew to Wichita Falls, Texas, to meet a girl friend. Early the next morning, I decided to hit some balls, so I looked in the phonebook in my motel room and dialed the number for the Wichita Falls Country Club. Professionals extend the use of their facilities to one another as a matter of courtesy and I anticipated no problem.

I got the pro on the line and introduced myself: "This is Doug Sanders calling," I said.

"What else is new?" came the reply.

"Well, nothing else is new," I said. "I'm just looking for a place to practice."

"Who's with you, Hogan or Snead?"

"No one's with me," I said. This was not the friendliest reaction I had ever gotten from a club pro. "Do you mind if I hit balls out at your place?"

"We don't have a range, Ben."

"I'm not Ben, I'm Doug Sanders," I said, annoyed. "Is there anywhere in town that would have a range?"

"Sure, try the public course. Not much of a place, but they're not fussy."

I hung up, dialed the public course, and got the pro there on the line.

"This is Doug Sanders," I said. "I'm looking for a place to hit a few balls."

"Sure, Doug," the pro replied quickly—too quickly it seemed to me. "Shall I send my car over for you?"

"No, no, I can take a taxi."

"Fine. I'll get Arnie and Jack and we'll make a foursome."

"That won't be necessary," I said, "and as a matter of fact they are playing in a tournament this week."

"Well, so is Doug Sanders according to the paper."

"No, Doug Sanders withdrew after his round yesterday and is now in town trying to get a goddam place to practice."

Long silence. Then a subdued voice: "Doug, I'm afraid there's been a misunderstanding."

When I got out to his course, the pro explained: The two pros were good friends and mutual kidders who often phoned each other under fictitious names. After I finished practice, he offered me $100 if I would just drop by the shop at the private club. He figured my appearance would shock the hell out of his friend. I said I'd be happy to do it for nothing. In fact at this point I was looking forward to meeting the first guy I had talked to.

I walked in his shop, told the assistant who I was, and waited. Out came the pro, thinking his pal had stopped by. When he saw me, he stopped dead in his tracks, his face blanched, and he said, "Oh shit, I've done it."

Of all forms of travel, flying in advanced aircraft has been my special favorite, though technically I have never gotten anywhere in such aircraft—we land back where we take off from. Sometimes I feel overstuffed with experience, with all the different places and people I've met. The sensation of something new doesn't really come until I feel it in the tremendous speed and reflexes of these catlike machines.

I have hopped rides in the Navy F-4 fighter-bomber, also known as the Phantom, in the F-106, which is an Air Force interceptor, and in the T-38, the basic trainer for Air Force pilots. Whenever my pilot-guides let me handle these planes in flight for brief periods, the feeling that came over me was extraordinary. I felt as though I had my hands on the steering wheel of a hurricane or some other great natural force.

Shortly before my first flight in one of these planes, the T-38, I was discussing the various safety preparations required with a couple of Air Force officers.

At one point James R. blurted out, "Just one goddam minute! What happens if something goes wrong up there? I am going to be put out of honest work."

"Well, James, let's see, anybody have a piece of paper?" Somebody handed me a slip of paper and I wrote on it:

TO WHOM IT MAY CONCERN:
Give James R. $25,000.

I handed it to him and he said, "Not enough. I'd say one dollar per foot of altitude would be closer to a just settlement of your estate."

I crossed out the $25,000 figure and wrote in $50,000. Colonel Gus Taute, now General Taute, signed it as a witness and James R. was at last satisfied.

We did reach 50,000 feet in the T-38—fast. We rolled, zoomed, dipped in the cloudless Texas sky, ran across the golf course at Odessa at 1,000 feet and went up again. The pilot let me handle the control stick briefly. Then, while we swam through the high sky, he ruined it by asking me for golfing tips.

In the F-106, three years later (it took time for me to run into and befriend generals in a position to arrange such flights for me), I got up to 65,000 feet with a pilot who had completed over a hundred missions in Vietnam. When we were at our ceiling, with what seemed like all of Kansas below us, the pilot asked me to try to lift my feet, but I couldn't because as he went into a banking maneuver the force of gravity became enormous. I managed to lift my hand to keep my oxygen mask on my face, for it seemed to be drawing off. I became the fourth civilian ever to have gone up in an F-106, and the pilot even let me handle the controls on and off for the forty-five delicious minutes we were aloft.

My excitement was the same as I felt when I went up in the T-38 and, at a still later date, when I would go up in an F-4 in San Diego. Besides feeling something new, which came as a special surprise to a jaded sort, I liked the sense of mastering flight a lot. At times when playing golf, I have felt that the club was as much a part of me as was my arm, and that I could direct it, and create shots with it, just as confidently as I could reach out with my arm and touch a spot on the wall. To ride the metal and thrust of an airplane and feel it as though it were part of yourself was even more dramatic.

The last airplane story I will tell is one in which I never got off the ground. My thirty-fourth birthday fell on Sunday, July 24, 1967. The week before, I had spent a few days in Minnesota fishing with my son Brad. In the course of showing him how to handle firecrackers safely, I had managed to practically blow off one of my thumbs. I came into Akron, Ohio, with the thumb badly swollen and bandaged. I did play in the American Golf Classic that week, but I told Jack Nicklaus that I would not be able to play in a one-day affair he was promoting in his home town of Columbus for the following Monday. I decided I would go to Chicago instead where a friend was planning a birthday party for me late Sunday night.

Meanwhile an insurance company I represented at the time begged me to change my plans and play in the Columbus event for business reasons—the company was seeking better representation in that area. So I decided to stay and play after all.

But on Sunday the thumb still felt sore, and I decided I really didn't want to play. Furthermore I was offered a good way to get out of town. The airlines were on strike at the time, but Tony Lema had hired a private plane. He and his wife Betty were going to fly into Chicago right after the American Golf Classic was over. He invited me to come along and I accepted.

Then I called one of the organizers of the Columbus event to explain why I couldn't participate after all. He immediately talked me back into playing by pointing out I would really look like a heel in Columbus if, after having withdrawn and then re-entered, I dropped out once more.

Finally I decided to stay in town. At the last minute, I called up Tony to tell him not to save a seat for me on the plane, and I called up my friend in Chicago to cancel the birthday party.

I went to another party that night in a home in suburban Akron. There were a number of golfers and people in the golf business at the party. One of them was the first to get the news on the telephone about eight o'clock, and to make the numbing announcement that the Lema plane had crashed and that there were no survivors.

10 / Sex and the Single Golfer

When I was practicing for the 1956 Canadian Open in
Montreal, I met a pretty English girl named Lynn. Her voice
was Shakespeare to my country ears and her figure was even
better. But she wouldn't go out with me.

"I'll give you a date—a long date—if you win the tournament," she finally told me.

"But no amateur has *ever* won the Canadian Open," I said.
The last professional tournament won by any amateur had
been the 1954 San Diego Open, which Gene Littler captured.
Now Littler was one of numerous pros in the field at Montreal
—pros like Arnold Palmer, Billy Casper, Doug Ford, Fred
Hawkins, Art Wall, Gardner Dickinson, Gay Brewer, and
Bob Rosburg. I had no illusions about a twenty-two-year-old
amateur's chances. I figured they were good (I was playing
well at the time) but not great.

To make a long story short, I was the only player to break 70 all four days of the tournament, and with a 68 on the final round, I picked up two strokes on the leader, Dow Finsterwald, forcing a play-off which I won on the first extra hole when Dow bogeyed. I owe my victory to two things: a new tranquilizer called Miltown which I took each night to maximize my rest, and the prospect of having Lynn. On Sunday night I had Lynn and left the Miltown in the bottle.

If nothing else, the story suggests to what preposterous lengths I would go as a bachelor to catch a woman I desired. Neither miles nor money nor modesty could ever get in my way—not to mention feats like winning pro tournaments as an amateur. I have flown from Miami to Atlanta and gotten off the plane to buy a ticket to New York, to be with a girl I had just met. Once I flew from London to Los Angeles just to have dinner with a girl, flying over Montreal, where I was supposed to play in a tournament, on the way.

"Goddam, I've got to come back here tomorrow!" I exclaimed.

Once, flying from Chicago to Toronto, an hour-long hop, I seduced myself into joining a young woman who was traveling to Miami and to Havana, two of my favorite nightspots in those days.

I never felt ashamed of my sex drive and never tried to conceal it or dress it up as something else. My openness offended more strait-laced members of the golfing community, I suppose, but it was something I could not help. I grew up in a town where, like many other country places in the south, sex was part of the landscape just like haystacks and Coca-Cola signs.

Not that I became a show-off—just the opposite. When I was seven a little girl used to lure me into the crawl space under our house. We would disrobe and hug until our backs ached and my penis stuck out wondering what to do next.

Once we walked into my house in that state, clothes in hand, and my mother walloped me. I learned discretion and decency then and there.

I was officially initiated into sex when I was eleven. A fourteen-year-old girl led me into a roadside ditch outside of town and explained we were going to act out a game called "Doctor and Nurse." After checking each other's heartbeats and giving a few other tests, she said, "Now here's the fun part," and she guided me inside her. It was over fast, I noticed, but wondrous while it lasted.

After that I was sold on sex and nobody could have made me believe there was anything wrong with it even if they tried. In grammar school a couple of boys and I located a trysting place beneath the gym—it was actually a crawl space—and we would take our girl friends there during recess when we could sneak away. In seventh grade, a girl and I once made love standing up behind a Hammond's Map of the World when the teacher was called from the room for a few minutes.

In high school I was just as bad, or just as good if you look at it my way. By this time I was pretty experienced in shot-making, so to speak, and there weren't many times or places not conducive to lovemaking if I tried. One girl and I used to get to school early on a regular basis, and made love in a coat-room or broom closet before classes began. This versatility survived years later as I continued to get the game on in odd places, such as crowded swimming pools or eight miles high in a commercial jet.

Some of my expertise and daring came as a result of seeing what went on at the golf course at night. First there were the parties I helped at, which various groups and organizations in town gave from time to time. I was the only one with a key to the back door of the clubhouse, which led onto the golf course. A guy would come up and ask me to let him out with his girl friend or somebody else's wife and then to let him and her back in fifteen minutes later. Nobody at the party would be the wiser, except me, who would also be richer by the dollar or two the guy usually slipped me for the favor. Occasionally high school teachers were involved in these escapades and that eventually made the problem of my absenteeism at school much easier to solve.

I was also in charge of discouraging lovers who tried to park out on the course at night. I was supposed to go out there with a flashlight and run them off, or at least make sure no one parked on a green or in a bunker. But I usually just checked to see who was with whom and what they were doing to each other. When it was time for me to go home I would cautiously cut across the first fairway, amid the beer cans and Coke bottles and condoms of the night's reveling, making sure mainly not to stumble into any couple still in a clinch, and possibly get some local Romeo angry at me for interrupting.

By the time I got to college I was an out-and-out lover, different from many men in my nearly constant desire to have women, and also in my shrewd and diligent manner of wooing women. One woman in particular helped me make an important change in my attitude toward lovemaking during this period. She was as young as I was, and not greatly experienced in the subject, but somehow she and I confronted the question, "What is sex?" together—and came up with an answer that to this day seems both natural and correct to me. Sex is probably the fullest feeling of the life force that one can experience, and what our discovery amounted to was that lovers had to sincerely want to, and technically know how to, give that feeling to each other.

Both sexes have had a tendency to be at fault in this area, in my opinion. Women, though their capacity for enjoying sustained sexual relations is far greater than that of most men, have tended to be less than honest about their true feelings and needs regarding sex. For various reasons they have been too passive and close-mouthed. They have not *taken*. Men have been at fault principally in their selfishness and unwillingness to concentrate hard on making the woman feel wonderful. They have had a tendency to get what they can, and then get out. They have not *given*.

It has been a pathetic situation, this needless communications gap between men and women. It has been like a boy and girl fighting over who unwraps the Christmas present that is meant for both of them.

Anyway I felt I matured from child to adult in this area of handling the opposite sex, during this particular relationship I enjoyed at college. We learned how important it was to reach each other on levels that might be described as "separate but equal." In other words, if on a scale of one to ten, one person needs nine to be pleased, and the other needs five, the goal of both partners should be to be sure, after it's all over, each has reached the right level.

During this same period, I also began to realize how much I annoyed some men who either envied or disapproved of my passions. Only luck, pluck, and some friends got me out of the predicaments my life as a lover led me into.

The most dangerous plight for me as for any lover were those involving The Revengeful Boy Friend. My first serious clash in this category occurred when I was living a high bachelor life in Miami shortly after leaving college. A stewardess was encouraging my attentions though she had a regular male companion, who in addition to being large in size was jealous in disposition.

After dinner with her one night, she invited me back to her apartment, indicating that her boy friend was out of town on some business. Naturally I accepted and, in the immortal words of someone else, one thing led to another. An hour later, after making love a couple of times, we were sitting naked on her couch watching TV when we heard a voice at the door, "Open up this goddam door or I'll knock it down."

I whispered to the girl to run, turn on the shower, throw some water on her, and then answer the door. Meanwhile I grabbed my clothes and ran out the back door. Racing through her yard in the dark I ran into a clothesline that hit me just above the nose. If it had hit much lower I would have been decapitated.

Out in the street, I got into a cruising taxi. I had to slow down to board.

"Where'd you come from?" the cabbie said, surprised to find a customer in his back seat all of a sudden.

"Shut up and drive," I said. "I am headed home."

Years later I found myself in a similar trap, only this time I happened to have that .38-caliber pistol that I had inadvertently taken into South America one year. Actually, I had not intended to bring it with me this night, either; but it happened to be in the overnight bag I used to carry my son's dirty laundry. The young woman I was staying with was going to do the laundry for me.

Anyway, we were awakened at 3:00 A.M. by someone kicking in a screened-in window in the girl's game room. It was her boy friend. I hopped out of bed, got the gun, and waited as the man came up the long hallway from the game room. Then I stuck the gun in his back.

"Stand real still while I get on my clothes," I said, trembling like a leaf. "I could shoot you as a burglar and get away with it."

After I got my clothes on, I went into the kitchen and found the girl scrunched in a six-inch-wide space between the refrigerator and the wall.

"Look, go tell that grizzly bear to go home," I said.

"Why don't you put that gun down and show me how brave

you really are?" said the boy friend, who had boldly followed me.

"Who asked you to move?" I said, wagging the gun barrel at him as I had seen it done in Cagney movies. "You are lucky to be alive," I declared.

We finally got him out the door, but then he started pounding on it to get back in.

"If you don't get out of here by the count of three, I'm going to let you have it," I said.

He left, but telephoned a little later.

"I have my gun now," he said, "and I'm coming over there and I'm gonna shoot you full of holes."

"Oh yeah?" I answered brazenly. Before he had a chance to say anything else, we were in my place on the other side of Miami.

Once I woke up in a motel to what I assumed was gunfire. I also figured, by the way the woman next to me leaped out of bed and danced across the room, that it came from a boy friend of hers. "I'll tell you one thing," I cried, "if you are going to beat me to the door, you better hurry." And I started after her, stopping in my tracks, however, when I got a sudden strong whiff of orange juice. A quart bottle had exploded in my portable bar.

One year Norman Simowitz, a childhood friend who lives in Augusta, put on a blond wig and crept into bed with me in the house I was staying in during the Masters. Groggily I came awake hearing a falsetto voice saying, "Oh, kiss me, hold me!" and seeing flashbulbs going off and getting glimpses of this long blond hair next to me. Now in fact I had been with a girl earlier in the night, and she had gone home. But I was too sleepy to realize that and I figured somehow or other I was being framed good. All I could think, having caught a look of Norman's face in the strange after-light that a flashbulb camera creates in a dark room, was why, if I was going to be compromised, it had to be with such an ugly woman. Then all the lights in the room went on, and I saw Norman's wife, Annette, standing there with the camera, a partner in the most keenly felt practical joke ever played on me.

I used to keep an address book for which Frank Stranahan once half-seriously offered me $5,000. It had the names and numbers of my friends, the majority of them female, in all the cities on or near the tournament trail. Once I discovered it was missing.

James R. and I had spent a couple of hours visiting with Joanie, my second ex-wife, at her house in Denver. Then we had gotten on a plane to Los Angeles. Halfway across the Rockies, I realized I did not have my book with me. I jumped out of my seat.

"Wait till we land to get off," James R. suggested.

From the Los Angeles airport, I phoned my ex-wife and learned to my great relief that she had found the book under a sofa cushion. "Would you mind sending it registered mail?" I said. "There are a lot of business contacts in there."

"Then it must be worth $2,000 to you at least," my ex-wife said.

"It is not worth such a sum to me," I lied, but I quickly added, "I will give you $500."

And that's what I ended up sending—only I never got the book back.

Once I tried to combine travel arrangements for two separate liaisons by taking a girl to her departing flight at O'Hare Airport in Chicago, at the same time I was supposed to meet a girl coming in on another plane. The arriving flight was early, however, and as we turned a corner in the terminal on our way to the gate for the departing flight, I saw my arriving date walking jauntily up the corridor.

I gasped and bent over.

"What are you doing?" said my departing date.

"I've got to tie my shoelaces," I said.

"But you're wearing loafers."

"I mean I've got something in my shoe," I stammered. "A pebble or something." By this time the other girl had passed by.

The worst case of overlapping occurred one year in Florida. Somehow I had made dates with five women for a three-hour period one afternoon.

"James R.," I said, "I have messed up."

"That is standard operating procedure."

"I've got a date."

"What else is new?"

"I've got five of them. I need help."

"I'll be glad to help."

"Not that kind of help." (Actually James R. never messed with other women, only with liquor, and he even gave up on that eventually.) "I need help with the coming and going."

James R. rose to the challenge. The first girl arrived and I led her away. Then, as each of the other four dates arrived, James R. received her, sat her down at the bar, near the pool, in the lounge or in the lobby. He told one I was in a business meeting, the next with a doctor, the third at a PGA affair, and the last on the phone. For three hours he shifted from one date to another, ordering a drink here and a sandwich there, frequently excusing himself to make "an important call to the Coast."

After I had kept all five dates, James R. dragged himself up to my room, exhausted from all the walking he had put in, and grumbling about the silly conversations he had had. But he was most disgusted with me, when he found I was dressing for the dinner date I was supposed to pick up in twenty minutes.

Some predicaments one cannot escape from. In Oklahoma City once, a friend of mine found me in the shower with his date—it had been as much her idea as mine. He had pushed open the bathroom door and called, "Have you seen Nancy?"

"Nope," I called back from the shower.

Then he flung back the shower curtain and there we were.

"This is not what you think it is," I said.

"It isn't?" said my friend. Even in that situation he could not help being impressed by the weakness of my retort. He looked from Nancy to me. "Doug, what do you think I think it is?" he asked.

I once spent a couple of weeks in Crawford W. Long Hospital in Atlanta for an operation on my left knee that was long overdue. If I moved my leg a certain way a bone would slide up under a nerve in the knee and I'd break out in a sweat. This was happening more and more and I knew I had to get it fixed. I had a lot of girl friends in Atlanta at this time and I was actually looking forward to the hospital stay. For the first couple of days after the operation, I was under too much sedation to entertain anyone, however—though apparently I did amuse the nurses and orderlies raving about my amorous conquests of the past.

On the fourth day, the drugs had worn off and my knee had swollen so much they had to cut a vent in the pajama leg. A doctor came and drew off the fluids with a huge needle. By that evening I felt fine. I got on the phone and the parties began. Friends brought up steaks, beer, and whiskey every evening, and sent over their friends during the day. One of the nurses would run in periodically with a wet washcloth to wipe the lipstick off my mouth before my next visitor. Some of the other nurses ran in periodically to smear me with their own lipstick.

On the day before I was to be discharged, I decided I was fit enough to make love. My visitor was a petite Atlanta girl with bright red hair, and she was willing to try too.

I had my left leg stuck straight out on a kind of shelf attached to my wheelchair, and I had the wheelchair backed up against the door so nobody could get in the room. She hiked her dress up and I wiggled my pajamas down and we got started. I had just about figured out the correct geometry for the final movements when I got a little too excited and the wheelchair turned over.

When my left knee hit the stone floor I let out a scream that must have cleaned out the cardiac ward in the hospital that night. Moments later a herd of nurses buffaloed in while my girl friend, torn between getting herself respectable and helping me, stood there in dismay, and I, with bleeding knee and half-erect member exposed, lay crumpled on the floor waiting to die.

I had to stay in the hospital another week to repair the fresh damage to my knee and, as an older nurse said to me, "It serves you right."

It is almost as easy to find sex on tour as on a paperbook shelf, if you want it. I once jokingly suggested that women spectators be handled as follows: put the married women on the right side, the unmarried ones on the left, and the ones who don't care in the fairway. What I was suggesting is a touring pro can get himself into a lot of trouble if he accepts every mating call coming at him. If he is married—and it is harder to stay married these days than it is to stay single—then the trouble comes in the form of silent treatment from pious colleagues or poison pen letters from wives of colleagues. If she is married, the trouble comes from a jealous husband. A fellow pro once got a note from someone in the gallery threatening him with his life if he kept playing in the tournament. The pro was sure it was from the husband of a woman who had been chasing him around all week, and he wasn't going to take any chances; he hit his next tee shot out of bounds and withdrew.

At the Colonial in Fort Worth one year, I got a note saying

"I'll be dressed in yellow, look for me on the first tee." Naturally my curiosity was aroused, but when I went out on the first tee that afternoon, there were five women dressed in yellow, ranging in age from eighteen to eighty. I didn't know where or how to start, and I almost topped my tee shot thinking about it.

My favorite note story came out of a rape trial in Milwaukee a few years ago. The victim, a demure young woman, was being examined by the prosecuting attorney. He asked the woman what the accused rapist had said to her just prior to the assault. She was too embarrassed to repeat the line, so the judge told her to write it down. She did and the attorney presented it to the jury. What she wrote on the note was: "I want to fuck you."

The note went from juror to juror until it reached a stout mild-looking woman in her fifties. She read it, stiffened slightly, then passed it to the man on her left. Now this man had not been paying much attention to the proceedings. His mind had been on baseball or painting the house. When he got the note, he read it, looked at his neighbor oddly, nodded—and stuck the note in his pocket.

I used to be impersonated a lot, which I suppose is a kind of compliment, though I have never really appreciated it that way.

Two girls named Carol and Betty called me up in San Francisco prior to a tournament there one year and claimed we had all been together in Lake Tahoe. "But that is one of the few places I have never been," I pointed out. They didn't believe I was serious until I arranged for them to meet me in person the next day at the golf course. At least I found out the phony Doug Sanders had not spoiled my reputation: the girls had had a good time.

Another time I got an angry phone call from a man in Boston who claimed I had taken advantage of his sister. It was easy for me to prove that on the several weekends "Doug Sanders" had spent with his sister, I was actually in tournaments in other parts of the country. But it was hard for me to believe, as happened, that the man's sister really thought she was going to bed with a famous golfer just because the fellow had a couple of newspaper clippings about me in his wallet.

My wife, Scotty, was standing in the baggage claim area at the Los Angeles airport one year. Next to her, watching the ramp for the flight's baggage to appear, were two men. One was a tall, nicely dressed fellow with graying hair and a pleasant manner. He struck up a conversation with Scotty and finally asked her, "Do you know anything about golf?"

"Some," replied Scotty.

"Do you know who I am?"

"No, I'm afraid not," Scotty said. She had never seen him before in her life.

"I thought you knew something about golf?"

"I do, I don't know a lot."

"But you should be able to recognize me!" he declared. At this point the man's golf bag slid down the ramp. "See that?" he said. "Now do you know who I am?"

"Well, it looks like a pro bag," she said.

"That's right," he said. "I'm a pro. And see my initials?" There were the initials "D.S." stitched on the side of the bag. "Now can you guess who I am?"

"No."

"Ever hear of Doug Sanders?"

"Yes."

"Well, that's who I am."

"You are?"

"That's right."

"Well, first of all," said Scotty, somewhat annoyed, "you're old enough to be his father. And second of all, no matter how old you get, you'll never catch up with him."

And she marched off. Back of her she heard the impersonator's friend roar with laughter and say, "I told you someday you'd run into someone who knew Doug Sanders!"—which apparently meant the guy had passed for me on a fairly regular basis!

Men sometimes come to me for help with their romantic problems. You can't repair a faulty swing in one lesson, and you can't perfect the technique of seduction with one short conversation with an expert seducer. But here are some of the things I say again and again in my little sex counseling workshops.

Work at it. Most men are too lazy to be good lovers, in my opinion, which probably explains why there are so many unsatisfied and unfulfilled women around for the lovers to pick off. No seduction worthy of its name was ever achieved without a little sweat.

Take your time about it. You can't seduce a woman unless you make her feel good about herself and about her relationship with you, which usually doesn't happen overnight. A man can use liquor or lies to get his way fast, but he will create no lasting feeling and he won't be welcomed back.

Relax, you don't have to prove anything. During the first couple of meetings, the important thing is to establish the aura of intimacy, not the act itself.

Play it cool enough and she may end up rushing you into action.

Touch. One of the greatest barriers between a man and a woman is scarcely noticed by most American men—the barrier of physical space. Latin-American and Mediterranean peoples use their hands freely to express warmth. Frequently touching a woman—on her hands and arms, on her face and neck, on her back, on her knees—sets up a feeling of real intimacy.

As the ad for Yellow Pages used to read: "Let your fingers do the walking."

Talk right. Don't lie and don't be a phony. A woman can smell a dishonest expression from a mile off.

Disagree with what a woman says, if you like, but never argue with what she feels.

Direct your conversation to things concerning the woman, not yourself. Forget your business and your golf game and your views on the economy. The more you get a woman to reveal about herself, the greater will be the sense of intimacy between you and the more trusting and compliant she will become.

Talk about sex. Don't make it sound dirty, please. There are some people who can make the word "angel" smell like garbage, and others who can say "let's go fuck" with the sweetness of cream. If you're in the first category, practice conversations about sex with understanding friends or dumb animals until you start handling the subject more smoothly and naturally.

Talking about sex is good strategy because it puts into the woman's head, at least unconsciously, the notion of getting together physically with you. It also fills you in on the woman's past experience and her general views on sleeping with men.

A few questions or comments like, "You have pretty lips," or "I bet you're a good kisser," or "Are you warm?" or even "Are you a good lover?" can get your relationship into an intimate plane right away. Say it in a friendly, light manner and you won't insult or frighten her. If she hits you or goes running from the room it means your nostrils started to flare and your tongue came out. Go back to practicing conversations with the dog.

Pay attention to details. Work out transportation and lodging and eating and all the other logistical aspects of a date or a weekend trip in advance. Don't let the woman get worried about or involved in practical decisions. If you want her to pick a restaurant, give her a specific either-or-type question like, "Would you rather have lobster, at Captain Queeg's, or fine French cuisine, at Chez Herman?" Don't ask her a dumb essay-type question like, "Where should we go eat?"

Flatter her in absentia by sending a card, flowers, or a gift that shows your personal knowledge of her likes and dislikes. Carefully schedule these gestures so they look spontaneous.

Learn to say you're sorry. If you do something wrong, like forgetting to do a favor for her, or being late, don't make excuses or try to shift the blame. There's a difference between saying, "I had a meeting and couldn't make it by seven," and saying, "I'm sorry this happened. I had a meeting but that's no excuse." A forthright apology will make you seem bigger, not smaller, for your mistake. An evasive and prevaricating remark will keep the mistake in her mind that much longer.

Lovemaking itself always works better when you know what gives a woman the most pleasure from the start, and the best way to find that out is to ask. Otherwise you may navigate halfway around the globe before you discover America.

Make sure the woman knows what you are doing. Don't go off on sidetracks or meaningless forays that will only confuse and mystify her. Stick to your game plan and keep a steady course.

Don't please yourself unless or until the woman is pleased.

Do not leave a woman staring at the ceiling while you are snoring like a dying hog.

Leaving too soon afterward cheapens the experience as much as instant snoring does. As a general rule, afterward should take as long as before.

Get a vibrator.

Some of this advice has worked for some friends, some for others. No amount of technique, it appears, can overcome certain problems, such as mismatched sexual appetites.

A friend of mine found himself with an unusually demanding partner one night in Palm Beach. After what seemed like hours of relentless lovemaking, he crawled out of bed.

"Where you going!" she called after him.

"Get a drink."

"I'll get it for you!"

"No, you won't," he replied, pulling on his pants. "I'm getting it in Miami."

Then there was the young man who came to me complaining about "shooting off in the bushes"—premature ejaculation.

"Hell, you've got to get your mind on something else," I said. "Look out the window, study the wallpaper or something." Then I had a brainstorm. "I've got it, think about your golf game!"

"That's it," he said, "I'll think about golf!" That night at dinner before he went out on a big date, he said, "Boy, am I going to be super in the sack tonight! I played two rounds today and I didn't break 100 either time. That's 200 plus strokes I can think about."

I saw him next morning and said, "How'd you do last night?"

"I never played golf faster in my life," he reported glumly. "Thirty-six holes in three minutes and I remembered every shot."

11 / "Martial" Bliss

"I didn't pay $5.00 to see a pro hit a putter from off the green," I heard a lady grumble about my club selection one day during a Florida tournament some years ago. I walked over and said, "Ma'am, I will chip on with a full 2-wood from here if you will pay my alimony for one month."

Alimony and the uphill battle of making marriage work were on my mind a lot in the old days. My exact matrimonial record is:

> Leaped from cliff — three times
> Landed on rocks — twice

which is probably not much worse than average nowadays. In fact I consider myself lucky, in finding my present wife, Scotty, in faring as well as I have.

My first leap came on December 21, 1956, two weeks after I had turned professional. I married a pretty Cedartown girl named Betty Jane Estes, whom everyone called "B.J." My decision flew in the face of advice from Dutch Harrison and a Canadian businessman named J. Bradley Streit whom Dutch had introduced to me.

Dutch was particularly upset. Before the marriage, I tried to explain to him why I was going through with it.

"I got to settle down, Dutch," I said, not knowing what the hell 'settling down' was all about at age twenty-three. I was living a wildly scrambled life in Miami and I knew I could use a little more order and organization. I also noticed many of my friends from college were getting married and starting families.

"Settle down?" Dutch said, throwing his hands high. "Why don't you just get in touch with the undertaker now!"

I told him how pretty and popular B.J. was in Cedartown.

"But how do you know she's the right lady for you?" he demanded. Then he told me about his first wife. "She turned out to be dynamite, boy, and mean to boot. I ran away from her and she follered. One night I heard a knock on my door and went and opened it. I recognized her high-heeled shoes and my gaze slowly traveled up her legs all the way to the barrel of a .38-caliber pistol with the hammer cocked.

"I threw up my arms and started shaking and sputtering. Then I started leaning, trying to lean out of that line of fire, and pretty soon I looked like the Leaning Tower of Pisa. I said, 'Lookie here, take my $25,000 in war bonds, take my $35,000 home, take my $20,000 in cash, but do not let the hammer go.' She said, 'Dutch, I accept your kind offer.'

"But before she left she said, 'One day when you're bending over a little putt, I'm going to shoot you right in the spinal column!' Doug, boy, I missed more short putts that year, trying to hit them quick and get a look behind me. I did not get a good night's sleep until I went in the Army. I finally felt safe there in my barracks. I knew she could not get through the Military Police."

It wasn't too long after my marriage to B.J. that I began to wish I had listened to Dutch and to Mr. Streit, who had been much less colorful but just as firm in advising me against an entanglement at my age and stage. B.J. and I had a great honeymoon while I played the Caribbean tour. But when we returned and tried to set up an apartment in Jacksonville, I discovered I was not really cut out for the husband-and-wife routine of those times. I couldn't throw parties to introduce my old friends to our new furniture. I couldn't sit around of an evening and invent conversations for me and B.J. to have. I couldn't plan our future together because I didn't even know what our present was.

This was a sad awakening for me. Like the man who discovers one does not learn how to swim by jumping into a deep lake, I felt like crying out for help. B.J. got pregnant which was a mixed blessing for me under the circumstances. I fervently wanted a son of my own, but I also had hoped to bring up any children in a reasonably happy family atmosphere, which plainly—my instincts already had told me—was not going to come about.

Meanwhile, I went back on tour and began the virtually unbroken string of injuries and mishaps that shortly forced me off tour with that timid takeaway of mine. With so many things amiss in my personal and professional life, I began to think my Canadian Open victory as an amateur had been like catching lightning in a jug, to use a Georgia expression—nothing but luck. I even interviewed for a club pro's job at Selva Marina Country Club—where some ten years later I would win the Greater Jacksonville Open. Somehow I could not bring into focus an image of myself as "Doug Sanders, Socks for Sale."

After my son was born, on December 7, 1957—Pearl Harbor Day—I decided to split the blanket with B.J. Fortunately we did not make it formal right away or I might have ended up in the Army.

One day after I had gone back on tour I was called into the Selective Service office in Atlanta. An Army captain said, "There are about ten thousand people in your home town, is that right?"

"That's the population all right, sir," I said. "How did you know?"

"Because that's about the number of letters we have gotten from Cedartown wanting to know why you haven't been drafted."

I had been classified 4-F because of my knee, but the captain advised me that I was now considered by the Army to be in excellent condition, and that I was likely to be drafted sometime during the last six months of my eligibility for service, which would end on my twenty-seventh birthday in July.

I heard nothing for a while and figured that I was going to be passed over—as I believed I should have been, anyway. But one day when I was practicing at a tournament in West Palm Beach, a man came up to me, stepped into my swing plane and handed me a letter. It was not a draft notice as I first thought, but it was a letter from my board advising me to keep them informed of any change in my address, with the implication that my formal induction notice would arrive shortly.

I went to a lawyer who supposedly specialized in draft cases —at $500 a meeting.

"I don't see what can be done," he said after studying my presentation of the facts. "Too bad you got divorced so soon."

"We're not divorced yet. We're separated."

The specialist's eyes lit up and he told me to get B.J. on the phone. I made her an offer she could not intelligently turn down. I gave her a choice between accepting a percentage of my pay check on tour every month, or getting all of my pay check in the Army every month, which would have amounted to $75.

"What do I have to do?" she said.

"Come back with me for thirty days."

And that's what we did. I sent a letter explaining my reconciliation to my draft board and I had a photo taken of me, B.J., and Brad together and sent it to the Cedartown paper, so the letter writers in my home town would not have to worry about my draft status any more.

The most remarkable thing about all of this was that B.J. and I never were happier together than during those thirty days.

On the morning of July 24, she woke up and said,

"What should we do now?"

"A deal's a deal," I replied, and helped her pack.

The only thing worth remarking about the divorce proceedings, which did take place in spite of that curious month of bliss, was that I made a slight faux pas in the judge's chambers. My cigarette rolled off an ash tray and sizzled a dark groove into the gleaming mahogany surface of the table.

"Mr. Sanders," the judge said, eyebrows raised. "Is that your cigarette on my table?"

At the same time, I felt a nudge from Bob Toski, who was there as a friend to inform the judge about the nature of living expenses on tour.

"Yes, sir, your honor," I said, recovering the butt and sliding the ash tray over the scar. "I'll get it fixed, your honor."

"No, I'll fix it," the judge replied. And he probably did by increasing my alimony payment 20 per cent.

About a year later, just before the 1960 Masters, I got married again, this time to a stunning, dark-haired divorcée named Joan Fay Brown, who worked as a model and on a

team of water-skiing performers at Cypress Gardens in
Florida. I had met her at one of the numerous parties my
friends started inviting me to after my divorce, to help me
find "the right woman" at last. I drove Joanie home that night.
It happened to be chilly. She invited me inside her apartment
for a cup of hot chocolate. Leaning against the stove in her
kitchen, I kissed her for the first time. Moments later I smelled
something burning. My coat had caught on fire from the
burner under the pot of water. "I've gotten a lot of hot kisses
before," I observed happily, "but none that would ever burn
a hole in my coat."

That turned out to be an omen of how fiery things were going to be between us.

I think my initial interest in Joanie had nothing to do with
love in the sense I understand the word today. I felt an intense
infatuation and I longed to be with her all the time. When I
left Miami after our first meeting, and began playing tournaments again, I knew this right away.

So three months later, we got married. Then began the alternating periods of passion and tumult that did, I think,
eventually grow into love, but it was an unmanageable kind
of love.

We loved each other, but we never especially *liked* each
other. We fought about everything. If a woman called me on
the phone, Joanie assumed it was a girl friend. If a man called
me, she figured he was representing a girl friend. The only
telephone calls I could expect to receive without an argument
were from polar bears.

I hasten to claim a full 50 per cent responsibility for our
various difficulties. I was definitely no bargain as a spouse.
We tended to feed each other's fires, so to speak. For instance
once I offered her a raisin and she said, "I don't want a
raisin."

"You don't want a raisin because I asked you to have a raisin," I observed.

"I don't want a raisin because I'm not hungry for raisins," she explained.

"Why don't you eat this goddam raisin before I throw it at you?" I suggested.

And that's the way our arguments always began.

Joanie had a cute little daughter named Carrie, by a previous marriage. Whenever Joanie and I argued, Carrie and my son, Brad, who often traveled with me on weekends, would get into the act too.

Once James R. was driving all of us back from a tournament during a period of hostility. Joanie and Carrie sat in front. Brad and I sat in back. No one talked. The atmosphere was so tense that every time James R. needed gas for the car, he made sure to stop near a bar, so *he* could fill up for the next two hundred miles too.

Finally Joanie broke the silence.

"When we get to Miami, Carrie," she said, "I'm going to cook you a nice beef roast."

"That's nice, Mommy," said Carrie.

"Brad, Joanie can cook a beef roast," I said mockingly. "Isn't that wonderful?"

"Yuch!" said Brad.

"James R.," Joanie inquired, "who is that smart son of a bitch in the back seat?"

James R. grunted and pushed down on the gas pedal a little more.

Once in a while our difficulties surfaced in public. After I won the 1961 Colonial, we decided to take a week off the tour and relax with some friends in Acapulco. Joanie had been in the hospital for a few days with a suspected case of appendicitis, and though she didn't have it, she had been looking forward to the extra rest she could get on our spontaneous holiday.

We were in the airport at Dallas (in fact I had just picked out our seats) when a call came for me from Ed Carter, the tournament director, and Bob Rosburg, chairman of the players' committee at the time.

Both of them were mad at me for dropping out of the Hot Springs Open Invitational. As the most recent winner on tour, I was a big attraction and the sponsors had counted on my being in the field.

"Well, I can't play," I said. "My wife is just out of the hospital and we're going right now to rest some."

"Then we'll have to fine you."

"How much?"

"Five hundred dollars."

"I'll pay it."

"One thousand."

"I'll pay that."

"And suspend you for three months."

"I'll see you in Hot Springs."

Actually I had nothing against Hot Springs, though I had never counted it among the livelier spots on tour. Jimmy Demaret once asked Dutch Harrison, who was a native Arkansan, what there was to do in Hot Springs for entertainment. Dutch suggested he go down to a barber shop and watch a couple of haircuts. Joanie felt even more strongly that Hot Springs could not caddie for Acapulco.

When we landed in Hot Springs, we were met by newsmen. I was mad and Joanie was tragic. I kept trying to steer the microphones away from Joanie because in her state I knew she was ready to give our whole life story. Big tears rolled out from under her sunglasses as she said to one reporter, "You know, we never really had a proper vacation together. We never even had a *honeymoon*."

I ended up winning the tournament, which was a kind of poetic justice. Then I remembered that as defending champion I would have to come back next year too.

Our marital battles got bigger and better. At the next year's Masters she would not let me in the house we were renting when I returned late from visiting my Augusta friend Norman. Joanie had been impatient with my antics all week so I was not astonished at the development. However it was raining out.

"I'm going to kick the goddam door down if you don't let me in!" I cried.

"You won't kick any door down."

"Don't you tell me I won't do nothing!" I said, greatly insulted. And I started punting at the door.

"If you don't stop, I swear I'll call the police."

She had me there. The last thing I wanted for me and the grand, if a bit severe, traditions of the Masters Tournament, was police-blotter publicity.

As I pondered what to do next, the door swung open and my clothes started flying out. I was too surprised to do anything but stand there. By the time the door slammed shut again, a closet's worth of custom-designed slacks and shirts was piled in the grass and mud, at the feet of the Peacock of the Fairways.

Now I really had to get control of myself. I got into my car and called my friend on my car telephone.

"Norman," I said, "it is time for some compulsory arbitration over here at the Sanders house."

"What you talking about?"

"Joanie won't let me in."

Norman arrived, got inside to talk to Joanie for a few minutes, and came out again. "She says you can get the rest of your stuff and stay at my house," he said.

So I went in, collected my shaving gear and a few odds and

ends and started leaving again. Then I stopped, put down my kit and walked over to her. I said, half-seriously I suppose, "I think I'll just hit you one time before I leave."

But Joanie was too fast for me. She snapped off one of her spike-heeled shoes, swung it around, and zapped me on the arm. It made an ugly purple knot in the muscle of my left arm.

"Norman," I cried, demonstrating my takeaway with the injured limb, "I can't draw back but to here!"

"Hell, that's normal," Norman said. "Let's get out of here."

Our worst fight—in terms of damage done to me—came during the Tournament of Champions in Las Vegas in 1961. We got back to our hotel room late after an evening of dancing and drinking vodka martinis and arguing as usual. Those martinis especially were like forest fires in our relationship. At one point I was in the bathroom. She knocked but I wouldn't let her in. When I finally came out, I saw right away my contrariness had stirred up a hornet's nest.

Joanie was holding a lamp, one of those huge lamps put in hotel rooms to make guests think they are in stately surroundings. It was so big that the only way she could handle it was by running around the room a couple of times to build up momentum. That's what she did, and then let go of it—CRAACK! Suddenly I was seeing more stars than an astrologer. She had got me solid on the side of the head.

I stumbled into the bathroom and in the mirror saw blood streaming down the side of my face. I didn't like that movie, so I stumbled back out.

"Oh darling, I've killed you!" Joanie cried.

"Not yet," I said. "But you have ruined me a little."

"Oh, God, what am I going to do!"

"Just stay away from me," I said. "Go to a neutral corner."

I reached a friend of mine on the phone and he came over, having arranged in the meantime to take me to a doctor's private office rather than a hospital emergency room. Once again

I was trying to avoid any unpleasant publicity. This doctor apparently had been at a party too, because when we arrived he gave me an odd little grin and waved at me with his fingers.

"Hi, there!" he said. "Why don't you put your hands down?"

I was holding a towel to my head. "Well, Doc," I said, "I don't feel I have that much more blood to lose."

"Don't worry, everything will be all right." He directed me to sit up on a metal table, laid my head over a pan, and then pulled out two ten-inch needles.

"Can't you find any smaller?" I said.

"These were the first I came to in the drawer," he said nonchalantly.

"Please just stitch me together, I don't care what you use."

He was in the course of knitting one and purling another, when suddenly my friend, who had been sitting nearby talking to me, slumped over on the floor. The doctor dropped the needles and ran to my friend. To keep one of the needles from sticking me in the eye, I sort of tied it to my ear with the thread, wondering all the while how bad my friend was. At this point, with myself half-stitched, a doctor half looped, and a friend half dead, I figured it was the end of the world.

My friend turned out to be all right—he had just fainted at the sight of blood. And the doctor completed his patchwork job on me.

I did not go back to my room that night, however. And the next day, after the tournament was over, I left town directly, without Joanie. I took refuge from her in my friend Andy's apartment in Dallas.

The second divorce, and another onerous financial settlement for me, followed shortly. Once again I managed to annoy the judge in the proceedings. In presenting my 1962 financial picture to show how costly it is to be a touring pro, my lawyer mentioned that my telephone expenses ran to $14,500. The judge said, "Why, I don't make much more than that in a *year*,

Mr. Sanders," and I knew right then that he was not going to be bending over backward in my direction in deciding the present case.

I should add again that I do not pretend to have worn a halo during the years of my second marriage. Joanie's and my wants and needs were often conflicting, and I was as much responsible for the clashes, and the eventual break-up, as she was. We had many happy moments together, but somehow the disasters stick in the memory more clearly.

I got married again in 1968 but with an important difference this time. For one thing, I had been dating Scotty Kolb, a lovely and independent-minded young woman with a good ground job in public relations with American Airlines in Los Angeles, for four years before the marriage. We knew what each other was really like as well as two adults can. I had had a premature marriage and a rebound marriage. Now at last I thought I had the chance for a lasting—and a lastingly interesting—marriage.

The hardest part was getting together long enough to actually get married, as it happened. I had won custody of my son after a nerve-racking courtroom fight with my first wife. First I asked Scotty to come to Dallas to marry me and help me set up good living and schooling arrangements for Brad. She quit her job and came, but before we could get married, I was swamped with business and golf commitments. I was on the road constantly for the next month. Every night I called Scotty to discuss our options. One night I phoned from Ohio.

"Well, now if you come to Akron on Monday," I said, "we could get the blood test on Tuesday and then, let's see, wait three days, and get married on Friday. No, no, not this Friday, I'm getting a haircut on Friday."

"It is demoralizing to be shot down by a barber, Doug," Scotty remarked pointedly.

Meanwhile, a physician friend of mine in Dallas heard of

our difficulties and gave Scotty a blood test form filled in for both of us, and she stuck it in her purse. Then I had her move to Houston, because that is where I had finally decided to settle down, for business reasons and to be near friends in the area. She found an apartment and began house-hunting.

The day after I myself arrived in Houston, I went downtown to get a haircut. My friend Ken Schnitzer had driven me into the city, but he couldn't drive me back because he had an unexpected business meeting. I called Scotty from the barber shop and asked her to pick me up.

She arrived and I jumped in the car. We started back to the apartment, chatting idly. Suddenly a new possibility dawned on me and I exclaimed, "Wait a minute, do you realize we are both together? This may never happen again! Let's get married!"

"Oh, we can't just go get married like that."

"But you have the blood test forms, right? All we need is a judge."

We found a pay phone and I looked in the Yellow Pages under justices of the peace. I dialed the number for a Judge Treadway and a girl's voice answered.

"Do we have to make an appointment to get married?"

"No," said the girl, "but you do need a license and a witness."

Our nearest acquaintance happened to be the woman who was selling the house we wanted to live in, Vivien Flynn. We stopped at her real estate office and asked her to be our witness. She agreed to meet us at Judge Treadway's at 2:00 P.M. and toasted us with some brandy.

Then we went to City Hall. I had on golf slacks and a shirt and Scotty had on an everyday cotton skirt and blouse, and sandals, but we gave ourselves away as soon as we stopped in the middle of the lobby and started giggling.

A nearby workman took one look at us and called over,

"Marriage License upstairs to your left, third door on the right."

Upstairs we giggled again about filling out the forms and having to reveal our first names of George and Priscilla on the application. The farther we proceeded, the funnier and sweeter it got.

After we got the license, we were walking along the sidewalk toward Judge Treadway's office when I stopped short.

"Wait a minute!" I exclaimed. "Don't we need rings to get married?"

"I don't know," said Scotty. "You've been through this more than I have!"

"I think we better get some."

We came to a place that sold new and old jewelry, and also made loans. It was not Tiffany's but it would serve the purpose.

"I'd like to see what you have in wedding rings," I declared to one of the two clerks behind the counter.

The guy pulled out a tray of wedding rings. I pulled two off the tray and said, "I'll take them!"

"You don't even know if they fit," Scotty protested.

"I don't care," I replied. "We only need them for one night." Then I noticed the clerk's eyes narrow, and I added, "I mean, we're going to buy new rings when we get a chance."

I paid for the rings and then asked if I could use the bathroom. While I was gone, the other clerk came up to Scotty and said, "That man looks familiar to me."

Scotty remained silent. While we were in Vivien's office, I had specifically asked her to be sure not to let anyone find out about our private wedding caper until afterward.

"I just know his face from somewhere," the clerk persisted. "Isn't he a golfer?"

"I don't know," Scotty replied. "I don't know who he is."

"But . . . but the wedding rings . . ." the clerk stammered.

When I returned, Scotty said, "He wonders who you are."

"I am George and this is Priscilla," I said grandly to the poor bewildered clerk, as we began walking out. "And we are on our way."

Twenty minutes later we met Vivien and were escorted to an empty desk by the girl I had talked to on the phone two hours before. Moments later Judge Treadway himself bustled in, picked up a book and began reading from it, without so much as glancing at us.

"Do you, George Douglas Sanders," he began matter-of-factly, but as soon as he finished the brief ceremony, his head snapped up and he said, "I know you, you're Doug Sanders the golfer!"

"Just tell me this," I said, "are we married at last?"

12 / *Soul Food, Friends, and Fun*

I could not have gotten through the rough times in my first two marriages and assorted other scrapes without a little help from my friends. Actually there is an almost built-in occupational requirement for sidekicks on the modern pro tour. If a pro is at all successful, he finds himself bombarded by propositions and advice. He needs a circle of associates to filter out the unnecessary or unpleasant signals that start to come at him from the outside world. And since he is constantly under the stress of performance, he needs people near him whom he can trust with the innermost thoughts and feelings that from time to time he absolutely has to express. If the pro tour is a pressure cooker, then a pro's buddy is the little valve whistling jauntily on top.

James R. Greenway of Cedartown and Andy Smith of Dallas and later Memphis, as I've mentioned, traveled with me regularly on tour for some years and got me out of almost as many scrapes as they got me into. James R. is an explosive fellow, who wears thick-lensed glasses and moves around fast, like a badger in a pen. Andy Smith is tall, handsome, and velvet-voiced. He moves fast only in emergencies, for instance if his chair is on fire. Andy actually worked for me on salary, helping me with business deals as a kind of executive assistant, until he decided to return to a more tranquil job in sales a few years ago. Actually today both James R. and Andy are mature and responsible men with good positions, and I know they won't mind my sharing some of our adventures together.

We all three still see each other sporadically and it does not take long to restore our old atmosphere of mischievous good humor. Our particular spirit of togetherness was perhaps typified one time when I was playing in the Colonial at Fort Worth. In the middle of a round, the skies opened up and word came out to the players that the round was canceled. James R. and Andy had been following me, as they usually did when they were on tour with me. They would come up to me if I happened to be in contention and ask me whether they should deliver a full whammy or a half whammy to the current leader in the field. Then they would actually locate the leader on the course and bestow hateful glares on him as though it really made a difference. There was some self-interest too. The better I played, generally, the later tee times I was assigned. Andy once figured that every birdie I made was worth another fifteen minutes' sleep to him the next morning.

Anyway, the three of us began hurrying back to the club-house. We came upon a beer stand that had been abandoned in the deluge by the concessionaire. We looked at each other. How could we pass it up? The sodden galleries moved across the course like an army in rout, and we commandeered the tent. There we stayed for the next hour, sitting on damp cases of beer, watching puddles form out in the fairway and getting rosily intoxicated.

I trusted James R. and Andy more than I trusted myself. They had the key to my safety deposit box back in the days when I did not even know the name of my bank. In some ways we were interchangeable, they knew me so well. One hot, dusty day, I staggered off the course after winning the 1962 Oklahoma City Open, looking more like a corpse than a competitor. I stopped off at the bar to recuperate and sent James R. to the press tent to answer questions. He knew my round stroke for stroke, and described it better than I could. Another time I was relaxing in a tub when a call came from a client in Kansas City to tape a radio promotion. I could not move. Andy picked up the phone and gave the spiel for me.

James R. used to meet my dates at airports for me. One year a girl was arriving at Miami Airport on a plane that was going to be anywhere from thirty minutes to three hours late. He couldn't go too far from the airport and he had to check on the plane every half hour or so, so finally he decided to go to a drive-in theater nearby. He bought a bottle of whiskey, a six-pack of Coke and made himself watch the movie that was on that night—*Bambi*.

James R. tore the fender off my new Chrysler in Dallas one year, so he took it to a garage to get some quick repairs made.

"It'll take us a week," said the service manager.

"I can't wait a week, I can hardly wait a day."

"There's nothing I can do."

"What is the name of this place?"

"Hamilton Motors."

"Direct me to Hamilton himself."

Finally James R., arguing that a bashed-in Chrysler would

present a bad image over at the Colonial tournament, got Mr. Hamilton to supply us with a new Chrysler for the week.

James R.'s character like mine was molded in Cedartown where as a youth he enjoyed making trouble in elaborate ways, revealing the same complex mind of his uncle Red, the man I mentioned earlier. Once James R. and some friends caught a young bobcat and stuffed it into a suitcase. Then they set the suitcase out on the side of a local highway. To make sure the bobcat would be anxious for its freedom, they poked a few holes in the suitcase and prodded the beast a bit with a stick. Then they withdrew into the trees and waited for a car to pass by and notice.

Finally an old jalopy came bumping along with about eight black country boys in it who probably had no place to go and nothing to do. The car went past the suitcase maybe twenty yards, then screeched to a halt, shifted into reverse, and backed up. Out jumped two of the fellows, grabbed the suitcase and jumped back in, laughing and whooping about their sudden good luck.

The car started off again and went straight for another twenty yards or so, long enough for the fellows in the back seat to get the suitcase open. Then the car started swerving crazily from one side of the road to the other. Finally it ran down into a ditch, doors flew open and everyone poured out hollering and running for daylight.

James R. also got into a number of fights when he was younger, often losing. Once he reported such an outcome to me by saying, "I wore out my opponent's fist on my face." He gave up on fisticuffs after he finally decided he was hexed in that field. Once, for example, he got into a vicious match in a private club outside of town where men used to play cards and drink. James R. had been losing the fight until his opponent hurt his fist on a brick wall. Then James R. began to prevail for a change. He finally got his man down and decided to put the finishing touches on the bout. He reached into a barrel where the club's empty whiskey bottles were tossed, planning to whomp his opponent with one. Instead he pulled out a plastic Purex container—the club could not have used up more than one quart of bleach every three or four years—and hit his foe with that. The jug bounced thirty feet in the air and utterly disconcerted James R., who leaped up from the fray and cried, "Lord behold! How unlucky can a man get? I let him have it with a soft bottle!"

Once James R. tried to stop a fight by stepping between two young men. Moments later he felt part of his ear being bitten off. "I am being cannibalized!" he cried. He reached into the guy's mouth to get his ear back and the young man bit off part of his finger. "Oh Jesus, he is eating me up!" James R. cried, staggering away. They rushed him to the hospital.

"Where's your ear?" said the examining physician in the emergency room.

James R. displayed his finger and said, "I tried to get it back."

"Where's your finger?"

"It is still with my ear!"

On tour we got into moderate amounts of trouble but we never got into fights or wound up in jail. Once we were thrown out of a hotel in Dallas when I fell asleep waiting for the bathtub to fill up. By the time Andy came in and woke me up, the main room looked like the underwater world of Jacques Cousteau. There were pulsating bubbles under the green carpeting. The man occupying the room one floor below knew something was amiss when he noticed water spouting out of the outlet for his electric shaver.

"We weren't exactly thrown out of here," Andy explained when James R. returned and found us packing. "But they gave us only thirty seconds to move."

One year James R. preceded me to our hotel in Jacksonville

by three days, during which time he settled down comfortably in my suite and ingratiated himself with the staff. I discovered this the morning after my arrival when I tried to get the parking lot attendant to bring my car to the front. The attendant went to his phone and dialed a room number.

"Mr. Greenway," I heard him say in a low voice, "there's some young cat down here trying to get your vehicle."

"What does he look like?" I heard James R. inquire in cavalier fashion.

I grabbed the phone and said, "You rat-son-of-a-bitch, tell this guy to give me my car! *My* car, not your car!"

"Let me have a word with the doorman," James R. replied coolly.

Twice we had misadventures with money. One night in Dallas, I asked James R. to hold $16,000 for me. We returned to the apartment building where we were staying and, while I went upstairs to change for dinner, James R. walked into the bar on the main floor and had a few drinks. He had a few too many, apparently, because a half hour later he walked out of the bar and directly into a pool that was decorating the main entrance to the place.

I didn't mind James R. getting my shoes, my slacks, and my alpaca sweater wet (he had been in my closet again), but I was annoyed about the soggy bank roll. He made amends by hiring a laundress to iron the money and hang it out to dry on two clotheslines crisscrossing the main room of my suite. All those $20 and $50 and $100 bills wafting in the breezes of the air-conditioning were a strange sight.

Before I went into the hospital in Dallas one year, I gave James R. about $7,000 to hold, urging him not to lose it while gambling or drunk or both. The first night I was in the hospital, James R. and Andy threw a party for thirty persons in my hotel suite.

Early on the morning after the party, James R. awoke bolt

upright in a chair, holding a glass in his hand. Across the way from him was a forlorn-looking young woman, hands folded in her lap, staring at him. Her date had stranded her in the course of the night, she explained nervously, and she had no way to get home.

"Get you some cabfare on the TV set in the next room," James R. said and dropped back to sleep. When he woke up again, he sent for some Alka-Seltzer. He went into the other room to get a dollar to tip the boy from room service. His money, roughly $3,000, was in a pile on the TV set. But my $7,000 was missing. "I am short," he said. "Goddam, I am really short!"

He turned the suite of rooms upside down, thinking he might have hidden my $7,000 somewhere before the party had begun. His favorite place for storing $100 bills overnight in a strange location was the Yellow Pages, for he had always reasoned that men seldom consulted phonebooks during burglary attempts. But he had not put my money there this time, it seemed. Andy came over from his apartment to help in the search, to no avail.

"I know," James R. finally declared, thinking of the girl he had sent into the room for cabfare, "it was that shameless hussy!"

"But then why didn't she take your pile?" Andy objected.

"To throw us off the trail."

Andy drove James R. to the girl's apartment. "All right, be reasonable," James R. said to her. "Take a thousand, don't take it all. If you take it all, I'm going to get killed, and by God if I get killed you're going with me!"

"But I didn't steal any money," the girl said, looking pale and frightened. "I took only $10 for cabfare like you said."

"Stop crying or I'll make those tears run *up!*" James R. said harshly. "Stop or *I'm* going to cry!"

Finally they decided the poor girl was innocent and left.

For the next few days, James R. paced the suite of rooms, mentally combing over the hours he had spent before the fateful party. He stopped by the hospital a couple of times a day, acting somewhat but not remarkably subdued. Later he told me he kept expecting me to ask for some of my money back, or for my watch and ring which I had also given him for safekeeping, and which also were missing.

On the day of my discharge, James R. braced himself to reveal the bad news. He asked a maid to come clean the suite of rooms for my return—all week he had forbidden anyone access to the suite except Andy and himself. While James R. sat and thought glumly about telling me he had lost the money, and about running his head against a plaster wall, the maid changed sheets, swept, dusted, and polished. At one point she came out of the bathroom with a pitcher of water, and commenced to irrigate a rubber plant standing in one corner of the room.

"Hold that water!" James R. exclaimed, rising from his chair. And before the chambermaid's astonished eyes, he uprooted the rubber tree and pulled out my watch and ring and $7,000.

The pro tour is a life of room, board, and golf, which is why motels and restaurants crop up in a pro's conversation as often as putting strokes and purse money.

One year a motel in San Diego tried to get more players to stay there by offering everything free to the golfer with the low tournament round for the week. The deal attracted a couple of dozen pros and their families. On the first day of the tournament, Bob Rosburg shot 63. Right away everyone knew no one would top that score for the week, so we all started signing Bob's name to the food and drink bills. By the time we finished, it cost the motel an extra $1,500.

Next year the owner of the motel offered the same deal only this time, to prevent the same abuse, he based it on the low score for the *final* round of the tournament. Now it happened that I decided to invite a half-dozen friends to stay at the motel at my expense that week, not because of any possibility of special rates but because I felt like throwing a real long party. On the final day of the tournament wind and rain blew scores high. My score of 70 turned out to win the week's expenses. Again it cost the motel $1,500 or more. To no one's great surprise, the promotion was not renewed the following year.

Some of the pros liked to take advantage of challenges offered by restaurants too. There was a place in San Antonio that advertised a seventy-two-ounce steak for $10.75. If you could eat it in less than an hour, the restaurant picked up the tab. I saw Dean Refram and Joe Carr attempt it one night. Joe failed but Dean, a short, stocky fellow with a knack for outdoing himself, finished his plate in forty-seven minutes and then ordered dessert.

Al Besselink was a big eater as I discovered during our frequent double dates together. He would always be ready for dessert before any of the other three persons at the table had ordered their salad dressing. One night before a dinner date, I told him, "Bessie, if you finish before anyone else, you're picking up the tab for a change."

"Sure, palsie," said Besselink. "I didn't realize my manners were not up to your standards."

In spite of my proposition, he still wolfed down his dinner. Later, after the rest of us had finished, I slid the check over to him, whereupon he picked up his fork, stabbed a sliver of beef he had concealed beneath his potato skin, and delicately set it between his teeth.

"High society, palsie," he said, pushing the check back at me.

No one on tour could ever match a man called Buttermilk, from Boaz, Alabama, for staying power at mealtime, however. Buttermilk, whom James R. saw in action on several occasions, was not a large man but his stomach, it was said, produced an acid that burned through food like a goat in clover. On a bet, he would finish off a crate of eggs in the time it took to fry them, eat fifteen pounds of ham non-stop, or consume five gallons of peanut butter in forty-eight hours. In fact he supported himself by betting on his appetite in matches against other big eaters. He usually won but not always. Once some backers took him to Nashville for a $5,000 match. They put Buttermilk on a starvation diet for two days in a hotel room, then rented a suite for the contest, setting up card tables laden with turkeys, chickens, ham, and beef. But the morning of the match, Buttermilk snuck out for a large breakfast, spoiled his edge, and lost the contest by two chickens.

Once James R. walked into a place for breakfast with Buttermilk. James R. ordered his breakfast—coffee and Alka-Seltzer. Then he heard Buttermilk order.

"Give me three eggs, a double order of bacon, hash browns, and some grits," Buttermilk said. "And make that ten times."

My own tastes in food are simple but getting them satisfied on tour is sometimes complicated. I like country soul food, which is country-fried steaks, pork chops, fried chicken, even fried rabbit or squirrel, served in sweet thick gravies with dumplings or cornbread and fresh butter. My favorite vegetables are corn on the cob, collard greens, black-eyed peas, juicy tomatoes. For dessert I like something called banana pudding, which I get once a year, anyway—during the Greensboro Open when I visit my sister Stella and her husband, North Carolina highway patrolman Gerald Brewer, whom I address as Brother-in-Law.

Trying to find soul food instead of steak and salad on the road in this country is hard enough. Doing it abroad is next to impossible. The Japanese think cornbread is the name of a rock group, and collard greens are some kind of curious putting surface to the British. That's why, when I do travel, I often take a carton of soul food provisions with me.

Not that I always know what to do with the provisions. At the 1964 British Open, when Lema and I roomed together, I was trying to get our sixty-year-old freelance cook, known affectionately as Ma Wilson, to rustle up some of the black-eyed peas I had smuggled into her country. When I realized I did not know the exact cooking time, I called James R. in Cedartown.

"You mean to say you are waking me up at 4:00 A.M. to find out how the hell to cook peas?" he hollered from across the Atlantic.

"Now wait a minute, James R., don't get mad," I said. "I also am calling to find out what kind of sauce to put on the pork chops."

I never had soul food under more unusual circumstances than during the 1973 inauguration party at the Kennedy Center for the Performing Arts in Washington, D.C. The entertainer Vikki Carr and her husband, Dann Moss, had invited me to have some specially prepared country food with them beforehand at their hotel suite, but I couldn't make it. So they packed a carton of chicken, cornbread, and collard greens for me and took it with them to Kennedy Center. When I met them inside, they presented me with my "dinner" and I ate it then and there, relishing every bite. They had had to get the carton through various security checks on their way in, and there was a seal of the Secret Service on it which I have saved to this day.

My appetite varies according to my amount of play. I can consume more calories in a day than most people consume in a week, and still not gain weight. I burn it all up when I'm playing regularly. I tend to gain weight when I'm not playing and am eating only two or three times a day. I stay the same, or actually lose weight, when I'm eating five or six times a day during a tournament week. A doctor in Memphis told me probably the best way to burn up calories was through sex, and I didn't argue with him.

My experience with liquor goes back some too. There were about fifty "commercial" stills in and around Cedartown when I was growing up, some of them capable of producing as much as six hundred gallons of white whiskey a week. And there were countless other family-size stills, including one my father maintained for some years, used strictly for private purposes. Once an ex-friend of my father's threatened to report him to federal agents, so we moved the still. When the guy went out to check Dad's operation himself, he stumbled in the hole where the still had been and broke his leg.

The first time I got drunk I was seven. I was so skinny that my mother had taken me to a doctor who had prescribed a beverage for giving me energy and greater appetite for food. It consisted of a raw egg, some milk and flavoring, and a spoonful of whiskey. I was supposed to take it every day. One day when my mother was busy doing something else, she told me to go ahead and mix the drink for myself. I did, but instead of putting in a spoonful of whiskey, I nonchalantly poured in about four ounces: I held my nose and drank it down. Then I went outside, climbed into a tree house we had built in the yard and promptly went to sleep. What I had done, more accurately, is pass out. They shook me awake about seven hours later, and I staggered back to the house on rubber legs, with absolutely no idea why I was feeling the way I was.

A few years later, cleaning up at the golf club the day after a party, I drank down half a bottle of champagne which I thought was flat and harmless. It reminded me of 7-Up, and I figured it could not have a much worse effect. A little later I was seized with a thirst so I drank down a glass of water. The water somehow transported the alcoholic content of the champagne to my senses, because almost immediately I felt woozy. I climbed up on the pool table in the club and fell into a profound slumber. I was aroused some hours later by Maurice Hudson, the professional whom I respected so much, and I didn't know how to explain what had hit me that time either.

I have drunk sufficiently since those days to know bourbon from scotch, as is well known, but I have rarely lost the capacity to take care of myself as happened those two times when I was a youth. My single accident as an adult drinker was the time I ran off the road in Augusta on the eve of the opening round of the Masters Tournament.

I had spent the evening at my friend Norman's house, where I shared a bottle of scotch—apparently I shared it with myself. Anyway toward midnight I decided to go back to my apartment and get ready for my eleven o'clock tee-off time.

"Are you sure you don't want me to drive you?" Norman asked.

"Of course not!" I said, teetering across his hallway and out the door.

Ten minutes later the phone rang in Norman's house and Norman answered it and heard me say, "Noooorrrrman, this is George Douglas."

"Where are you at, what is the matter?"

"I am in a lot of trouble."

"Tell me where you are at, George, quick."

"Well, when I look out the car window I see a sign that says Murray Hill."

"Are you at the Murray Hill intersection?"

"No, I am on top of the sign."

Two cars had been racing on the narrow road and when I saw them coming, I had overreacted and run my brand-new Lincoln convertible off the road, through a street sign and into a pole. After it happened, I barely felt capable of using the car telephone, let alone getting out and assessing the situa-

tion. After I talked to Norman, I dialed a girl friend in Los
Angeles and fell into a discussion of a book called *The Prophet*,
and the upcoming baseball season. Shortly Norman arrived
and said, "George, get off the phone and get out of this wreck.
Tomorrow is the Masters."

Playing with a hangover can be a challenge. A couple of
years ago in Las Vegas, George Knudson had attended a party
or two the night before the first round of a tournament. He
arrived at the first tee feeling fair to bad, teed up his ball, and
took a practice swing. Then he stared down the first fairway
for several long moments. Finally he picked up his ball and
said to an official, "Send in a substitute."

Obviously that fairway looked far too long to walk that day.
It was a considerate action in a way, too, because it permitted
one of the alternate players to get into the tournament. If
George had hit his tee shot and then walked off, the alternate
could not have gotten in.

Another year, at New Orleans, George barely made his tee-
off time. He had left a wake-up call for 7:00 A.M. but it never
came and by the time he reached the course, his group was
teeing off. He jumped out of his car and teed off in his street
shoes. James R. parked the car for him. That night George was
back in his hotel room when the phone rang. He picked it up
and heard a sweet voice saying, "Hello, Mr. Knudson, this is
your seven o'clock wake-up call."

Andy Smith happened to be visiting me in Houston on his
thirty-eighth birthday one year. We celebrated at breakfast
and again at lunch. After a round of golf together, we celebrated some more. By the time we were supposed to go to a
barbecue at Ken Schnitzer's house, we had celebrated his birthday so much we didn't know how old he was any more. But
we went anyway, thinking somebody might offer us a drink
there.

A little later, I was talking to Miss Texas by Ken's swimming

pool, and Andy was talking to Mr. and Mrs. Howard Lee
(Mrs. Lee is the actress Gene Tierney) over by the outside
bar. Fortunately for Misses Texas and Tierney, these two conversations came to a merciful end at almost exactly the same
time. This happened when Andy politely bowed out of his
talk and came over and pushed me into the swimming pool.
Then he pushed the host and hostess, Ken and his beautiful
blond wife, Joan, into the pool as well.

For the first time all day, I felt reasonably sober and I called,
"Andy, you are supposed to be the one in the pool." It had
become a kind of tradition, if any of us happened to be with
Andy on his birthday, to find some way to push him into a
swimming pool. So, after helping Joan out of the pool—she
went directly to change out of her sopping wet $600 silver
lamé pants suit and to do something with her ex-hairdo—I
grabbed Andy and did my duty. But the moment I pushed
him, I remembered I had loaned him my $3,000 Piaget wrist-
watch earlier in the day. As soon as he surfaced I called out,
"Andy, what about my watch!"

"Don't worry about it."

"But are you wearing it?"

"No, I took it off, I tell you, it's safe."

"But where did you put it?"

"In my pocket!"

Well, on a warm summer night among friends, my $3,000
Piaget watch and her $600 outfit were not really that im-
portant. At least that's what I tried to tell Joan Schnitzer after
she had got herself into something dry and combed out her
coiffure. We were standing on the terrace watching Andy and
Ken still splashing around in the pool. Then I overheard a
deep voice saying to someone else behind me, "Who is that
ill-tempered young man in the pool, the one who pushed in
our host and hostess?"

"Why, that is Andy Smith," I said, turning to the stranger

who had made the remark, and not liking his tone about my
friend at all.

The man glared at me, sniffed, and said, "Mr. Smith would
not get away with such a thing at my house."

"Well, I'm sure he wouldn't," I replied, more annoyed. "For
one thing he would not be invited to your goddam house, and
for another he would not go even if he were invited, and
neither would I!"

A few weeks later I discovered that the same man, who was
a baron in some titled European clan, owned a house in Houston that was ideally suited for the family I was trying to as-
semble with my new wife, Scotty, and my newly recovered
son Brad. The house had been on the market since the break-
up of the baron's marriage, but when he discovered I was the
uncouth party interested in buying it, I think he tried to prevent its sale.

It took months of unpleasant negotiations to finally get it.
The first thing we did after moving in, of course, was invite
Andy Smith over and push him into the pool.

13 / Mixing Pleasure with Business

If Arnold Palmer's business symbol is the umbrella, mine should be the sieve. That's because I have lost so much money in my business deals. Don't get me wrong—I have earned a lot of money in outside interests too. But I think my difficulties are more interesting in that they reflect the curious vulnerability of the professional athlete, and particularly the pro golfer, in recent years, who like anyone else sometimes has a hard time telling a con artist from an honest man.

Why are golfers so vulnerable? First of all, when a pro wins a tournament, he finds himself with enough cash capital to finance any number of quirky schemes or insane inventions. Second of all, his victory brings him myriad offers of endorsement fees and appearance money because his winner's image is believed to help sell products and services. And finally the pro exists in a milieu where wheeling and dealing is the order of the day, anyway.

He runs into many more business opportunities than the professional football player, for instance, because he is always mixing with well-heeled gents and shrewdies in pro-ams and at parties on or near tournament sites. Unless he is a man of very sour personality, or has a noticeable skin disease, he is bound to receive approaches and overtures, and some of them are bound to be good.

Of course others are bound to be rotten. A Kansas man talked me into investing $10,000 in his golf course project one year. I had played a round with him and knew his family and I thought his idea sounded great too. I even talked fellow pro Bruce Devlin into giving the guy $10,000. But he ran with our money and we never saw him again.

Another time, a fellow in Florida got my ear and extracted a check for $7,100 from me for an oil well he was digging. He guaranteed me in writing that I would not lose a penny on the deal. Then he moved to Argentina.

"Bruce!" I said, next time I saw Devlin. "I have just saved you $7,100!"

My single worst business decision, for which I risked losing as much as half a million dollars, is still in litigation and probably will be for the next decade. And I am only a minor figure in the drama, at that, which involves charges of bribery and multimillion-dollar stock frauds and has already affected the careers of various high-level political leaders in Texas.

I became involved when I signed a contract to become touring professional for Sharpstown Country Club, a course near Houston where Morgan Baker was the club professional. Morgan had recommended me for the position simply because of a little thing I had done for him during the Houston Open which was played at Sharpstown. During the tournament I spent a half hour behind the counter in his pro shop casually drumming up sales for him. When a few years later the offer came through—to my great surprise, for I had had little contact with Morgan in between times—I was especially pleased because it seemed to confirm my basic outlook that being nice pays off. Actually it did, only a happy ending just did not materialize.

The contract I signed stipulated that as playing representative for Sharpstown, I would receive $25,000 a year for the next ten years. Eventually Morgan Baker planned to retire and I would take over his golf shop and golf cart concession for additional income. The place was near my home in Houston, so I could play and practice there conveniently. Plans called for upgrading the course, erecting a new clubhouse and attracting a solid membership—it was presently operated more as a semi-public course. The various features of the position greatly appealed to me. I thought it would be ideal for me in future years, too, when I would begin to cut down on my play on tour.

Anyway I signed the contract, but my real mistake was to agree to let Frank Sharp, who was owner of the club and chairman of the now bankrupt Sharpstown State Bank, invest money for me with the idea that the profits from the investment would help the club pay for my $25,000 annual salary. Sharp was a highly successful businessman, a benefactor of various Houston area charities and civic causes, a recent visitor to the Pope, and I figured it was safe to go along with anything he suggested. Unfortunately our loan-investment arrangement and the subsequent stock purchases made in my behalf, got me into hot water with the Securities and Exchange Commission and the Federal Deposit Insurance Corporation when Sharpstown State Bank suddenly failed in early 1971.

As my friend Ken Schnitzer has repeatedly told me, my main fault in business has been a tendency to see Santa Claus in every new entrepreneur I shake hands with.

"You are too gullible," he told me once. "That's why sometimes you find nothing in the stocking on Christmas morning. That is why sometimes the stocking itself is missing!"

I have learned to protect myself better by using a friend like Schnitzer as a kind of intermediary and objective viewpoint in any discussion of "new business." This has a couple of advantages. The outsider retains perspective during the give and take of negotiations because he has nothing to gain or lose in the matter, either in money or in ego. And he can ask for terms that the involved party may be too embarrassed or shy to demand.

It has taken so long for me to tell a con artist from an honest man because my first real dealings with a business figure were so favorable and so helpful in getting me firmly started in my golfing career.

As I mentioned elsewhere, when I was still an amateur, Dutch Harrison introduced me to a Canadian financier named J. Bradley Streit, a real lover of golf and supporter of young amateurs in the game. He had helped Dynamite Goodloe and Harvie Ward as youngsters. His own nephew, Doug Streit, was married to Marlene Stewart Streit, who became one of the world's top amateur woman golfers in the 1950s.

Streit invited me to visit him in Toronto after Dutch introduced us over the telephone in 1955. We played nine holes at Yorktown Country Club. I shot 33 and answered his frank questions about my financial status (then non-existent) and my aspirations in golf (then barely formed). At the end of the nine holes, he asked me to stop by his office next day.

In all I spent three days in his office, mostly doing nothing but listen to him calling Paris for four million shares of one thing and London for two million shares of something else, and rattling off buy and sell orders in gold and copper and nickel. It all went over my head. Aside from setting terms for golf matches, at which I was adept, the only involvement in business in my life to date had been collecting $2.00 for every one hundred pounds of cotton I picked. But I was naturally impressed with the magnitude of some of Streit's transactions, and with the integrity of the man himself, which came across clearly to me in overhearing various conversations he had with clients and associates in his investment firm.

"It's time to open up an account for you," he announced on the third day I spent in his office. Then he pulled out his wallet and counted out with his left hand—he was left-handed —five $100 bills. He called in a broker. Streit introduced me to him as "a new customer with $500 to invest."

I went home on a cloud. Ten days later I phoned him, as he had asked me to do. Only I did not make the call collect, so Streit hung up and made me do it properly. I told him I wanted to play in the Mexican Amateur and ticked off the approximate travel expenses. A few days later I got a check in the mail for $750, with a note from Streit saying, "So far your investment is doing fair."

During the next few months, I kept getting slips of paper from the broker in Toronto saying I now owned five thousand shares of one stock purchased at $.10, and twenty thousand shares of another purchased at $.25, and by the middle of 1956, I was drawing what amounted to about $2,000 a month in dividends, all supposedly out of the original investment of $500. Obviously Streit had fattened my account from time to time with his own money. I know he was not making any money out of this operation. But he was making it possible for me to see how far I could get with my talent in making a career in golf.

About this time I got a letter from the U. S. Golf Association inviting me to a conference on my amateur status. Someone, I assumed, had been questioning the manner in which I was supporting myself as an amateur golfer, so I called Streit. He put me in touch with an attorney of some note—former

New York Governor Thomas E. Dewey. I spent a few days
with Governor Dewey at his home in Pawling, and came away
with the belief that I had nothing to worry about. I had properly filled-out tax return forms (which Streit's office had prepared for me) to present if needed to show that my income from investments in stock and from a job with a public
relations title for a Puerto Rican plastics firm was legitimate.

So I visited with a half-dozen elders of the USGA in a room
at Knollwood Country Club in Illinois, two days before the
1956 Amateur was to begin. In fact I did not have to show my
tax return, simply to answer some polite questions about my
means of support. Nevertheless, afterward I decided I had
not really liked being put on trial even in the USGA's gray
clubby splendor. A few things bothered me in retrospect. I
realized I would not have gotten J. Bradley Streit's financial
help if I had not been a fine golfer to start with, so in a way I
was making a living off golf, in violation of the rules of amateur
status. But I also knew Mr. Streit's dedication to golf was as
honorable as the USGA's. And I believed what others had told
me—that not a few insurance agencies and other businesses
had thrived in this country partly on the basis of an "amateur"
golfer's sharp game.

The incident drew my eye to some contradictions about
myself—and also about the institution of amateur golf—that
I could not put away again. Finally I decided to notify the
USGA I was turning pro.

I also felt I should no longer depend on Streit for help. My
true love was golf, not the stock market, anyway. He had been
disappointed in me for turning professional, and then for getting married right on top of it, but he offered to keep "investing" for me during my six-month waiting period. After I won
some $6,000 on the Caribbean tour that winter, I told him,
"I've done it now, Mr. Streit. I want to try it on my own."

His selfless support of me was something I would never

forget, however, and when my son was born a year later, I named him after my benefactor with pride and gratitude.

I came on tour at the onset of the big-money era, the "gilded age" as I called it earlier. In my opinion, three men turned the touring pro into a valuable business proposition during that time, and their activities symbolize three distinctly different ways in which the touring pro grew into a solid economic entity.

First was George S. May who promoted what some critics disparagingly called "the Hot Dog Opens" at his Tam O'Shanter Country Club, since leveled for housing in suburban Chicago. May singlehandedly jacked up the level of tournament prize money when he started offering $100,000-plus purses, including first prizes of $50,000 at his World Professional Championship beginning in the early 1950s. He made other tournament sponsors look like pikers, for the average purse of the day was little more than $15,000. At the same time, by getting newspaper and television (still in its infancy) advance promotion for his events, he drew large crowds to watch the golfers. Some of his Barnumesque views did not stick, for instance his desire to get the golfers to wear big name tags on their backs for the sake of the galleries. "Why should I stick pins through my $15 golf shirt?" Jimmy Demaret once objected. But he did succeed in converting the weekly pro tour event into a major sports spectacle.

The second influential figure in behalf of the pro was Jack Harkins, founding president of First Flight Company. Harkins was a gruff, well-liked, Irish-born sales type who set a new tone in player-industry relations. He had a great and amiable respect for the touring pros, whose talents he genuinely admired, and he was prepared to put his money where his mouth was, in the form of generous endorsement fees. I got $10,000 for signing with First Flight in 1960 after three years with Wilson, where I began at $2,500 per year. Wilson, to give that old and fine firm its due, had been on the golfing scene for years and at this time had almost all the top players. While it did not pay golfers so highly in their prime, in this period, Wilson loyally retained their staff pros long after their playing years on tour ended. Harkins knew the only way to get name players away from Wilson was with a lot of money up front.

Like George S. May, who startled golf purists when he kicked out caddies and introduced a fleet of powered golf carts at his course instead, Harkins was an incurable innovator. In the 1930s he aided in the development of the steel shaft and the concept of swingweight. In the 1950s he introduced steel-centered balls. Early in the 1960s he put the first major line of left-handed clubs on the market. After developing First Flight into a major club manufacturer, he founded in succession two more companies that would eventually grow in stature and finally merge: Professional Golf Company and the Arnold Palmer Company.

In my view Jack's major contribution was his placing the touring pro in such high esteem and setting an example for other firms, not just in club manufacture but in golf apparel and other goods and services. He signed on people like Demaret, Gary Player, and me for business reasons too, obviously, but he was able to be a warm friend to all of us as well as a business colleague. You never had to ask what room Harkins was staying in at any of the motels along the tournament trail. All you had to do was listen for his booming brogue of a voice from the lobby. Once he collared me by the ice cube machine (a good place to run into like-minded spirits) and told me about a hot stock. In voice that must have been heard down by the swimming pool, he said, "NOW YOU BETTER BUY 10,000 SHARES OF THIS, DOOG, BUT REMEMBER MY ADVICE IS STRICTLY CONFIDENTIAL!"

As Lew Oehmig, who succeeded Harkins as First Flight president, said when Jack died, at age sixty-three in 1964,

"Knowing Jack Harkins was one, long, humorous adventure."

The third behind-the-scenes pioneer in behalf of the touring pro was Mark McCormack, the energetic and creative attorney and administrator who gave the pro the contractual integrity he enjoys today. By his own admission McCormack would not have succeeded so well or so soon if his aims and his personality did not match so completely those of his long-time friend and client Arnold Palmer. Negotiating legal and economic advantages for somebody as charismatic and marketable as Arnie gave Mark a lot of practice in success. McCormack happened to hitch his wagon to a star.

He was the first to really broaden the pro's earning potential by developing more outlets for his play and personality in corporate and media activities, by involving him in travel and publishing ventures and by getting him into the ripening golf markets abroad, particularly in Great Britain, Western Europe, and Asia. But the heart of his achievement, I think, was getting the pro and his rights into the small print of a contract—protecting the pro at the same time that he helped him to grow. He and his associates became so handy with a contract that the party of the first part was happy to get out of the office with his belt buckle on. Years after McCormack first came on the scene numerous other individuals and firms started in the business of managing the economic life of the pro, and to varying degrees have rooted themselves in the life of the modern tour.

After Jack Harkins died, I left First Flight and went with Ram Golf Corporation, the equipment firm I still represent on tour in America; in Great Britain I represent Ben Sayers. My first clothing endorsement contract was also with First Flight, who briefly marketed a Doug Sanders shirt with a bulldog embroidered on the breast—which had no connection with Red Greenway's trained bulldog of Cedartown fame. Later I represented Jaymar-Ruby, then Catalina, then McGregor-

Doniger. I had a contract with Stylist shoes for some years, then Doug Sanders Country Club.

My main resort affiliations have been Ojai Country Club in California, Shamrock in Tulsa (briefly), the aborted Sharpstown deal, and Ironshore Golf and Country Club in Montego Bay, Jamaica. Right now I'm connected with Devil's Nest, a three-thousand-acre resort and vacation home development in the famous Nebraska Badlands where Jesse James and various other outlaws of the Old West used to hide out.

I have the distinction of having starred in the longest running "greasy kid stuff" commercial in the Vitalis series a few years ago. My spot ran periodically on TV for two years. It was one of the few times I got through a "one-shot" with relatively little effort. After only three tries (compared with fifty-six tries for Jack Kramer, the tennis great), I managed to flawlessly recite, *"Here, you take a couple of swipes with my comb, and I'll take a couple of swipes with mine. See, you can even feel that greasy kid's stuff."* The odd thing is the only oil I had ever put in my hair for years before doing that commercial was Brylcreem, the "greasy kid's stuff" we were trying to run down.

I had trouble with commercials as a rule because I have never been a good memorizer of lines. I enjoy speaking in front of large groups as long as I don't have to stick to a script. In fact not long ago some group named me one of the top three after-dinner speakers among athletes in the country. Yet once I had to say only five words for Chrysler and I couldn't do it. In response to an off-camera voice saying, "Doug, you have a lot of class," I was supposed to say, "And so does my new Chrysler." While setting up for the first take, I happened to start watching a cat across the road. Sure enough, when I got my cue to speak—"Doug, you have a lot of class"— I said, "And so does my black cat." We had to do take after take after that, before getting it right. All I could think of were rainbows and cats and spots on the collar and airplanes and greasy kid stuff.

To make another Vitalis commercial, I had to fly from Orlando, Florida, to Los Angeles on the Sunday evening following an exhaustingly humid tournament. I got into bed in Los Angeles about 2:00 A.M. and got up again at 4:00 A.M. to reach the course in time for the shooting. The script called for a 40-foot putt and the first one I stroked rolled straight into the cup. Then the cameraman cried out he had no film in his box. It took another half hour to sink the same putt.

After Byron Nelson won the Masters one year, he was asked to do a promotional film during which he actually holed out his tee shot on a par-3 hole at Pinehurst. The camera had the remarkable event recorded until it ran out of film when the ball was twelve inches from the hole.

Lew Worsham's famous wedge shot, which won May's World Championship in 1953, was caught on Chicago television. Jimmy Demaret was commentating for television at the time. Lew hit the 140-yard shot to the elevated eighteenth green at Tam O'Shanter and Demaret narrated, "He's hit it fat . . . it will probably be short . . . it just hit the front edge of the green . . . it's got no chance . . . it's rolling but it will stop . . . it's rolling toward the cup . . . well I'll be damned!"

More than anything else, the one-day pro-amateur event that precedes each week's tournament on tour is the symbol of how well golf and business go together. Here men who run giant corporations, or who speak in public on weighty matters, mingle boyishly with the touring pros they admire so much. And in many cases—more than we are given credit for —the pros mingle respectfully with the hackers who the *pros* admire for their success in business and industry or whatever. The younger college-educated pros in particular, I think, are aware of the potentially valuable contacts that exist among their partners of a day early in the week when competitive pressure is at a low. The pro who grunts and swears or just plain ignores his amateur partner in the pro-am is more the exception today than the rule, I think. I know I still collect the business cards of my pro-am partners today as I did when I first came on tour.

To be sure, there are moments in pro-ams that would try a saint. Dutch Harrison lost patience with a congenital duck-hooker he played with one time. Toward the end of the round, the fellow, who had been extracting lessons from Dutch all day, asked about a shot that had landed in a bush.

"How should I play it, Dutch?" he said.

"Under an assumed name," Dutch replied.

A man playing in a Florida pro-am one year became so nervous that he decided to get drunk beforehand. He must have had a dozen glasses of beer before he teed off. Then all during the round he kept ducking into the woods to relieve himself. At one point, curious about his score for some reason —he had been shooting tens and twelves with pretty good regularity—he asked one of his partners, "How am I doing?"

"So far the dog is two trees up on you," his partner replied.

One year I played with a sixteen handicapper named Leroy in the Hope Desert Classic. He was another one of those rare amateur players who justify the outbursts of pain and anguish among pro partners from time to time.

In four days he never won a hole for the team, though of course I didn't hold that against him. He did have one pretty good chance when he reached a par-3 on his tee shot, but then he four-putted. On the day we played the Indian Wells course, he put his first shot in the water; to avoid the water he would have had to hit the ball 150 yards, which was decidedly beyond his means. He collected five balls instead of his one from the lake with his aluminum extendable ball-snatcher before any of us could proceed down the fairway. Nobody would ride with him in his cart after the first two days because he began to smell. In fact he wore the same clothes for four days, and brought his lunch in a brown paper bag.

The pro-am is a curious institution—part hero worship, part clinic, part competition, part joke-telling, and part wheeling and dealing. The wheeling and dealing is the part I like the best, I think, because, just as my amateur partners like to think they have a pro's distance off the tee, or a pro's touch around the greens, I like to think I know my way around a business deal once in a while. Unfortunately my follow-through in business is about as undistinguished as some of my amateur partner's follow-through in golf. More than once, for example, I have gotten a tip on a certain stock, gone out and bought thousands of dollars' worth of it, and then thrown the certificates into a box or my golf bag or a jacket pocket and forgotten about it for six months instead of selling it at a profit when I was supposed to.

One year I played in a pro-am with a broker who told me about a surefire boom stock priced at $9. I ordered $15,000 worth. Next year, in the same pro-am, I spotted my tipster in a neighboring fairway playing in another group, and I called, "Hey, how's our stock doing?"

"You mean you didn't sell?" the broker called back.

"No, was I supposed to?"

"Hell, yes, I told you to sell when it went up to $25!"

"I forgot. Where is it at now?"

"Eighty cents."

14 / How to Smile, Wink, Whistle, and Tip

It pays to be nice, at least that is my theory. Sometimes it doesn't work out right. You forget the second half of the hot tip on the stock and end up losing money instead of making money. You get involved in hopeless boondoggling fiascos like my Sharpstown contract. You are polite to people like Leroy and they keep coming back because they think you love them.

Those are the bad hands and unlucky bounces, and if you build your life philosophy on them you might as well establish residence on a deserted island—and wait for a coconut to drop on your head or a tidal wave to sweep away your grass shack. That is the melancholy view which I will leave for cynics and other ill-tempered sorts to further develop.

Here is what I say to prove my theory of being nice.

Popular, well-liked touring pros score better, sometimes

unfairly so, than the unknown or disliked players. No golfer hitting into a green packed with his fans has to worry about taking too much club for instance. If he hits too long, the shot will bounce off the shins, elbows, and foreheads of admirers and back onto the putting surface. Occasionally—I have seen it done—it will deliberately be kicked back onto the green.

Popular players also score better because of the collective moral support in their galleries. You can almost feel a surge of energy carrying you along the fairway sometimes, when the fans are behind you, almost willing you to succeed. Gene Cernan, the astronaut who is a good friend of mine in Houston, once described the lift-off experience at Cape Kennedy in that way. He said he felt that the millions of people watching on TV lent their oomph to the blast and helped get the craft moving into space. The favored golfer's chance to win are better for more definable reasons too; he has more confidence in his shotmaking ability, and his opponents are demoralized.

I think this theory may apply to any enterprise involving other people, such as business. You are better off in the long run by acting nice because you obtain the advantages of both individual support (a co-worker recommends you for promotion or covers up your mistake) and collective support (employees smile at you when you walk into your office and you feel a psychological boost). Or is being nice a weakness? Our usual image of the effective leader in business, industry, and the various professions is a stern one. But maybe it is a case of too many middle-level exec types playing the role of ruthless tycoon, just as there are too many touring pros pretending to be hard-bitten Hogans. Most of the corporation presidents I know are relaxed and pleasant-mannered individuals, anyway. And even if there really is a "law of the jungle"—dog-eat-dog, survival-of-the-meanest, etc.—I know there is no law against breaking it.

A fellow pro, whom I liked and respected, came up to me one day in the locker room after seeing me fooling around with the galleries one day and said angrily, "What are you doing out there? What do you think we are, a bunch of clowns?"

I have a basic difference in outlook with many of the touring professionals in that I do not regard our competitive golf exclusively as a business. I think like any other spectator sport it is also an entertainment, and part of its vitality comes from its color and dash and unpredictability. I have great respect for it and for its role in the life of the nation. At certain times, when an individual like Joe Louis, Mickey Mantle, or Arnold Palmer emerges in a particular sport, it goes even beyond business and entertainment, and seems to me to serve an emotional need as basic to a culture as the medical profession, for instance, or the political process.

So I am just as proud to be a professional golfer as the man who criticized my clowning. But I feel strongly we have an obligation to share our personality as well as our skill with the fans, and to communicate on a friendly basis within the limits of our own natures. I'm not suggesting that a quiet, inward-looking man like Billy Casper or a fierce competitor like Bruce Crampton should be singing and dancing down the fairways— not at all. Nor was I disappointed when Chi Chi Rodriguez announced a couple of years ago he was no longer going to amuse the galleries with wisecracks and antics on the course. Obviously Chi Chi had recognized he had a more serious nature and that is really how he should come across, not play-acting as a jester.

Furthermore I know it is harder on the modern pro tour *not* to be intensely serious. In Demaret's era, if you were having an off day and were more or less playing for fifth place, the money riding on your performance would be so insignificant that it was perfectly acceptable—in fact practically inevitable—to let up and just finish the round for fun. Today there's so much at stake on every stroke that golfers are much more reluctant to relax their concentration even if they're playing for twentieth place.

What has to be understood, though, and repeated apparently every twenty-four hours so that some of my colleagues will be sure to remember the fact, is that the PGA tour, like any spectator sport, is ultimately the property of the people —the fans—and that while none of us on the fields of play has an obligation to be a clown, none of us has the right to be surly and rude, either.

That said, I will now describe how surly and rude I felt like acting one day at the Greensboro Open, to show I am not foolish or sentimental on the fan issue.

It was an unusually hot day and the combination of sunshine and cold beer must have gotten to more than the usual number of spectators. My usual strategy with drunks is to kill them with kindness, but I wasn't in the mood to do it this round because I was in contention and preoccupied.

It started on the fifteenth green, where I was preparing to putt from about two feet off the fringe.

"Hey, you!" came a booming man's voice behind me, "you can't use a goddam putter unless you're on the green."

I backed away from my ball, smiled without conviction in the direction of the heavens, then returned.

"Now wait a minute, there," called the voice again. "I paid good money to see you cats play golf and I want you to chip that ball on the green like you're supposed to."

Finally two tournament marshals dragged my coach away.

On the next hole, I was about to take my club back for my drive when suddenly I heard a loud rattling sound. I stopped, looked up and found another drunk staring at me. This one had a strange grin on his face. He was shaking an empty beer can in which he had evidently poured some rocks.

"You should've chipped that ball on the green like my buddy told you," he said.

"Marshal!" I cried.

On the next hole, I was taking a shortcut through a throng of fans when I tripped over a fellow passed out under a tree. And last, walking along the eighteenth fairway, an older man broke away from the gallery lining the hole and weaved his way to my side.

"Sanders!" he said, peering at me intently. "All the money you make and there you are with a patch on your sweater. Awful! Shameful!"

"What patch?"

"Right there," he said and with an unsteady finger he indicated my D.S. monogram.

I was hitting balls on the practice range at Rancho Park before the 1972 Los Angeles Open when another drunken voice came drifting from the crowd at me.

"You don' thin' you could knock that li'l ball all the all the all the way to th' fence as small as small as you are, do ya?"

I turned and saw a fortyish fellow glaring at me from the middle of the crowd. He was nicely dressed but his head had a telltale tilt to it and his professorial goatee seemed a little unkempt.

I smiled tentatively and said, "Well, I'm just going to try, sir. That's all."

"Well I jus' don' thin' as little as you are and with that silly li'l swing, well you don' carry it back far far far far enough to hit it forty forty yards!"

"Maybe you could do better?" I suggested.

"I thin' I could hit it over the fence wi' one hand!"

At this point I decided to withdraw from the discussion; I saw no way of winning it. My tormentor made a few more cracks and finally wandered off.

After I finished practice, I was surprised to find the guy

seated at a table in the sponsors' tent—a special accommoda-
tion for high-paying supporters of the tournament. For added
surprise, he was sitting with a friend of mine, who saw me and
called me over. I approached the table wary of the new abuse
I fully expected to get about my ridiculously short swing. My
friend stood up and said, "Doug, you must know Foster
Brooks, you know, the comedian who plays the drunk on TV
a lot?"

Brooks seemed abashed and I was speechless.

"I'm sorry I upset you down there," he said.

"That was the greatest drunk act in history," I said after I
regained my voice. "I want to buy you a drink."

"No thanks," he said. "I don't drink."

Obviously dealing with the public sometimes is trying, but
except for such rare cases as the belligerent drunk, it is
usually easy for a fast-thinking person to handle the situation. It really amounts to learning to manage your own feelings
under stress and tension.

One year, paired with Frank Stranahan, I hit two unusually
good fairway wood shots on two consecutive holes. Each time
I wound up with less than a three-foot putt for birdie, and I
missed both putts. After walking off the green after missing
the second putt, a man appeared at my side, boisterously
threw his arm around me, and said something about how we
had met eight or nine years ago. I couldn't remember his name
and if I could have placed his face it would have been in my
fist—that's how mad I was after missing those putts. But instead I said, "Come over here and I'll tell you a joke."

A little later, Stranahan, whose relationship with the galleries was always on the cool side anyway, said wonderingly,
"How could you do that? How could you go tell a joke after
spoiling two sensational shots?"

"It wasn't his fault I missed the putts," I said, shrugging

though I was still greatly annoyed myself. "And what else could I have done?"

Sometimes you can anticipate distraction and do something about it early. Whenever I see a small child near me in a gallery, I try to figure out some way to con him into standing still while I make my shot, such as offering him a ball or a tee or a dollar.

More unusual problems you can't rehearse for. A man once innocently stepped into a chemical toilet in a deserted wood off the fairway at a tournament. Moments later a mass of humanity descended on the spot—Arnold Palmer had just hit his shot into the trees.

When the fellow opened the Port-o-Let door, he was astonished to see the huge crowd, and aghast to see Palmer studying his lie ten yards away. Palmer looked up sharply when the door creaked open, and the man was so flustered that he slammed it shut again.

Palmer addressed his shot, then stepped away. He walked over to the toilet and knocked on the door. "Look," he called. "Take your time and don't get upset. I'd just as soon wait for you to finish and then make my shot."

"Oh no, Mr. Palmer," the man called out, acutely embarrassed. "You go ahead with your game. I'm so sorry."

Arnie shrugged and went back to his ball and tried again. No use—all he could think of was the guy trapped in the toilet. He went over again and said, "Really, I won't be able to concentrate on my shot. Don't worry, just come out when you get finished."

At last the man came out, crimson-faced, feeling a thousand eyes on him, wishing he were dead. Palmer fixed it up, though. He shook his hand and gave him that famous man-to-fan smile of his.

I was playing in the San Diego Open one year when a similar incident occurred. A California highway patrolman acting as a security guard for the tournament had stepped into the portable toilet a few yards behind the sixteenth tee at Torrey Pines. Just as I was about to hit my drive, a sudden gust of wind from the ocean blew the toilet door open with a clang. The patrolman was helpless to stop urinating or to reach the open door, so he just finished his business in the open. I held up my shot as the gallery went into convulsions of laughter about the poor cop. Finally he stepped out of the toilet to a big round of applause.

Dave Marr told me he found out how much salesmanship there can be in a smile when he was walking down a fairway one day during a tournament. A spectator stepped out of the crowd and came toward Marr, nodding his head and smiling beamingly.

"Well, I'll be darned," Dave said, extending his hand and wondering where and how they had seen each other before.

"You probably don't remember me, Dave," said the man gleefully, "because we've never met."

Introductions can be a trying experience but I learned it is usually better to act like a friend than a foe during them, no matter what the circumstances. Once I was in Las Vegas at a cocktail party I didn't want to attend, tired and irritable from a lot of unexpected travel in recent days, a $15,000 loser in blackjack that afternoon, and generally not fit for human consumption.

I was standing in a circle of guests when a middle-aged gentleman poked me in the arm and said, "Hi, I bet you don't remember me."

I turned and confronted this latest interloper in my social life. "You're goddam right I don't remember you," I was about to say. I wanted to cut this stranger down to size and send him crawling, psychologically, from the room. Then I felt a hand on my arm and woman's voice saying, "You remember my husband, don't you, Doug?"

"I certainly do!" I exclaimed, grabbing the guy's hand so fast he jumped back in surprise. I was trying to make up for my rotten intentions fast, because the man's wife had done more favors for me in Las Vegas over the years—getting me hotel rooms and finding me seats on flights in and out—than all the travel agents in town combined. If I had insulted her husband I would have been the one to crawl from the room. That's why, every time I'm tempted to be rude or surly with strangers since then, all I have to do is remember that close call in Las Vegas and I usually can ride through the most anxious social moments.

Jack Nicklaus recounted a similar experience once. A couple of years ago, during the Crosby Pro-Am, someone called him to the phone on his birthday and insisted on singing "Happy Birthday" to him—all the verses. When it was finally over, Jack said somewhat coolly,

"All right, who is it?"

"Bing Crosby," was the reply.

From such run-ins as these, I have formed some views and opinions about being nice to other people, also known as etiquette.

"Excuse me, but please say thank you."

Human intercourse is more mannerly in the South, which is not to say people in the North are less well-intentioned. They just hide their pleasant natures better. The first trip I made of any size was to Ames, Iowa, to play in my first National Junior Jaycee Championship in 1950. During one of the practice rounds, I stopped at the snack bar between nines for a soda. The place was jammed with contestants and the fellow running the place looked a little harried. I went to the counter and said, "When you get a chance, sir, could I have a Coke, please?" Then I went and sat down at a table, figuring I would have to wait ten minutes or so for service. To my astonishment, the man came along almost immediately with the soda.

"Where you from?" he barked.

"Georgia, sir," I replied.

"Well, you're the only goddam kid in here who knows the word 'please' and that's why you're first."

And he stamped his way back to the counter and the mob.

Remembering Names

People should identify themselves right away when they approach someone who is likely not to remember their names.

Why let your ego, or your ignorance, turn a simple hand-shake into a war of nerves? Typical of such exchanges, a man came up to me once and said challengingly, "I bet you don't remember me."

"Well, your face looks familiar," I replied lamely.

"You gave my little girl a golf ball in 1958 in Philadelphia."

"Oh yes, the one with the pretty hair," I said. The man evidently had not bothered to guess that I might give away more than one golf ball a year (I give away about 150 a month), so I had to play conversational hide-and-go-seek with him for another five minutes before I found out who he was —and by then I really didn't care.

I always say my name as I approach someone I have not seen in some time, and I have more reason to expect to be recognized, I suppose, than most.

Remembering Numbers

I use "golf arithmetic" to implant important numbers in my head, a system any golfer could use effectively. For example, I would commit the telephone number 665-4242 to memory by saying to myself, "I started with two double bogeys, then made a par-5, and ended up shooting two 42s for the round, and I should have stayed in bed."

Keeping Appointments

Being on time is another form of being nice to people, which makes being late an affront. Possibly because touring pros have had to make precise tee-off times all their careers, we are more conscious of promptness than others. Sometimes when I make an appointment with someone, I do it in the spirit of scheduling a tournament, by making the time of meeting an odd hour like 10:17 A.M., say, instead of 10:15 or 10:30. For some reason the other person tends to show up at the exact time that way, and not ten minutes early or late.

Keeping Up Correspondence

Postcards are like interoffice memos—easy to write and cheap to send. In twenty minutes you can reach a dozen friends or business associates this way, whereas on the phone during the same amount of time, for many times the cost, you would be lucky to reach more than one.

Money

Handling money properly in social situations has a lot to do with being nice to others. It is a ticklish subject, though, because money is worshiped according to so many different and ingrained sets of beliefs. A tight fist is a closed fist, in my opinion. And I know one thing for sure, teaching generosity to a cheapskate is like cooling down a hothead—the lesson sticks for one time only.

I have established a kind of peaceful coexistence with the cheapskates on tour after years of trying to reform them or make fun of them, neither tactic having had the slightest effect.

During the San Diego Open one year, I noticed a young pro stocking up on doughnuts and cupcakes that were set out gratis in the locker room as snacks for the players.

"What are you doing?" I said.

"I'm bringing some TV snacks back to the room for the family."

"Well, what about some of this potato salad?" I said, picking up a big cut-glass dish and handing it to him. "And how about a case of Coke?" I added sarcastically.

"I don't like Coke," he said in all seriousness. "But I'll bring the dish back in the morning."

Once I had to give another man's caddie $20 so the caddie could pay his own motel bill for the week and get to the next tournament site—he hadn't even made expenses on what his own pro had paid him. The pro himself had won $3,700 that week and paid him only $80.

Another pro and I sat down once for a cup of coffee together. When the waitress came after we finished, the other pro said to my great surprise, "Separate checks, please."

"No," I said facetiously. "I believe I can swing this one."

Luckily for waiters and little match girls, for every born cheapskate there is a born spendthrift, like myself. Most people, I hope, aspire to some happy medium.

Borrowers

I handle persistent borrowers the way I handle drunks—I try to kill them with kindness. If a man asks me for a loan of $50, I give him $20 outright and tell him I don't expect it back. That takes the wind out of his sails on the next occasion he would have liked to borrow from me. Chances are he won't ask, because he'll be too embarrassed to get another handout.

Beggars

Beggars I always acknowledge with a dollar because I think it would bring me bad luck if I passed them by, and I have enough bad luck without developing new sources.

Tipping

Tipping separates the good skates from the cheapskates, I guess. Actually I don't tip for philanthropic reasons, though I am conscious of the fact that human beings occupy the various service positions.

I tip to pay for the service given to me and, more selfishly, to get that service done as well and as fast as it can be done. A consistently intelligent tipping policy pays off for anyone for whom time is money. When I get off a plane, I know I'm not going to have to trot all over the airport to find somebody to tote my bags for me. When I go to a crowded restaurant, I know I won't be asked to stand in line for twenty minutes drinking a whiskey sour, before a table opens up for my party in front of the swinging kitchen doors. If my car is in a parking garage, I know it will always be ready for me at the time I have stipulated, not a half an hour early or twenty minutes late.

Maybe one reason service has fallen off in this country is that Americans don't really appreciate it any more. In fact I think many of us don't even approve of one person waiting on another person. And when we do acknowledge service, we tend to be undiscriminating. We are a nation of ten per centers—no matter what speed or quality we get in our service, we figure out what is ten per cent of the bill and that's what we tip.

A deliberate attempt to evaluate service usually produces a fairer tip. Also it makes you aware of other ways in which service is rendered, often without a tip of any kind. Sometimes I tip a service station attendant, looking at him as a worker who spends a lot of time out in bad weather on my behalf. I saw Frank Sinatra slip $5 to a busboy scrunched up in the corner of a restaurant where we ate together once, and it made me aware of that usually untipped service for the first time.

He paid him on the sly, Sinatra explained later, so the waiter would not try to get a cut of it after we left.

Tipping in Foreign Countries

I travel overseas so much that I have devised an easy system for tipping correctly in spite of currency differences. All I do is bring along a wad of U.S. singles. I reckon the value of the service I get and then I pay for it in multiples of that $1.00 unit. That way I don't ever make the mistake of leaving a shilling when I meant to leave a pound.

Sometimes I get my bills mixed up. I flew into Frankfurt, Germany, in 1966 to film a "Shell's Wonderful World of Golf" TV show and gave $5 to the fellow who carried my bags and clubs to the taxi. At least I thought it was $5. When I reached my hotel room, I checked my wallet and discovered I had given him a $500 bill.

That is to date my grandest gratuity.

Not Tipping

The only time I left no tip at all was in a bar in a Los Angeles hotel where a waiter kept sitting down in a corner whenever I needed another drink. I had to serve myself at the bar three times and when the hour came to sign the check, I conspicuously dropped one dime on top of it for the waiter.

"Sir," said the man in a neutral tone, "tipping is not mandatory."

"Very good, give me back my goddam ten cents," I said and I grabbed my money and left.

Tipping with Gifts

There are some people I deal with regularly—such as my liquor store dealer, whom I have made one of the ten wealthiest men in Houston—whom it is not proper or convenient to tip, yet who render me real service. I include them in other forms of recognition, such as a gift of a dozen golf balls and a thank-you card at Christmas.

Thoughtfulness sticks out like a sore thumb, and so does ingenuity. One summer years ago I got a Christmas card from Elmer Hawkins, a pro who ran the driving range in Gainesville, Florida, where I used to hit balls. I mentioned getting the card next time I stopped by there. I said, "Your wife or your secretary or somebody is a little mixed up."

"Hell no," he explained. "I always send my Christmas cards in July. That way everyone notices."

Telephone Operators

Whenever I check into a motel or hotel, I make a point of saying hello or at least winking at the switchboard operator, because I know she is the one who is going to make sure my phone calls and messages get through to me.

Once I sent a long-distance operator in Miami a dozen roses for placing several complicated calls for me. I didn't know her name so I had them sent to her operator number and signed my own billing number. The florist figured me for an espionage agent or a nut, or both.

Older Women

I slip compliments to older women when I get a chance on the assumption that no man may have told them they are cute or well proportioned or beautifully coiffed in forty years, sometimes because all those assumptions may be true.

Highway Patrolmen

I keep my license and registration papers in the trunk of my car. If I am stopped for speeding, I have to open the trunk and then the cop sees my pro bag with my name emblazoned on the side. If he is a golfer or has a golfer in the family, he will usually soften a bit in meting out punishment to me for speeding, especially if I give him a putting lesson as once happened. If he is not a golfer, I follow him to the station as once happened too.

One-day Affairs

There are two distinctly different attitudes among the pros toward the one-day minor money-maker known as the exhibition match. One is to fly in, play, and fly out. The other, which I follow, is to linger for an hour or two after the exhibition and attempt to reach some of the sponsors on a personal basis.

Exhibitions of course usually are held in towns and cities that are too small in population or resources to hold a regular pro tour event, yet are fan for fan just as enthusiastic about golf as the regular tour stops. So I feel a responsibility to share my skill and my personality with the people just as I do during tournaments before big galleries.

I also believe in comporting myself, no matter where I am or who I'm with, as though I'm going to be in that place and with those people again some time. That is a tough test to pass all the time but I think it forces me to act more responsibly and decently. This is what the smart business executive does on the odd sales call too. If you act like yourself, and like a pro, all the time, and not just for the big customers, it is bound to pay off eventually.

In a way, of course, being nice cost me the Pensacola Open title in 1966—the year I forgot to sign my scorecard in the confusion of autograph seekers after my round. But even in that situation I won eventually. A few months after the tournament, the Pensacola Sports Association got in touch with me and asked if I would be willing to appear in a one-day exhibition, which they hoped would help them make up for the loss in gallery receipts they said my disqualification caused in the tournament itself.

I told them I would. I went down there one weekday, and dragged Vic Damone and Bob Hope along with me. Some 2,500 locals paid $5.00 each to watch us fool around for eighteen holes. The Pensacola Sports Association got their money back, and I got an unofficial moral victory out of the turnout.

15 / Raising a Son

One day around Christmas a couple of years ago, a two-year-old girl accidentally drowned in a swimming pool near where I was sitting with some friends. We had been playing cards and watching a boat race off shore from the Miami home where I was a guest. The father of the little girl happened to be in his own boat leading the race when this tragedy struck his family.

Later that day, as I drove to Miami Airport to meet Scotty, who was joining me for a trip to Morocco later in the week, a fearful incident flashed through my mind from more than a decade before. On December 7, 1957, while I was drinking champagne from a golf trophy in Bogota, Colombia, my son Brad was born in Cedartown. When I finally learned about this coincidence of events (two cables to me about the birth had failed to get through), I was haunted for weeks by the possibility that something might have gone wrong when I had been in the midst of celebration. Now, driving to the airport, I realized this is what happened to the father in his boat. He had found a bitter horror beneath his victory.

The idea that Brad could have been born dead while I was drinking champagne had seemed so real to me at the time. The pregnancy had been very tough on his mother, Betty Jane, in the first place. At five and a half months she had to undergo emergency surgery to remove an intestinal blockage. At that time I just assumed the fetus was lost, and it was not until two days later that I found out from the doctor that the unborn child had not been affected by the operation. Two months later, B.J. began hemorrhaging and we became pessimistic again. Thankfully the birth went all right, but all the prior difficulties had made me insecure and a bit morbid.

I was struck hard by this reflection of another time and by the events of the day—I had carried the limp body of the little girl to the ambulance, after all our efforts to revive her failed. When Scotty got off the plane I found I could hardly speak. It was like the time I had been penalized for my disagreement with a tournament official—only worse. I took Scotty off into a corner of the airport and stammered an explanation of what had happened, then wept.

Afterward I asked myself why I had taken it so hard. Obviously my long-time desire for a son—a desire that went back to my own youth—was at the base of it. But then I decided that this desire was part of my even more fundamental desire to have some small but real share in the future.

So the painful moments at least helped me bring into focus such things as my lifelong affection for kids of all kinds, my struggles to develop a scholarship program in my name, my efforts to befriend and help young pros on tour, as Dutch Harrison and Bob Toski had helped me when I was starting out.

And of course my fighting for and eventually winning custody of my own child—an unusual action for a father caught in divorce, especially back then.

I don't want to bring back in detail all the unpleasant and elaborate process of the custody battle, except to point out that it was easy to prove I was a devoted parent because I went to such length and expense to see my son whenever I could—when Brad was six, he flew over fifty thousand miles on various trips to join me on tour.

I wanted a close, honest relationship with my son. I had not been close to my own father, who died in 1956. We were not distant, either. Mainly, he was just too busy scratching out a living to be able to get to know me well. Without ever holding it against my own father, I wanted my son to have something better from me, and I think we achieved that. When Brad was fourteen, he gave me a card for Father's Day on which he had written:

> "Dads are called many things—
> dads, pops, and fathers—
> and I've called my dad all of these—
> dads, pops, and fathers . . ."

And on the back side of the card, he finished with:

> ". . . but above all, I call him my friend."

In those first years before I won custody, Brad's mother would not permit the boy to ride on airplanes alone, understandably. But playing in tournaments as I was, it was not easy for me to fly to Jacksonville (where Brad and B.J. lived) on Friday night, fly back with Brad to the tournament site, and then bring him home on Sunday after the last round. That is where my friend James R. came to the rescue, performing a kind of Berlin Airlift emergency service between father and son.

I played golf better when Brad was with me, as a rule, mainly because I tended to go to bed earlier at night. In a way visits to me were lonely for him, since I had to play golf every day and usually there were few children out on the course for him to fool with. I tried to arouse his interest in following me around by paying him $1.00 for every birdie I made. I also gave him $2.00 for a new toy each week. Once, when he was three or four, I sent him into my pants pocket for his weekly toy money. Later in the day, after we had picked out a toy in a store for him, he pulled out two $100 bills to pay for it with.

"Son, that toy's going to cost more than $2.00," I said, repossessing my two $100 bills, "so let me pay for it!"

My spoiling him with money came to a head one day when James R. was driving Brad home from St. Petersburg after a tournament. They came to a ten-cent toll station and James R. discovered he did not have anything smaller than a $100 bill. Brad had at least $15 in coins because he had been with us all week, and as usual he had ended up with all the small change left over at mealtimes and other occasions where money changed hands.

"Let me have a dime, Brad," James R. said when they stopped at the gate.

"No. You can't have my money."

"Let me borry a dime, Brad. Borry it, that's all. Come on now, the nice man is waiting here."

Brad jammed his fists into his pocket, protecting his bankroll. Meanwhile, cars backed up behind James R., who started alternating between smiling nervously at the toll gate attendant and glaring angrily at Brad.

"I'll pay you right back, Brad, soon as we stop for some ice cream like you asked for."

Brad shook his head violently.

"Well, if that's the way you feel," said James R., discreetly shifting the car into park. Then he lunged at the boy and wrestled him down on the floor. But he couldn't extricate Brad's hands, which were stuck into his pants pockets like corks in a bottle.

Car horns began blowing and finally the attendant said, "Why don't you go on through this time, sir."

"Thank *you*, sir," said James R. "Son of a friend of mine," he added by way of explanation.

"I'm sure he is," said the attendant, probably certain Brad was James R.'s son.

A little later they stopped for ice cream as James R. had promised. He was in no mood to please little Brad, but as usual he felt he had to make a special effort to be calm and fair-minded with the boy since he was my son. After buying an ice cream cone for him, James R. set off again.

They were racing along the highway when Brad, as a somewhat perverse joke, let James R. have it with the ice cream cone. He started laughing, but almost immediately stopped again, realizing he had made a serious mistake. He knew this because James R. showed absolutely no reaction. He simply kept driving at the same rate of speed, eyes fixed ahead of him on the road, with the lump of ice cream on his face slowly dripping into his lap.

At the next exit, James R. pulled over and stopped. Then, without a word, he proceeded to whale the daylights out of the boy. It is a beating Brad vividly recalls to this day. In fact he and I are inclined to agree with James R. about the incident—that it marked the day Brad began to grow up.

Spoiling and spanking are techniques for raising more dust than children, I suppose. My own faith is in incentives and education. Incentives, such as I received from Maurice Hudson, J. A. Gammon, and E. J. Duggan in Cedartown, get a youngster moving toward a goal smoothly and on track. I've seldom known it to fail. I've told a dozen boys—sons of friends

or relatives mostly—when they were ten or eleven and shooting maybe 130 for eighteen holes, that I would buy them a
new set of clubs if and when they broke 80, and most of them,
by the time they got to be sixteen or seventeen, managed to do
that. I got a letter from Bucky Ayers, a Cedartown youth, a
few years ago, and it was pretty much in the form most of the
boys broke the news to me. The letter went:

> Dear Mr. Sanders,
>   The family says to say hello. Everybody is getting
> along real fine. Just wanted you to know I shot 38s
> back to back, sure hope I can get my new clubs in
> five days so I can play with them in the high school
> tournament coming up.
>
>   Bucky

My faith in education is a little trickier to explain because
of my indistinguished record in that field. As I mentioned
before, I was never much of a student after grammar school
days. In high school I frequently skipped classes to play or
practice golf. When I did make class, I was either thinking
about golf or catching up on my sleep. When I went to the
University of Florida on an athletic scholarship, neither I nor
the college had any illusions about my business on campus.
I was there to win matches for the golf team.

These were the days of the "good hands—no brain" variety
of scholar athlete, and colleges throughout the country ac-
commodated themselves to it. Jocks had preposterous ways to
meet the terms of their free-room-board-tuition-books-laundry
contracts with the schools, and the schools usually tolerated
it all with winking good humor. Bribery and conniving were
blatant—some teachers were softened up with gifts, whiskey,
even dates with girls. Cheating was widespread and doing it
was considered normal, like taking a drink during Prohibition.
Athletes had spies among the girls working in the various ad-

ministrative and faculty offices, who obtained advance copies
of major exams.

"Studying for a test" in those days meant reading the test
before you went in for the test. Jocks wrote the correct answers
on their shirts or stencil-typed them on a seemingly blank
sheet of paper. I knew one fellow who replaced his watch-
works with a little scroll-like device on which he had all the
answers. As the test proceeded, he casually wound the watch
on his wrist from time to time—thus unwinding the scroll and
revealing more answers.

Sometimes natural stupidity triumphed. Once a fellow
golfer carefully etched his advance answers into the six sides
of his pencil, then absent-mindedly sharpened the pencil at
the start of the exam, completely upsetting the order of his
answers.

In a final exam for an English course, I sat next to a football
player who was pale with worry about passing. He took my
casual manner for confidence—in fact I was dropping out of
the course and didn't care how I did on the test—and asked
me if I would mind sharing my answers with him.

"Be my guest," I said, and during the test I sat so that he
had a clear view of my paper. I checked off my answers to the
multiple-choice questions as though I had studied all week for
the thing, and the football player copied the answers off my
paper as fast as he could write them. In fact I did not even
consult the questions, but I figured my guesses were as good
as his guesses, and I knew I saved him a lot of worry.

Once I hired a tutor to write a psychology paper for me—
another common practice in those days—and the teacher called
me in, it turned out, to discuss the implications of the theory
I had presented.

"Mr. Sanders, the point you made about Pavlov and indus-
trial cafeterias was quite interesting, and should be developed," he said.

"I certainly will develop it!" I exclaimed, having no idea who Pavlov was or what the paper was about. I had assumed I was called in because the teacher disliked the paper, or had caught on to the fact that I had not written it.

I did not finish college—though I was sincerely pleased to get an honorary degree from the University of Florida a few years later—because my education simply was not taking place there, it was taking place on the practice tee and in tournaments and matches. So when people joke about my supporting education today, I point out that what I am really trying to support is the learning process in young people, wherever and however it occurs. I happen to believe that it is more likely to occur for more people in schools than anywhere else, but I am not impressed by any academic degree unless there is real personal growth behind it.

My formal involvement in support for education began late one night in the fall of 1966, when I got a phone call on tour from James R., who had identified himself to the hotel operator as my brother so he could get through my "do not disturb" instructions.

"When are you coming home?" he said.

"Why, before Christmas, James R., as usual," I answered sleepily. "What is on your mind?"

He explained: That day, he had played a round of golf with Cedartown attorney Lamar Gammage, a friend of mine, and the superintendent of the Georgia School for the Deaf located near Cedartown. In the course of the round, James R. had volunteered my services to help raise money for the school's athletic program.

"I just wanted to be sure your services are available," James R. said after describing the planned golf exhibition.

"Well, I guess they are available if you have made them available, James R.," I said.

"Well, if they are not available, say so and we can forget the whole goddam shooting match."

"No, no, no, James R., don't get hot. I'll be glad to help."

James R. and Lamar arranged the exhibition for a day during the week I spent in Cedartown that December. Three other Georgia pros—Hugh Royer, Wayne Yates, and Emory Lee—joined me for a match on my old course, now called Cherokee Country Club, which drew a good crowd on a sunny winter day and raised about $4,000 for the school.

"Do you suppose there is any way we could do something like this every year?" I asked Lamar afterward. I had played in many exhibitions for charity before, visited hospitals and clinics, and tried to help people out of jams on an individual basis. But this event felt different to me, mainly, I suppose, because I was involved in planning it, and because it was for the benefit of local kids. "I always come home Christmas week anyway," I pointed out, "and it would be easy enough to take a day to do it."

"The only trouble is the weather is kind of unreliable this time of year."

"Well, then," I said, "I could take a week off from the tour in the spring and do it. But we need something to do it for, something for kids."

"That's no problem," said Lamar. "Plenty of kids could use help and money."

As an afterthought, I said, "Maybe I could get one of my entertainer friends to come along too."

"That would be dandy!" Lamar said.

Returning to the tour in January, I started asking some of my friends on the celebrity circuit if they might ever be able to appear with me in a benefit back in my home town.

"How busy would you be next spring, for instance?" I asked Phil Harris.

"Hell, I'm never too busy," he said. "Except that one day a year I have to fly into Kentucky."

"Kentucky? What do you do in Kentucky every year?"

"Lay a wreath on Jack Daniel's grave."

I asked Dean Martin if he could see his way clear to making an appearance as a favor to me.

"Only if you get a hold of a piano player who drinks too much," Martin replied.

But behind the joking façade of the various entertainers whom I approached, I began to realize there was a serious, almost solemn commitment to helping me. I was thrilled—and also overwhelmed by the notion of bringing so much talent into Polk County.

That was how we ended up with what became an annual celebrity benefit show, instead of a golf exhibition. One spring night in 1968, in a modest, 1,700-seat auditorium in the town of Rome, twenty miles north of Cedartown, the first show took place. When Dean Martin came out, he stared into the auditorium's only spotlight and said, "Look out, you all, there's a train coming through!"

In two and a half hours, a million dollars' worth of talent appeared in front of that lone spotlight. Besides Martin there were Keely Smith, Pat Boone, Phil Harris, and Andy Williams.

The show was such a success that we moved it to much larger quarters for the next two years—the Civic Auditorium in Atlanta. Among the talent showing up for those shows, free of charge and no strings attached, were Bob Hope, Andy Williams, Danny Thomas, Pat Boone, Phil Harris, Chuck Connors, and Keely Smith in 1969, and Dean Martin, Buddy Hackett, Nancy Ames, Vic Damone, and Mike Douglas in 1970. Andy and his 28-piece orchestra put on a show that would break attendance records in Caesar's Palace in Las

Vegas a week later. In fact this amounted to his dress rehearsal
for the big opening.

Bob Hope machine-gunned the audience per style with such
jokes as:

"Sanders told me how to keep California from slipping into
the sea—replace my divots."

Each year I was amazed that so many of the world's greatest
entertainers would troop into my home region and put
on a free show for a minor benefit. I realized these were men
and women with hearts as big as their talents.

We raised enough money to put eighty Georgia youngsters
into college. We set up a fund administered by my friend
Norman Simowitz of Augusta, Lamar Gammage of Cedartown,
and former Georgia Governor Carl Sanders—no relation to me
though he always called me "cuz."

I had a chance to meet some of the youngsters when I appeared for the signing of a special bill that had been passed
by the Georgia Legislature to authorize my scholarship program. Later, in the posh Hyatt House in downtown Atlanta,
we had a press conference and I shook hands with a dozen
youngsters who would be attending college next year on a
Doug Sanders scholarship.

I remember a gangling black boy in particular. He came up
to me in a borrowed suit that was two sizes too small for him
and a frayed white shirt. But he had a sharpness in his eyes
and enormous strong hands. While his hand swallowed my
hand as we were introduced, he mumbled something about
appreciating my program and I was suddenly too moved to say
anything at all. All at once I felt so privileged to be giving
those hands of his a chance to do something besides pick cotton or push a broom.

Which is a way of passing along some of the help I got as
a kid, I suppose, and getting that share in the future I mentioned before. After one of our Atlanta benefits, Phil Harris

appeared on the Johnny Carson Show and mentioned the benefit. "It's a side of Doug Sanders that the public doesn't know about," he said on TV. I believe he is right. There is a side of me that lives for the future, and it balances off that side of me that lives for the pleasures of the moment. I see my future in those scholarship students as well as in my own son, of course, and in the kids I've equipped with golf clubs or the ones I meet on tour who send me notes and letters.

I also see my future in the sons of friends of mine who have been named after me—thirteen boys at last count. I heard one of them recently chopped down a tree and blamed it on a neighbor. I'm told another one, at age four, picked up the family poodle and tossed it in the swimming pool just for the hell of it.

Plainly my future is going to be full of mischief and difficulties, just like my past. But that's me, and I'm ready for it.

Appendix

Doug Sanders

PLAYING RECORD 1951–72

WINS AS AMATEUR

1951   National Jaycee

1953   Southeastern
        Florida State Intercollegiate

1954   Southeastern

1955   Mexican Amateur
        Florida State Intercollegiate
        World Championship of Golf
        All-American

1956   Florida State Amateur

Canadian Open   Beaconsfield G.C., Montreal, Que-
July 5–8   bec, Canada

1st* 69 – 67 – 69 – 68 – 273

Eligibility to play U.S. tour began June 12, 1957.

---

* Defeated Dow Finsterwald in sudden death play-off on first extra hole.
Becomes first amateur to win event in its fifty-three-year history.

WINS AS PROFESSIONAL

1957

WINS

BARRANQUILLA OPEN   Bogota, Colombia, South America
Dec. 4–7

BIG FOUR FINISHES
(winner's name in parentheses)

MASTERS   Augusta National G.C., Augusta, Ga. (Doug Ford)
April 4–7

    Tied 31st   76–72–75–77 – 300 $300

FINISHES IN TOP TEN

Events played 12   Earnings $2,893
  Win   0   Rank   63rd
  Place 0
  Show 0

Top Ten finishes 3
  T – 4   Carling
  T – 6   Erie
  T – 7   Miami Beach

1958

WINS

WESTERN OPEN   Red Run G.C., Royal Oak, Mich.
May 29–June 1

1st   69 – 68 – 70 – 68 – 275 $5,000

BIG FOUR FINISHES

U.S. OPEN   Southern Hills C.C., Tulsa, Okla. (Tommy Bolt)
June 13–15

75 – 70 – cut

FINISHES IN TOP TEN

Events played 23   Earnings $13,739
  Win   1   Rank 23rd
  Place 0
  Show   0

Top Ten finishes 5
     1 Western
     4 Greenbrier
   T – 8 Carling
   T – 10 Gleneagles-Chicago, West Palm Beach

1959

WINS

CORAL GABLES OPEN   Biltmore C.C., Coral Gables, Fla.
Dec. 3–6

    1st   68–71–69–65 – 273 $2,800

BIG FOUR FINISHES

PGA   Minneapolis G.C., St. Louis Park, Minn. (Bob Rosburg)
July 30–Aug. 2

    Tied 2nd   72–66–68–72 – 278 $3,562

FINISHES IN TOP TEN

Events played 26   Earnings $20,794
  Win   1   Rank 14th
  Place 1
  Show   0

Top Ten finishes 15
      1   Coral Gables
    T – 2   PGA
      4   Los Angeles
    T – 4   Tucson, Tournament of Champions, Carling
    T – 5   Sam Snead Festival
    T – 7   Kansas City
    T – 8   San Diego, Miller, West Palm Beach
    T – 9   Rubber City, Dallas, Portland
    T – 10   Hesperia

1960

WINS

None

BIG FOUR FINISHES

MASTERS   (Arnold Palmer)
April 7–10

    Tied 29th   73 – 71 – 81 – 73 – 298 $500

U.S. OPEN   Cherry Hills C.C., Denver, Colo. (Arnold Palmer)
June 16–18

    Tied 46th   70 – 68 – 77 – 82 – 297 $260

PGA   Firestone C.C., Akron, Ohio (Jay Hebert)
July 21–24

    Tied 3rd   70 – 71 – 69 – 73 – 283 $3,350

FINISHES IN TOP TEN

Events played 31   Earnings $26,740
  Win 0   Rank 10th
  Place 2
  Show 4

Top Ten finishes 14

    2 Pensacola
  T–2 Baton Rouge
  T–3 New Orleans, "500" Festival, Western, PGA
  T–4 Houston
    5 Utah
  T–5 De Soto
  T–6 Yorba Linda, Dallas
    7 Tournament of Champions
  T–9 Greensboro, Oklahoma City

1961

WINS

GREATER NEW ORLEANS OPEN   City Park G.C., New Orleans,
March 2–5   La.

    1st   68 – 65 – 69 – 70 – 272 $4,300

COLONIAL NATIONAL INVITATION   Colonial C.C., Fort Worth,
May 11–14   Tex.

    1st   69 – 75 – 67 – 70 – 281 $7,000

HOT SPRINGS OPEN   Hot Springs C.C. (Ark.)
May 18–21

    1st   68 – 68 – 69 – 68 – 273 $2,800

EASTERN OPEN   Pine Ridge G.C., Baltimore, Md.
Aug. 3–6

    1st   72 – 66 – 68 – 69 – 275 $5,300

CAJUN CLASSIC   Oakbourne C.C., Lafayette, La.
Nov. 16–19

    1st   67 – 67 – 67 – 69 – 270 $2,000

BIG FOUR FINISHES

MASTERS   (Gary Player)
April 6–10

    Tied 11th   76 – 71 – 68 – 73 – 288 $1,666

U.S. OPEN   Oakland Hills C.C., Birmingham, Mich. (Gene
June 15–17   Littler)

    Tied 2nd   72 – 67 – 71 – 72 – 282 $6,000

PGA   Olympia Fields C.C. (Ill.) (Jerry Barber)
July 27–30

    3rd   70 – 68 – 74 – 68 – 280 $3,600

FINISHES IN TOP TEN

Events played 35   Earnings $57,428
  Win 5   Rank 3rd
  Place 4
  Show 2

Top Ten finishes 16
    1 New Orleans, Colonial, Hot Springs, Eastern, Cajun
    2 Palm Springs, Phoenix
  T–2 U.S. Open, Dallas
    3 PGA
  T–3 Mobile
  T–4 Texas, Insurance City, Denver
    5 Western
    6 Seattle

1962

WINS

PENSACOLA OPEN   Pensacola C.C. (Fla.)
March 8–11

    1st   67 – 67 – 67 – 69 – 270 $2,800

ST. PAUL OPEN   Keller G.C., St. Paul, Minn.
Aug. 16–19

    1st   66 – 69 – 69 – 65 – 269 $4,300

OKLAHOMA CITY OPEN   Quail Creek G. & C.C., Oklahoma
Aug. 23–26   City, Okla.

    1st   70 – 69 – 74 – 67 – 280 $5,300

BIG FOUR FINISHES

MASTERS   (Arnold Palmer)
April 5–8

    Tied 33rd   74 – 74 – 73 – 75 – 296 $500

U.S. OPEN   Oakmont C.C. (Pa.) (Jack Nicklaus)
June 14–16

    Tied 11th   74 – 74 – 74 – 69 – 291 $1,325

PGA   Aronimink G.C., Newtown Square, Pa. (Gary Player)
July 19–22

    Tied 15th   76 – 69 – 73 – 69 – 287 $1,225

FINISHES IN TOP TEN

Events played 34
  Win 3
  Place 3
  Show 3

Earnings $43,385
Rank 7th

Top Ten finishes 19

1	Pensacola, St. Paul, Oklahoma City
2	Mobile Sertoma, West Palm Beach
T-2	Texas
3	Buick, New Orleans
T-3	Baton Rouge
4	Tournament of Champions
T-4	Portland
T-5	Panama, Houston, Dallas
T-7	St. Petersburg, Coral Gables
T-8	Beaumont
T-9	Colonial
T-10	Eastern

1963

WINS

GREENSBORO OPEN   Sedgefield C.C., Greensboro, N.C.
April 11–14

   1st   68 – 65 – 68 – 69 – 270

BIG FOUR FINISHES

MASTERS   (Jack Nicklaus)
April 4–7

   Tied 28th   73 – 74 – 77 – 73 – 297 $750

U.S. OPEN   The Country Club, Brookline, Mass. (Julius Boros)
June 20–23

   Tied 21st   77 – 74 – 75 – 78 – 304 $525

PGA   Dallas Athletic Club C.C. (Tex.) (Jack Nicklaus)
July 18–21

   Tied 17th   74 – 69 – 70 – 75 – 288 $1,075

FINISHES IN TOP TEN

Events played 28   Earnings $28,202
  Win 1   Rank 17th
  Place 0
  Show 0

Top Ten finishes 10

     1 Greensboro
   T – 4 New Orleans, Colonial
   T – 6 Seattle
     7 Tournament of Champions
   T – 8 Crosby, Utah
   T – 9 Pensacola, St. Petersburg, Texas

Also won: Japan Open

1964

WINS

None

BIG FOUR FINISHES

U.S. OPEN   Congressional C.C., Washington D.C. (Ken Ven-
June 18–20   turi)

    Tied 32nd   74–74–76–74 – 298 $375

BRITISH OPEN   St. Andrews, Scotland (Tony Lema)
July 8–10

    11th   78–73–74–68 – 293 $335

PGA   Columbus C.C. (Ohio) (Bobby Nichols)
July 16–19

    Tied 28th   71–73–76–68 – 288 $800

FINISHES IN TOP TEN

Events played 30   Earnings $34,474
  Win   0   Rank 14th
  Place 3
  Show 0

Top Ten finishes 6
     2   Greensboro
   T – 2   Tournament of Champions, "500" Festival
   T – 4   Pensacola
   T – 6   Seattle
  T – 10   Whitemarsh

1965

WINS

PENSACOLA OPEN   Pensacola C.C. (Fla.)
March 4–7

    1st*   68 – 71 – 65 – 73 – 277 $10,000

DORAL OPEN   Doral C.C., Miami, Fla.
March 11–14

    1st   65 – 71 – 71 – 67 – 274 $11,000

BIG FOUR FINISHES

MASTERS   (Jack Nicklaus)
April 8–11

    Tied 11th   69 – 72 – 74 – 74 – 289 $1,550

U.S. OPEN   Bellerive C.C., Creve Coeur, Mo. (Gary Player)
June 17–20

    Tied 11th   77 – 73 – 69 – 71 – 290 $1,650

PGA   Laurel Valley G.C., Ligonier, Pa. (Dave Marr)
Aug. 12–15

    Tied 20th   71 – 73 – 74 – 74 – 292 $1,450

* defeated Jack Nicklaus in sudden death play-off on third extra hole

FINISHES IN TOP TEN

Events played 27   Earnings $72,182
  Win   2   Rank 4th
  Place   2
  Show   2

Top Ten finishes 11
     1   Pensacola, Doral
     2   Seattle
  T – 2   Philadelphia
     3   Tournament of Champions
  T – 3   Phoenix
  T – 4   Sahara
     6   Buick
  T – 8   Jacksonville, Colonial
  T – 9   American Golf Classic

1966

WINS

BOB HOPE DESERT CLASSIC   Palm Springs, Calif.
Feb. 2–6

    1st*   70 – 72 – 68 – 73 – 66 – 349 $15,000

JACKSONVILLE OPEN   Selva Marina C.C., Jacksonville, Fla.
March 24–27

    1st   71 – 65 – 66 – 71 – 273 $13,500

GREATER GREENSBORO OPEN   Sedgefield C.C., Greensboro,
March 31–April 3   N.C.

    1st*   65 – 70 – 71 – 70 – 276 $20,000

BIG FOUR FINISHES

MASTERS   (Jack Nicklaus)
April 7–11

    Tied 4th   74 – 70 – 75 – 71 – 290 $5,700

U.S. OPEN   Olympic Club, San Francisco, Calif. (Billy Cas-
June 16–20   per)

    Tied 8th   70 – 75 – 74 – 71 – 290 $2,800

BRITISH OPEN   Muirfield, Scotland (Jack Nicklaus)
July 6–8

    Tied 2nd   71 – 70 – 72 – 70 – 283 $13,215

PGA   Firestone C.C., Akron, Ohio (Al Geiberger)
July 21–24

    Tied 6th   69 – 74 – 73 – 71 – 287 $5,000

---

* defeated Arnold Palmer in sudden death play-off on first extra hole.
* defeated Tom Weiskopf in sudden death play-off on second extra hole.

FINISHES IN TOP TEN*

Events played 29   Earnings $80,096
  Win 3   Rank 4th
  Place 1
  Show 0

Top Ten finishes 15
     1 Hope, Jacksonville, Greensboro
     2 PGA National Team (with Al Besselink)
  T–4 Masters
     5 Minneapolis, Hawaiian
  T–5 Crosby
     6 Houston, PGA
  T–6 Tucson
  T–8 Buick, Cajun, U.S. Open
   10 New Orleans

* excluding showing in British Open, not an official U.S. PGA tour event

1967

WINS

DORAL OPEN   Doral C.C., Miami, Fla.
March 2–5

    1st   68–71–66–70 – 275 $20,000

BIG FOUR FINISHES

MASTERS   (Gay Brewer)
April 6–9

    Tied 15th   74–72–73–73 – 292 $2,100

U.S. OPEN   Baltusrol G.C., Springfield, N.J. (Jack Nicklaus)
June 15–18

    Tied 33rd   76–72–74–70 – 292 $940

PGA   Columbine C.C., Denver, Colo. (Don January)
July 20–23

    Tied 27th   72–71–76–73 – 292 $900

BRITISH OPEN   Hoylake, England (Roberto de Vicenzo)

    Tied 18th   71–73–73–73 – 290 $690

FINISHES IN TOP TEN

Events played 30   Earnings $109,455
  Win 1   Rank 6th
  Place 4
  Show 2

Top Ten finishes 14
     1   Doral
     2   Hope, Greensboro, Western, American Golf Classic
     3   Pensacola
  T – 3 Hawaiian
  T – 4 Tournament of Champions, Dallas
     6   Westchester
  T – 7 Crosby
  T – 8 Phoenix
  T – 10 Florida Citrus

RYDER CUP matches, Champions G.C., Houston, Tex., Oct. 20–22
    Foursomes: Jacklin/Thomas df. Sanders/Brewer 4 & 3
    Four Ball: Sanders/Dickinson df. Will/Huggett 3 & 2
                Sanders/Dickinson df. Alliss/Gregson 3 & 2
    Singles: Coles df. Sanders 2 & 1

1968

WINS

None

BIG FOUR FINISHES

MASTERS   (Bob Goalby)
April 11–14

    Tied 12th   76–69–70–68 – 283 $2,850

U.S. OPEN   Oak Hill C.C., Rochester, N.Y. (Lee Trevino)
June 13–16

    Tied 37th   73–72–73–74 – 292 $950

PGA   Pecan Valley C.C., San Antonio, Tex. (Julius Boros)
July 18–21

    Tied 8th   72–67–73–73 – 285 $3,405

FINISHES IN TOP TEN

Events played 25   Earnings $38,131
  Win 0   Rank 44th
  Place 1
  Show 0

Top Ten finishes 4
  T–2 Jacksonville
  T–5 Greensboro
  T–6 Kemper
  T–8 PGA

1969

WINS

None

BIG FOUR FINISHES

MASTERS   (George Archer)
April 10–13

    Tied 36th   72–71–76–77 – 296 $1,425

PGA   National Cash Register G.C., Dayton, Ohio (Raymond Floyd)
Aug. 14–17

    72–79 – cut

FINISHES IN TOP TEN

Events played 32   Earnings $30,311
  Win   0   Rank 64th
  Place 0
  Show 0

Top Ten finishes 3
    8 Monsanto
  T–8 Texas
  T–9 Heritage Golf Classic

1970

WINS

BAHAMAS ISLANDS OPEN   King's Inn & G.C., Freeport, Ba-
Dec. 10–13   hamas

   1st*   66 – 70 – 68 – 68 – 272 $26,000

BIG FOUR FINISHES

BRITISH OPEN   St. Andrews, Scotland (Jack Nicklaus)
July 8–11

   2nd*   68 – 71 – 71 – 73 – 283 $8,950

PGA   Southern Hills C.C., Tulsa, Okla. (Dave Stockton)
Aug. 13–16

   Tied 41st   75 – 74 – 71 – 74 – 294 $750

FINISHES IN TOP TEN*

Events played 31   Earnings $47,891
  Win   0   Rank   47th
  Place 0
  Show   0

Top Ten finishes 2
   1   Bahamas
 T – 6   Hartford

---

* defeated Chris Blocker in sudden death play-off on second extra hole
*lost to Jack Nicklaus in 18-hole play-off round, 73 to 72
*excluding showing in British Open, not an official U.S. PGA tour event.

1971

WINS

None

BIG FOUR FINISHES

PGA   PGA National G.C. (East Course), Palm Beach Gardens, Fla. (Jack Nicklaus)
Feb. 24–28

    79 – 75 – cut

U.S. OPEN   Merion G.C., Ardmore, Pa. (Lee Trevino)
June 17–20

    Tied 37th   68 – 75 – 71 – 76 – 290 $1,080

BRITISH OPEN   Royal Birkdale, Southport, England (Lee Tre-
July 7–10   vino)

    Tied 9th   73 – 71 – 74 – 67 – 285 $3,720

FINISHES IN TOP TEN*

Events played	30	Earnings	$24,891
Win	0	Rank	86th
Place	0		
Show	0		

Top Ten finishes   0

---

* excluding showing in British Open, not an official U.S. PGA tour event

1972

WINS

KEMPER OPEN   Quail Hollow C.C., Charlotte, N.C.
June 1–4

    1st   71 – 68 – 68 – 68 – 275 $35,000

BIG FOUR FINISHES

U.S. OPEN   Pebble Beach Golf Links (Calif.) (Jack Nicklaus)
June 15–18

    81 – 79 – cut

BRITISH OPEN   Muirfield, Scotland (Lee Trevino)
July 12–15

    4th   71 – 71 – 69 – 70 – 281 $7,150

PGA   Oakland Hills C.C., Birmingham, Mich. (Gary Player)
Aug. 3–6

    Tied 7th   72 – 72 – 68 – 73 – 285 $6,383

FINISHES IN TOP TEN*

Events played 26   Earnings $102,252
  Win   1   Rank 16th
  Place 1
  Show 0

Top Ten finishes 7

     1   Kemper
   T–2   Houston
     5   Memphis
   T–5   L&M
   T–7   PGA, Atlanta
  T–10   Sahara

* excluding showing in British Open, not an official U.S. PGA tour event